JIM CARMODY

BIG NASTY

MISSISSIPPI'S COACH

RONALD F. BORNE

Introduction by Rick Cleveland

ISBN: 978-1-936946-59-4

The Nautilus Publishing Company
426 S Lamar Blvd., Suite 16
Oxford, MS 38655
Tel: 662-513-0159
www.nautiluspublishing.com

First Edition

Front cover and interior design by Deborah Freeland

Library of Congress Cataloging-in-Publication Data has been
applied for.

Printed in the USA

10 9 8 7 6 5 4 3 2 1

DEDICATION

For Deborah — Accomplished artist, photographer
par excellence, creative graphics designer, vibrant
videographer, musician, astute football fan,
devoted mother and perfect partner.

AND

To Earlyn Regouffre "Noonie" Carmody, beauty
queen and dedicated wife and mother — the rock
upon which the Carmody family unit was built and
the glue that held the family together
during all the transitions.

CONTENTS

INTRODUCTION

BY RICK CLEVELAND

Mississippi's college football rivalries are fierce, bordering on savage. Ole Miss and Mississippi State fans almost seem to live to hate one another. Back in the day, back when both those schools played Southern Miss on an annual basis, all the Rebels and Bulldogs could agree upon was a shared disdain for USM.

At least one man has known the Magnolia State rivalries from all sides. Indeed, Jim Carmody was part of huge victories by all three over the other two. Indeed, Carmody, renowned as a defensive wizard known to many as "Big Nasty," was part of many of the most monumental victories in Mississippi history.

What's more, he served two different stints at all three universities.

"That's fairly unique, I would say," Carmody once told me. "Two different times at all three schools. I guess it shows I didn't burn any bridges."

Whether you like Carmody or loathed him, his track record was impossible to ignore. His was a case of, "If you can't beat him, hire him." Here's just a sampling of his achievements:

• As the first-year head coach at Southern Miss, in 1982, his Golden Eagles, led by Reggie Collier, defeated Bear Bryant and Alabama in the legendary coach's last home game at Tuscaloosa. The 38-29 USM victory ended a 57-game Alabama home-winning streak and marked the first time in 19 seasons a visitor had won there.

• As the defensive coordinator at Ole Miss in 1977, Carmody designed the game plan that helped the Rebels defeat eventual national champion Notre Dame 20-13 at Mississippi Veterans Memorial Stadium. Hall of Famer

Jack Carlisle was an offensive assistant on that Ole Miss staff but says his lasting memory of the game will be the inspired play of the Rebels' defense. "Jim Carmody's defensive plan was masterful," Carlisle said. "His players knew just what to do."

• After signing Brett Favre at USM and then coaching him in Favre's first season, Carmody wound up coaching the Mississippi State defense against Favre twice. Both times, the Bulldogs were victorious before capacity crowds.

In Carmody's 10 games against Mississippi State as a head coach and defensive coordinator at USM, the Golden Eagles were 8-2. In two games as defensive coordinator at State against USM and Favre, Carmody was 2-0.

Coincidence? Hardly.

Even later in his career, Carmody came back to haunt State, this time at Ole Miss. In 1992, the Rebels won 17-10 when Carmody's defensive front held State out of the end zone on 11 plays inside the 10-yard line on three separate goal-line stands.

"That was unbelievable, really," Carmody said. "I had never seen anything like that before, and I haven't seen anything like it since."

What made Carmody so successful? First and foremost, his intellect. The guy would have been successful no matter what occupation he chose. He just happened to choose football coach. Obviously, he knew Xs and Os and knew how to arrange his Xs to beat your Os. And he was also a master motivator, as you will learn in the pages that follow. He was extremely well organized and efficient.

In his first stint at Mississippi State (1964-66), he helped the Bulldogs to their first victory over a Johnny Vaught-coached Ole Miss team (20-17 at Oxford in 1964).

"Man that was a big deal back then," Carmody remembered. "The game was on national TV, and Vaught had just dominated State. It was a such a big deal the president cancelled classes the following Monday. I remember that."

Carmody was again part of Mississippi football history in 1987 when his USM Golden Eagles defeated Jackson State 17-7 before a packed house at USM's Roberts Stadium in the first football game that matched historically black and white Mississippi universities.

Carmody pushed for the game to be played because of his respect for Hall of Famer W.C. Gorden and his Jackson State program and because he knew the game would be a badly needed sellout. Not many coaches would have taken that risk. In 1987, Jackson State was loaded with future NFL standouts. Indeed, Jackson State outplayed USM, but the Golden Eagles won primarily because of attention to detail, particularly in the kicking game, a hallmark of Carmody-coached teams.

At USM, Carmody's defenses became known as the Nasty Bunch, and he was called "Big Nasty."

"That was the players' idea," Carmody said. "Hanford Dixon, J.J. Stewart, and Cliff Lewis all came to me with the idea, and I told them it was OK with me, but they better live up to it. Call yourselves whatever you want to as long as you live up to it. Over the years, I really believe they did."

Ben Williams, another Mississippi Sports Hall of Famer, played for Carmody as a defensive tackle first at Ole Miss and later for the Buffalo Bills. "Jim came in at Ole Miss my junior year, and we got better real fast," Williams said. "He was great on techniques and teaching you how to play."

Williams became an All-American and was voted Colonel Rebel.

Later, when Williams was playing in the NFL with the Buffalo Bills, then Buffalo-head coach Chuck Knox was looking for a defensive line coach. This was 1981. Williams suggested Carmody. "I told Chuck Knox, 'You hire Jim Carmody, and we'll go to the playoffs,'" Williams said. Knox hired Carmody away from USM where he was the defensive coordinator.

Buffalo not only made the playoffs, the Bills led the league in defense and set an NFL sacks record. Williams made All-Pro.

Nowadays, Carmody and Williams have a running joke. Williams says he made Carmody a great coach; Carmody fires back that he made Williams a great player. There's probably some truth on both sides.

After one season in the NFL, Carmody came back to USM to replace Bobby Collins. There, he coached his son, Steve Carmody, who was then a standout center for the Golden Eagles and is now a lawyer in Jackson.

"He treated me the way he treated everyone else," Steve Carmody says. "It was fun to see your dad at work every day. Not everybody gets a chance to do that. I thought he was successful because, No. 1, he was so smart, and No. 2, nobody was going to outwork him. He was always thoroughly prepared."

There's a photo both Carmody men treasure. It's of Jim Carmody shaking hands with Bear Bryant after the 1982 USM victory. In the background, Steve, No. 51, is shaking hands with then-Alabama assistant coach Paul Davis, who had hired Jim at Mississippi State way back in 1964, the year Carmody started making Mississippi football history, so much history.

WARM-UP

OVERLEAF PHOTOGRAPH
"Warm-Up"

Carmody and Bear Bryant at midfield following
USM's 38-29 upset of Alabama in 1982.
Son Steve center (there coincidentally),
congratulating Alabama's assistant
coach, Paul Davis
(Carmody Family Collection)

The GATA Bowl
USM 38 Alabama 29

The University of Southern Mississippi Golden Eagles football team entered the 1982 season on a highly optimistic note. Everything seemed to be in place for USM to be nationally ranked with a good bowl game awaiting them. They had a new head coach, Jim Carmody, who knew the program quite well, having previously served there as an assistant coach and defensive coordinator. They had probably the best quarterback in the nation, Reggie Collier, to spark the offense behind a stable, solid offensive line. Their defense had always been among the nation's best. *Sports Illustrated* magazine featured Carmody and Collier on a preseason cover, and *SI* ranked the Eagles in their preseason Top 20. But as the season progressed things did not go their way. They lost to Ole Miss in Oxford by 9 points and then had a game taken away from them at Auburn when the refs failed to call time on Auburn at the end of the game as the Eagles lined up for a game-winning field goal.

On Monday, November 8, USM received devastating news from the NCAA that could not have come at a worse time. — USM was found guilty of several violations, was placed on two years' probation, and was declared bowl-ineligible for two years. The 6-3 Golden Eagles were preparing to travel to Tuscaloosa to take on the legendary Coach Paul "Bear" Bryant and the 7-2 Alabama Crimson Tide that coming Saturday.

USM and Alabama first played in 1947 in a game that was dominated by the Crimson Tide. The series was suspended for ten years but was resumed in 1981. The game usually featured an underdog USM team taking on a SEC and national powerhouse Alabama football team. USM was surrounded by SEC members: Alabama and Auburn to the east and Mississippi State and Ole Miss to the west. The competition for Mississippi high school footballers was heated. Top recruits dreamed of playing for a SEC team, and most would list the Golden Eagles lower on their preference list than these other, more famous programs. The USM roster was usually full of players not heavily recruited by the three bigger programs — including several from the state of Alabama — so it was always a challenge to take of group consisting of less than heavily recruited players and mold them into a team that could compete with these powerhouse rivals. But this was the type of challenge that USM head coach Jim Carmody relished. Under Carmody USM enjoyed such success against Ole Miss and Mississippi State that the SEC schools refused to play them for many years, fearing they had more to lose playing USM than they would gain while risking recruiting losses in the process. The Alabama game gave USM the opportunity to show the nation and region that it could compete with the big shots. Historically, the Alabama game was perhaps the most anticipated game on the USM schedule, and USM was seemingly bowl-bound, so the news of NCAA probation came at the worst possible time for the Eagles.

The NCAA had concluded that the previous USM staff had committed several violations resulting in multiple penalties — one of which was that the 6-3 Golden Eagles were declared bowl-ineligible for two years. This was a crippling penalty for USM since at the time the football program did not belong to a conference (interestingly, USM was a member of the Metro Conference in all sports other than football), and a bowl game was the best measuring stick of a nationally successful program. The team was obviously dejected when they heard the news. But Carmody would not let the team stay down for long — he was a master at motivating his teams. At practice the early part of the week the team mood was quite somber. At mid-week Carmody, nicknamed a few years earlier by his defensive players as "Big Nasty" when he was USM's defensive coordinator, called a team meeting and announced that the Eagles were going to a bowl after all — the "GATA Bowl." Players were stunned and began to look at each other and at Big Nasty as if he had lost his mind. Carmody said, "Not the G-A-T-O-R Bowl, the G-A-T-A Bowl." Carmody spelled it out on the blackboard and said, "Come on, guys, help me. What does the "G" stand for?" Several guesses ensued until someone said, "Get." Right — what about the "A" — someone else said "After." Then it became obvious. The Eagles were going to the "Get After Their Ass" Bowl!

The players thought this idea was a stroke of genius and got fired up again.

In reaction to the news of the NCAA probation the Hattiesburg campus worked itself into a fever pitch. The mood was "Us vs. Them." On Thursday night USM staged the largest pep rally in the school's history. The team was as fired up and emotionally ready to play the game as any other team fans could remember.

Steve Carmody, Jim's son and starting USM center, remembers the USM-Alabama rivalry as being very intense. "We had a lot of native Alabama players and also Panhandle (Florida) players who were overlooked in the Alabama recruiting process. The game was personal for them. On offense, Sam Dejarnette (RB) and Freddie Richards (RG) were both Alabama natives. On defense, Alabama native Mark Carmichael (LB) had a helluva a game. Rod O'Barr also played at linebacker. Our punter, Bruce Thompson, was from Alabama. Backups Mike Poulin (C), Chris Haag (G), Scott Seay (G), Lehman Alley (G), and Mike Justesen (DL) were also intensely involved in the preparation and the game."

Under Bear Bryant the Crimson Tide had won 57 straight games at Bryant-Denny Stadium (honoring Bear Bryant in 1975 by renaming Denny Stadium the Bryant-Denny Stadium), over a 19-season range. The Tide had not lost in Tuscaloosa since Florida beat Alabama there 10-6 in 1963. Bear Bryant was a legend in collegiate football and had never lost a game to a rookie head coach. Despite being a huge underdog the Eagles had been optimistic since they played tough against Southeastern Conference opponents earlier in the season, losing close games to Ole Miss and Auburn but defeating Mississippi State. The GATA Bowl gave them renewed incentive.

Both coaches were aware of the importance of this game. Alabama had lost to LSU 20-10 the previous week and was unaccustomed to losing two games in a row. Bryant, though, was wary of this USM team and their outstanding QB. He knew how tough USM could be because the two teams played to a 13-13 tie in Birmingham in 1981. Bryant himself was nervous about this game, having said, "I think the last two years, not only has Mississippi Southern been a tough football team, but Reggie Collier has been harder for us to do anything with than any team we have played."

Steve Carmody remembers, "We had tied Alabama the year before. I thought they were going to be out for revenge because of the embarrassment. When I walked into the stadium at Tuscaloosa for warm-ups and then back on the field to start the game, I knew we were facing a great challenge. They had a great team that year. Alabama was rated #2 after drilling Penn State to start the year 5-0. They had lost the week before to LSU and a nail biter to Tennessee the week before that. However, they were in the top twenty with two losses and a dang good team. We caught them before the season-ending match with Auburn."

Fans on both sides wondered how USM would react to the NCAA penalty. Carmody said, "People ask me 'How's probation going to affect you?' I don't know because I have never been on probation before." He knew how powerful Alabama's offense, led by elusive Walter Lewis, had been. "Defensively we have to be patient — they will get some yards. We'll bend some, but we can't let them make the big play."

On Friday the team had lunch at the USM cafeteria and then boarded the buses for the 180-mile trip to Tuscaloosa. Hundreds of Eagle fans showed up and surrounded the buses to see the team off. The team arrived in time for a 3:30 walk-around practice at Bryant-Denny Stadium and checked into the Ramada Inn. Following dinner at 6:00 the team assembled to watch a movie. Carmody had chosen an Arnold Schwarzenegger film, "Conan the Barbarian," for the Friday night movie, hoping his team would get even more motivated. No one really knows how much sleep the coaches and players got that night, but after breakfast and team meetings at the motel, they boarded the buses at 11:30 for the short trip to the stadium for the 1:30 p.m. kickoff. Not a whole lot was said by the players on the way to the stadium.

It seemed as if a classic struggle was at hand since USM was coming off of two straight shutout victories, and Alabama was averaging nearly 30 points a game offensively. Besides, Carmody had earned a reputation of being a defensive genius, and the Eagles were now playing like a typical Carmody-coached defensive unit led by Jearld Baylis. But USM was not without a potent offense, guided by its brilliant quarterback, Reggie Collier; running back, Sam Dejarnette; and wide receiver, Louis Lipps. Alabama was led by its versatile quarterback, Walter Lewis, and running back, Paul Carruth, and its defense by All-American defensive back, Tommy Wilcox. But Carmody felt he had an ace-in-the-hole. His son Steve was the senior center who glued his offensive line together.*

It was an ideal fall day for a football game. Skies were clear, and the temperature was a nice, cool 47 degrees. A sellout crowd of over 60,000 fans, 5,000 of whom were USM fans, filled Bryant-Denny Stadium. The USM fans, decked out in their gold and black attire, were seated across the field from the USM bench between the goal line and the 15-yard line and were easy to pick out among all the Alabama fans wearing their Crimson Tide red and waving their red and white pom-poms.

As expected, the game was quite intense. The Crimson Tide was embarrassed by last year's tie and sought revenge coming into this game. For 'Bama the tie was the same as a loss; for USM it was like a victory for the program.

The Golden Eagles came out fired up. USM captains for the game were defensive tackle Larry Alford, fullback Neal Alexander, and offensive tackle Glenn Howe. Reggie Collier was the star of the show. USM's offense ran the veer option out of the I-formation. For this game Carmody and offensive co-ordinator Keith Daniels tweaked the veer with a QB counter after the initial step on the option. The fired-up Eagles scored on their first four possessions and did not punt in the first half. They scored their first touchdown with 10:28 left in the first half — Collier ran a QB counter option off of the tweaked veer and scored after a 22-yard run. Alabama had fumbled on their own 48 yard-line, and USM scored eight plays later. Carmody later said that USM had not used the counter-step veer play all season. Alabama linebacker Robbie James said, "That was the first time I've ever seen that play." Minutes later USM drove again and ran the same play, but this time Collier pitched to RB Sam Dejarnette, who raced 11 yards for the second TD. Collier, a 6'4", 205-pound senior QB, constantly baffled the Alabama defense on that option

---

*Another Carmody son, Keith, was a redshirt freshman on the team and did not make the bus trip to Tuscaloosa. Keith began his Golden Eagle career wearing No. 91 jersey but switched jersey numbers to No. 50 — the closest he could get to his dad's and brother's numbers since No. 51 (his dad's number) was already taken by another player who did not letter.

play, either keeping the ball or making a last-second pitch to Dejarnette. Collier did not have overwhelming statistics for the game — rushing for 81 yards and passing for 149 yards — but he controlled the game. Dejarnette ended up rushing for 152 yards.

USM did not commit a turnover, while Alabama had four. Most fans expected a defensive struggle, but it was a day for offense. The Eagles led 21-7 at the end of the first quarter and scored in every quarter — as did Alabama — and took a 28-14 lead to the locker room at halftime.

The game became more and more intense. Carmody's son Steve recalled that he had "pancaked" the Alabama defensive end near the end of a play in the first half. "The next time we were in a pileup he tried to hit me in the family jewels." Steve was upset and went after the end when the pileup cleared, and a fight nearly ensued. "At halftime my dad pulled me aside and told me that I need to control my temper and if I got kicked out of the game that I would never play a down for him again." Vintage Big Nasty.

Through the first three quarters Collier scored on runs of 22, 8, and 5 yards, and Dejarnette scored twice on runs of 11 and 3 yards. With ten minutes left in the game and USM leading 35-29, the outcome was still on the line. No one seemed to leave the stadium. Offensive coordinator Keith Daniels said he was satisfied to just control the ball. Starting on their own 41, Collier engineered a time-consuming 51-yard drive in 11 plays and faced fourth down and inches to go on the Alabama 8-yard line. The temptation to go for it never entered Carmody's mind. "I never thought of going for it. A field goal was the only thing that entered my mind." But Collier wanted to go for it and stayed on the field. Finally he was coaxed off the field, and Steve Clark kicked a field goal to ice the game. Carmody told his team not to celebrate too early but felt he had the game in control. USM had scored the most points on a Bryant-coached team in Bryant-Denny Stadium.

Despite yielding four touchdowns the defense had a great day. Baylis made an amazing 18 tackles, and defensive backs Bruce Miller and Bud Brown had 12 and 11 tackles, respectively. Bruce Thompson punted four times all day and averaged 49.3 yards per punt. As Carmody predicted before the game, his defense bent but did not break.

As the sun was beginning to set over Tuscaloosa, 55,000 Alabama fans, clad in their proud Crimson Tide Red, were slowly and gloomily exiting Bryant-Denny Stadium while the Eagles fans cheered their team. The 'Bama fans were stunned. The University of Southern Mississippi Golden Eagles had just defeated their beloved #17 nationally ranked Tide, 38-29. They had just witnessed the end of a 57-game Bryant-Denny winning streak and had not seen 'Bama lose at home since they lost to Florida almost 20 years ago. In addition to seeing the Eagles end this streak they also saw the first time a rookie opposing head coach defeated their beloved Bear Bryant in his last game in Tuscaloosa.

At the end of the game Carmody and Bryant met at midfield for the customary post-game exchanges. True to his reputation, Bryant congratulated Carmody and said, "If we played again next week, you would win again. You have a helluva quarterback." Carmody reportedly returned the compliment, "Well, Coach, we don't want to play you all again." Following the game Alabama linebacker Robbie James told the press, "I can sum it up in three words: Collier, Collier, Collier."

Collier said, "Alabama is human too, and it gets old people making excuses for Alabama and downplaying us. Just give us credit."

Bryant repeated, "They are for real. This was no fluke."

Carmody told the press, "There was a great deal of character on that field today." He added, "offensively we're one of the better teams in America. We had proven that before this game. I felt we could move the ball. It didn't totally surprise me." He credited USM fans for their support and then added, "This is the greatest victory in Southern Miss history."

The photograph taken of Carmody and Bryant shaking hands at midfield following the game is a family treasure — and is the cover of this biography. By pure accident, Carmody's son Steve was framed between the Bear and Big Nasty. Steve was on his way to shake hands with Alabama assistant Paul Davis, with whom his dad had coached at Mississippi State. "I shook his hand and introduced myself. I regret not removing my helmet, but they told us to keep them on after the game. I also shook the hand of another Alabama assistant before I shook coach Bryant's hand."

Jackson *Clarion-Ledger* newspaper columnist Orley Hood noted that Alabama had not lost in Tuscaloosa since 1963 — "The Beatles hadn't hit shore yet" — and that Carmody worried all week about the effects of probation almost draining the life out him. "'Bout bled him dry," Hood wrote. Big Nasty, rookie head coach, had just defeated the legend, Bear Bryant — and on Bryant's own turf.

The bus ride back to Hattiesburg took on a celebratory mood, and the players had a great time — especially the players from Alabama. When the Eagles pulled up to their dormitory they were met with a huge reception by a thousand fans. People were on top of the dorm cheering and waving flags, and the enthusiastic crowd mobbed the team as they got off the bus. The fans had not underestimated the importance of this game.

On Sunday, the USM coaching staff had a meeting. The jubilation was evident since five of the coaches had Alabama connections. Carmody said, "We were just talking about what a bunch of good kids we have. I know every coach talks about what a great bunch of kids he has, but I don't believe many programs could do what these guys did yesterday."

USM finished the season with a 7-4 record, good enough under most circumstances to earn a bowl bid. But that possibility was squashed by the NCAA probation.

Death of Bear Bryant

The following week USM suffered a letdown and lost to Billy Brewer-coached Louisiana Tech, 13-6, in a game played in a steady drizzle. USM committed six turnovers (three interceptions and three fumbles). Carmody said, "We just ran out of gas." Alabama that same week lost to Auburn, 23-22, and on December 15, 1982 — almost one month exactly from the USM victory in Tuscaloosa — Bryant announced his retirement as head football coach effective after the Liberty Bowl. He would continue to serve as athletic director. After the LSU loss and just before the USM game Bear had hinted that he was thinking of retiring. Obviously the USM and Auburn defeats convinced him that the time had come for him to step down. Two weeks following his coaching retirement announcement, Alabama defeated Illinois in the Liberty Bowl, 21-15. On January 26, 1983, just two and one-half months after the USM game, Bear Bryant suffered a massive heart attack and died.

But the GATA Bowl was not over. Many Alabama fans, grieving over the incomprehensible loss of their Bear, placed the blame for the death of their leader partially on Jim Carmody's shoulders. He began receiving hate mail from "loyal" 'Bama fans accusing him of causing damage to the Bear's heart by beating him back in November.

Bear leaving the field following the MSU-Alabama game.
(Carmody Family Collection)

First Quarter

OVERLEAF PHOTOGRAPH
"First Quarter"
Jim Carmody at Holy Cross, 1951
(Carmody Family Collection)

Bema, Ted, Jim, and Elizabeth
circa 1939

1

GROWING UP IN NEW ORLEANS

Whenever the topic of great American football coaches comes up, especially great defensive coaches, and especially Mississippi legendary coaches, the name Jim Carmody always seems to enter the discussion. Carmody is the only coach to have coached and recruited at Mississippi's Big Three universities: Mississippi State University, the University of Mississippi, and the University of Southern Mississippi — and twice at each place at that. He coached at the high school and professional levels as well. His defenses have led the nation, and he has coached some of the best players in football. He was a player's coach. During the six years he served as a head coach at USM no student athletes who played for him ever became academically ineligible. Carmody initiated an athlete agent bill designed to regulate sports agents, and that bill was passed in the Mississippi legislature. He earned the nickname given to him by his players — "Big Nasty" — but more on that later.

If you were to ask Jim Carmody where he was from, in all likelihood he would say New Orleans. But James Edward Carmody, Jr. was actually born in Shreveport, Louisiana, on August 24, 1933 — during the first year of President FDR's first term as the nation was slowly beginning to emerge from the Great Depression. Jim's sister, Elizabeth, was born three years later in Natchitoches, Louisiana. His father, James Edward (Ted) Carmody, was born on June 24, 1900, in Zanesville, Ohio, one of six children of Michael Byrnes Carmody and Elizabeth Kennedy Carmody, who was born in Ireland. Ted was the fifth born of six children and had three brothers (Francis M., Arthur R., and Frederick E.) and two sisters (Genevieve and Marie) — all born in Ohio. The family was staunch Irish Catholic. Jim's father was given the nickname "Ted" when Vice President Teddy Roosevelt became President following the assassination of President William McKinley in 1901. Jim's grandfather, Michael B. Carmody, was born in Brady's Bend, Pennsylvania, in 1859 and married Elizabeth Kennedy in 1890. He worked in the oil and gas business and moved to Youngstown, Ohio, in 1889. Michael and Elizabeth lived in various cities in Ohio (Marietta, Zanesville, and Columbus) from 1890 until 1908, when they moved to Louisiana. Ted Carmody was born in Zanesville, Ohio. Jim's mother was born in Colfax, Louisiana.

Jim's grandfather, Michael, eventually was employed as field manager for the Caddo Gas and Oil Company of Shreveport and was publicly hailed in 1911 for stopping a gas well that had been running wild for several years, wasting hundreds of millions of cubic feet of natural gas daily. Had the well not been stopped, the entire Caddo field would have been drained. Michael implemented a plan suggested by A.G. Curtis of the Shreveport Gas, Electric Light and Power Company. A Shreveport newspaper stated, "Mr. Carmody has done something for which he will have the thanks of the citizens of Louisiana for generations to come."

Ted worked as a land leaser for an oil company in north Louisiana, primarily Shreveport and Monroe, and married Bema Stewart, who was born in Colfax, Louisiana. They had two children, Jim and Elizabeth Carmody Gonzalez, who now lives in Baton Rouge, Louisiana. Jim's mother played a key role in teaching Jim discipline. She also began saving newspaper articles of all of Jim's athletic achievements starting with his playing football for Holy Cross High School.

Ted was a talented musician, and he was known as "Banjo Ted." Somehow Ted's family managed to send him and his three brothers to Notre Dame, from whence he graduated after majoring in journalism. In fact, all four of the Carmody brothers graduated from Notre Dame. Ted was a writer for a year or two for a small newspaper in Ohio. The yearbook at Notre Dame had this to say about Ted Carmody: "Scarcely anybody calls Carmody by his real name, James. But everybody knows 'Ted,' the man of banjo fame who played in the orchestra with Harry Denny. Ted is almost like Buster Keaton. He doesn't smile much. But when he does, you are sure that the joke is a good one. Or when he doesn't you imagine the joke is on you, and maybe he's laughing at you up his sleeve. In philosophy class Ted used to look intense, and when Prof. Mercier quoted a lot of Latin, Ted looked around and nodded gravely as if to say, 'That makes it much clearer.'"

But a degree from Notre Dame was no guarantee of financial success. The effects of the Great Depression were felt throughout the 1930s, especially in the South. Jim recalls living in Shreveport for two years and Monroe for two years. Bema's parents lived in Campti, Louisiana, and her father, Doc Stewart, worked for a sawmill company in Campti and was provided with a house to accompany the job. When Jim was five years old his family moved to Campti to live with his grandparents to save money, and he started Catholic school. Ted was an independent oil and gas businessman but never hit it big. When Jim was eight years old his family moved to nearby Natchitoches (where his sister, Elizabeth, was born in 1936 while the family still lived in Campti — Campti did not have a hospital at that time) located ten or so miles from Campti where his family rented a home. Jim attended third grade and vividly remembers the Japanese bombing of Pearl Harbor and a neighbor saying that we would "wipe out those Japs in no time." Since paying the rent was still a problem because of low wages the family moved back to Campti, where Jim attended fourth and fifth grades.

The Carmodys then moved to New Orleans in 1943 where his father worked for the Consolidated-Vultee Aircraft Factory, helping to build the PBY-5 Catalina "flying boat" aircraft. The PBY became an important factor in anti-submarine warfare, escorting convoys, and conducting patrol bombing and search and rescue missions. The plant had just been built on Lake Pontchartrain so the family moved to the Gentilly area of New Orleans. Ted was determined to give his son a Catholic education, and Jim went to the St. James Major Catholic Grammar School for the sixth grade. He would take a public bus back and forth to school. At that time bus fare in New Orleans was seven cents each way. He then transferred to Gentilly Terrace public school to which he could walk, saving his family the Catholic school tuition and the fourteen-cents-a-day bus fare. He attended Gentilly Terrace for the seventh and eighth grades.

The pre-integration high school system in the New Orleans area, which was predominately Catholic in the 1940s and 1950s, was quite complex. When Jim reached high school age, a strong Catholic school system separated by gender and race and run by different orders of Catholic priesthoods — schools with long traditions of high quality education — existed. If the parents of a young man wanted their son to achieve a high quality, private, Catholic education — and could afford the tuition — there were many choices in the late 1940s and early 1950s. All-male schools such as Holy Cross (founded in 1849), Jesuit (founded in 1847), and St. Aloysius (founded in 1869) existed. Other Catholic all-male segregated high schools such as De La Salle (1949) and Redemptorist (1937) were opened later. At the time there were also segregated all-male public schools in the greater metropolitan area such as Warren Easton, Alcée Fortier, and Francis T. Nicholls. Private, non-denominational high schools such as Isidore Newman and Country Day also existed.

Additionally, segregated all-girl Catholic high schools included Ursuline Academy, Sacred Heart Academy, and St. Joseph Academy. The Catholic high school system also included all-male black schools such as St. Augustine and Xavier Prep. Each had their strengths, but strong academics, strong athletics programs, and strong discipline particularly characterized male Catholic high schools.

High School Career at Holy Cross

Being of Irish descent, and Ted's having graduated from Notre Dame, it is no surprise the Carmodys were Fighting Irish devotees. Ted wanted his son to have an education under the Brothers of the Congregation of Holy Cross, who founded Notre Dame, so he sent him practically across town to Holy Cross High School in the Lower Ninth Ward of New Orleans, despite the high cost of a private education (tuition then was around $100/year) and the distance from Gentilly to the Lower Ninth Ward. Although Ted was multi-talented, playing banjo and joining a band, Jim did not inherit his father's musical talents. Jim's days at Holy Cross were long. To help the family pay tuition he took on a New Orleans Times-Picayune morning newspaper route. At 5:00 every morning he would pick up the 150 papers he threw on his paper route, fold them into his bicycle basket, and deliver the papers to the subscribers in his neighborhood. Since he lived such a long distance from Holy Cross he would leave for school at 7:30 a.m. or so. He would take the Elysian Fields bus, get a transfer, and then take the St. Claude Avenue streetcar across the Industrial Canal. He then got off the streetcar at a stop on St. Claude Avenue and walked five blocks to Dauphine Street in the Lower Ninth Ward to Holy Cross. Classes began at 9:00. During football season he would get home around 7:30 p.m. Getting to and from Holy Cross was not an easy task, but it helped Jim develop self-discipline — a characteristic that marked his life.

High school football, especially in Louisiana, in the 1940s and 1950s was an extremely popular sport. In 1929 the Louisiana High School Athletic Association allowed non-public schools to become members, and the popularity of high school football flourished. The New Orleans Prep League, consisting of a mixture of six male Catholic and public schools, had been formed and was particularly competitive. The league initially represented the top football programs in the city, and members included the Holy Cross Tigers, Jesuit Blue Jays, St. Aloysius Crusaders, Warren Easton Eagles, Fortier Tarpons, and Nicholls Rebels. These high schools featured some legendary high school coaches: Lou Brownson at Holy Cross, Gernon Brown at Jesuit, Harold "Hoss" Memtsas at Warren Easton, and Eddie Toribio at St. Aloysius. Intense rivalries formed.

The rivalry between Holy Cross and Jesuit dates back to 1922 and is one of the longest and most intense high school rivalries in the country. The two schools have played every year since — despite the Great Depression, World War II, and hurricanes such as Katrina — making it the fifth-oldest continually played high school rivalry in the nation. In 1940, this rivalry game attracted a record 34,345 fans to City Park Stadium, an indication of the popularity of high school football, and particularly this rivalry, at the time. Over 1,000 fans had to be turned away. The game has been played annually, and without interruption, in spite of Hurricane Katrina's totally destroying the Holy Cross campus in 2005. Jesuit was significantly damaged as well, so teams were hurriedly put together literally at the last minute. The prevailing spirit of the players and fans was that "we are not gong to let a little hurricane break the consecutive-games-played streak." Holy Cross won the "Katrina Game" 20-10 — played at Joe Yenni Stadium in Metairie — an area relatively less affected by Katrina than other parts of the city — but Jesuit leads the series 56-38-1.

Carmody started attending Holy Cross in 1947 and went out for football. He slowly developed as a football player and did not advance beyond the "B" team during his freshman, sophomore, and junior seasons. Jim says that the Carmodys were an athletic family — all the brothers played football, basketball, and baseball in high school. The best athlete was Ted's older brother Michael who played baseball at Notre Dame, signed with the Pittsburgh Pirates, and played in the Texas League for several years as an infielder. (The Official Encyclopedia of Baseball does not list him as having played in the major leagues.) Lesser players would probably have given up trying to make the varsity, but even at that age Carmody never knew the word "quit." He matured physically in his senior year, made the varsity team, and had a great season playing right tackle on offense and defensive end and linebacker on defense. He weighed 175 pounds.

At the time Jesuit was coached by Gernon Brown, who hired fellow Jesuit alum Lou Brownson as his assistant coach. Brownson spent two years as an assistant coach at VMI and became head coach at Holy Cross in 1942. Brownson had earned a reputation of being an astute strategist. Beating Jesuit was Coach Brownson's number one priority. In fact, beating Jesuit was almost an obsession. In 1944 Holy Cross defeated Jesuit and then went on to win the Louisiana high school championship. While Carmody was there, Holy Cross beat Jesuit 55-0 in 1948, 33-13 in 1949, and 18-14 in 1950. Following the 1950 victory, Holy Cross went on to play Fair Park in the state championship game, which Fair Park Won, 12-7.

In an unusual academic move Brownson talked Jimmy, as he was called back then, out of graduating in 1951 as anticipated and persuaded him to stay at Holy Cross for the fall football season. Brownson was impressed with the progress Jim made during his senior year and his aggressive style of play in his first year on the varsity team. Brownson did not want to take the chance of having the string of victories over Jesuit snapped in the 1951 season. Since Jim was only 16 years old when he finished his senior year, Brownson convinced him that he still had eligibility left, and he could play another year as a post-graduate. Brownson convinced the Holy Cross registrar to drop two courses from Carmody's academic record, and Jim was told that he would have to complete those courses before graduating. So Carmody re-enrolled for the fall 1951 semester. He does not regret that decision to this day.

On Sunday, November 18, 1951, the Tigers played their best game of the year and upset the heavily favored Blue Jays 20-13 before a crowd of 22,500 at City Park Stadium. The Times-Picayune reported, "Ray Willhoft, Donald Masinter, Jack Carmody, Jack Kuchler and Bill Nuckley were other Tigers that stood out." Reporting Jim's first name incorrectly and misspelling his last name would be a problem throughout Jim Carmody's career. His first name was variously reported as Jack, Tom, Bill, Tommy, and John. The victory should have given Holy Cross the district title, as they were the only undefeated team not only in the district but also in the state. But in a stunning upset the Tigers were defeated by the 2-5 Nicholls Rebels (who began their football program only in 1950) the following week in the "battle for the Ninth Ward," putting Jesuit and Holy Cross at one loss apiece. Jesuit defeated Warren Easton, and Holy Cross defeated Fortier on a Friday night, setting up a Tigers-Blue Jays rematch. Holy Cross and Jesuit then played once again, this time on short notice, the following Wednesday night. Trailing Jesuit 14-6, Holy Cross staged a big comeback and again defeated their rivals 18-14, eliminating the Blue Jays from state championship contention. Carmody was still undefeated against Jesuit. This victory set up a Holy Cross playoff game against Istrouma (the high school that would later produce the famous and infamous running back, Billy Cannon) for the Louisiana South Championship. Counting the Nicholls game Holy Cross played four games in a thirteen-day stretch. The worn-out Tiger team lost to Istrouma, 38-20. Carmody was not to be blamed for the loss, according to the *Times-Picayune* newspaper, who reported that he was a pillar of strength.

Both Gernon Brown and Lou Brownson are members of the New Orleans Prep Hall of Fame. Brown retired from coaching in 1952, and Brownson retired in 1956. Brownson coached all four major sports at Holy Cross and won a total of eight state championships in those sports. Brownson ended his career with a winning record against Jesuit — winning nine of the seventeen games he coached.

The Holy Cross-Jesuit rivalry continues and has become more than just a football game — it is a celebration.* The Jesuit Alumni News magazine, "Jaynotes," described the rivalry as a Mardi Gras-type thing. The game is a festival that combines tailgating with a parade (this is New Orleans, after all!). In October 2015 the 96th meeting of Holy Cross and Jesuit took place. The Tigers and Blue Jays set up tailgate parties outside Tad Gormley Stadium that concluded with the Krewe of Rivalry parade. The two schools honored their "Katrina teams" on the tenth anniversary of Katrina and recognized both

Coach Brownson and Holy Cross, 1951 - Carmody, last row center

*Three of my Jesuit Class of 1956 classmates, Jim Moore, Ronnie Gravois, and Dick Daigre, have developed a web site detailing the 97-year history of this rivalry. The web site can be found at www.bluejaystigers.com.

schools for not letting the rivalry die. "That the game was played stands as a testament to resilience, determination, and survival and marks the squads as two of the schools' most memorable and important teams." Carmody was pleased to learn that Holy Cross won the game, 28-21.

2

PLAYING COLLEGE BALL

Carmody's play at Holy Cross in 1951 earned him second-team All-Prep honors and attracted the attention of several college recruiters in the area. Midway through the 1951 season he was recruited by Raymond "Bear" Wolf, who was an assistant to Henry Frnka, head coach of the Tulane Green Wave. Jim graduated from Holy Cross at the end of 1951 and on January 15, 1952, received a letter notifying him that he had been awarded an athletic scholarship to LSU by head coach Gaynell Tinsley. He went to LSU shortly thereafter and checked into spring football training. Jim and several others participated in a few drills and scrimmages but had little opportunity to impress the coaches. Carmody met John Meibaum, who played football at Kenner (Louisiana) High School (they would later become roommates at Copiah-Lincoln Junior College). Both were told that they would have to gain weight to play at LSU.

Copiah-Lincoln JC

After a summer of working in New Orleans Carmody reported back to LSU, and assistant coach Dick Flowers told Carmody and Meibaum that they had not gained enough weight over the summer and wanted them to go play at a junior college for one season and gain some weight. Flowers told them to go get their clothes and then took the pair to the Greyhound bus station and put them on a bus to for a 115-mile ride to Wesson, Mississippi — the home of Copiah-Lincoln Junior College. Coach Flowers told them, "We'll send you to Co-Lin for a year then bring you back." They never heard from LSU again. Jim and Meibaum had no real idea where Wesson, Mississippi, was located

(145 miles north of New Orleans). They arrived after dark — it seemed like midnight — and when they got off the bus they did not see anyone around. Finally they saw a car parked in the dark, and a man behind the wheel of the car identified himself, between spits of tobacco, as Coach J.W. Waites and told them to get in the car. Waites had torn the pocket on his Hawaiian print shirt to enlarge the pocket where he could a put a spit cup. Waites would talk a little then spit into his pocket. He drove them to a dormitory and told them he would see them tomorrow. "Boys," he said, "we are going to scrimmage tomorrow." No doubt Carmody and Meibaum wondered what they had gotten into. Meibaum recalls Waites as a really rough guy. After the first scrimmage Waites told Carmody that he was impressed with Carmody's play and hoped he would stay.

On this inauspicious note Carmody began his Co-Lin career that would be recognized by the college when he was inducted into the Co-Lin Hall of Fame in 1993 and was one of three Co-Lin alumni to be named Alumnus of the Year at Co-Lin in 2014.

At Co-Lin Carmody was coached by Waites his first year and by John Gregory his second year. During his first year he played offensive tackle and defensive end and was switched to center and linebacker his second year. He lettered both years and was named co-captain of the Wolves his second year. Co-Lin went to a bowl game on December 5, 1953 — the Laurel Bowl — and played Perkinston Junior College to a 6-6 tie.

While at Holy Cross Carmody had tried out for the baseball team but did not make the squad. He tried baseball again at Co-Lin and pitched for the Wolves one year. He also pitched CYO overhand softball in New Orleans and was an effective pitcher during the summer of 1954. Undoubtedly influenced by his dad, Carmody thought he would major in journalism, and he wrote a couple of articles for the Co-Lin student newspaper: "Home Coming Finds These Wolves in Other States" and "Wolf '5' Wins Opener."

After he completed his second year at Co-Lin he had received offers from Tulane and Memphis State. He decided to go to Tulane where he had been offered a scholarship while at Holy Cross. His Co-Lin roommate, Meibaum, also decided not to return to LSU and transferred to Tulane with Carmody.

Meibaum was never really happy at Tulane. A third member of that Co-Lin team, Milton Robichaux, transferred to Tulane with Carmody and Meibaum. Robichaux was an outstanding athlete. He was a star football and basketball player from Hahnville, Louisiana, lettered in both at Co-Lin and, like Meibaum, did not like Tulane. He transferred once again, this time to Trinity College in San Antonio, Texas, where he starred in football and basketball. He was selected as an All-American in football at Trinity and played in the Canadian Football League for two years. Robichaux, like Carmody, is a member of the Copiah-Lincoln Athletic Hall of Fame.

Meibaum said he knew he would not be at Tulane very long because he did not like the food or the way they served it piled high on a table. Meibaum signed up for R.O.T.C. and was told to report to a trigonometry class. Meibaum admits that Carmody was a better student, and he knew he did not belong in a trig class. He quit going to class but kept practicing football in the afternoons and going to Bourbon Street at night. Meibaum eventually left Tulane and transferred to Memphis State where he played the 1954 season as a left tackle and the 1955 season as a left guard. When he graduated from Memphis State he joined the Marine Corps and was stationed in the Philippines. He became a 2nd lieutenant and watch commander for Air Squadron 1. Among those who reported to Meibaum was a young man named Lee Harvey Oswald. Meibaum is now retired and lives in Ripley, Tennessee.

Facing an athletic budget deficit, Tulane University President Rufus Harris began the process of de-emphasizing football in the early 1950s by decreasing the number of football scholarships available, eliminating players majoring in physical education, and requiring all players to follow normal university B.A. or B.S. academic tracks for fields of study. Tulane also had tougher admissions requirements for players than opposing schools laid out to attract players. While these moves enhanced the academic reputation of Tulane, they had a devastating effect on the football program. In 1953 — the year before Carmody transferred to Tulane — the Green Wave compiled a miserable 1-8-1 record and between 1954 and 1965 enjoyed only two winning seasons. Tulane eventually dropped out of the Southeastern Conference in 1966, supposedly preferring to play a national schedule as an independent.

But success did not immediately manifest itself. Between 1966 and 2013 Tulane has enjoyed only twelve winning seasons.

Tulane head coach Andy Pilney offered Carmody an athletic scholarship. Pilney replaced "Bear" Wolf, who in turn had replaced Henry Frnka. Wolf was let go by Tulane after leading Tulane to a 1-8-1 record in 1953. Pilney was the running backs' coach on Wolf's staff.

Pilney played football and baseball at Notre Dame and had a brief professional baseball stint with the Boston Bees in 1936. Pilney was a star in the 1935 "Game of the Century" (of which there are several on various lists) between Notre Dame and Ohio State University. Both teams were undefeated when they met in Columbus. With the Fighting Irish behind 13-0 in the fourth quarter, head coach Elmer Layden (fullback of the famous "Four Horsemen of Notre Dame") called Pilney off the bench. Pilney returned a punt 47 yards to the OSU 13-yard line, and two plays later the Irish were on the board. Pilney pulled the Irish back to within one point at 13-12 with 1:30 left. Notre Dame tried an onside kick, but it was recovered by Ohio State. Taking a knee was not particularly popular in those days, and Pilney and teammate Henry Pojman forced a fumble that was recovered at the Notre Dame 45-yard line. Pilney "became the stuff of Irish legends" when he faked a

Jim Carmody at Tulane, 1954.

At Tulane (l-r) Otis Gilmore, Byran Burnthorne, Head Coach Andy Pilney, Tony Sardisco and Carmody. (Photo provided by Curtis Akey, Tulane Sports)

handoff, turned upfield through the center of the line, evaded eight Buckeye tacklers, and ran for 30 yards to the OSU 19. But Pilney suffered torn knee ligaments when he was tackled. Nevertheless, with Pilney being carried to the locker room on a stretcher, Bill Shakespeare completed a touchdown pass to Wayne Miller, and the Irish scored with 32 seconds left to win 18-13. After playing professional baseball briefly and serving in the U.S. Navy in 1942, Pilney was in 1946 hired as an assistant coach at Tulane, where he remained until being named head coach.

In January 1954 Carmody moved from Co-Lin to Tulane, checked into his dormitory room, and learned that his roommate was Johnny Caruso, who was one year behind him. Caruso was a quarterback and also punted for the Green Wave. Carmody and Caruso would remain lifetime friends.

Tulane University

When Carmody finished 1954 spring training at Tulane he was listed as the Number 5 center on the team. Over the summer one center quit, so Jim moved up to the Number 4 slot. Because of injuries and Carmody's continued improvement, he moved up to Number 2 center. The Number 1 center, Jim Wilson, was then injured for the season, and Jim became the starting center. Two of the injured centers returned to the team but could not replace the much-improved Carmody as the starting center. His playing weight was listed at 190 pounds.

When Tulane played Ole Miss in the fall of 1954 Carmody was the only center listed on the Tulane depth chart. Playing both offense and defense against Ole Miss, he played 58 minutes of the game! He made the All-SEC checklist that week, but Ole Miss handily won 34-7 at Hemingway Stadium in Oxford. Ole Miss was ranked #7 in the nation in the Associated Press poll at the time. Carmody relates the time when he joined the Ole Miss coaching staff twenty years later and renewed acquaintances with Eddie Crawford, Ole Miss running back. He reminded Crawford that he had chased him down and tackled him from behind, ribbing him because a linebacker had run down a running back. Bill Keefe, a reporter for the New Orleans morning newspaper, the Times-Picayune, in his usual colorful language wrote, Crawford went on a "55-yard jaunt that would have landed in Tulane's Kings Row had not Jim Carmody knocked him out of bounds on the Greenie 24." Crawford told Carmody that the only reason he caught him was because "I was tired from running all over Tulane's ass." Tulane ended up with another losing season, finishing 1-6-3, defeating only Vanderbilt. But the following year, Carmody's senior year, head coach Andy Pilney and the Greenies made a major turnaround, and Tulane enjoyed its first winning season since 1950.

During the spring of 1955 Carmody tried out as a pitcher for Tulane baseball and made the team under first-year coach Ben Abadie, an outfielder on the 1948 Tulane SEC Championship team. Tulane's baseball program had fallen on tough times, and the 1955 team was trying to bounce back from a disappointing season in 1954. Tulane turned to Abadie to restore the program to one of respectability. Eventually, Abadie and Tulane enjoyed moderate success, but the 1955 team finished last in the SEC. Newspaper accounts of Carmody's baseball exploits included the following description of his start against Mississippi State University in the second game of a doubleheader: "A

Tulane Line — 1954

bad opening inning ruined a fine pitching effort for Jim Carmody in the second game. Two walks and an error let in two runs for State and it was enough to win." In another account of the game the newspaper wrote, "Rangy Jim Carmody threw a three-hitter in his Wave debut. But it went for naught in a 2-0 nightcap loss to State." Prior to Carmody's start against Alabama, another newspaper report stated, "Jim Carmody, a big right-hander whose chief claim to Tulane athletic fame has been an aggressive game as a football center, gets his chance Tuesday to stop the Southeastern Conference's hottest team — Alabama's Crimson Tide."

Carmody enjoyed a fine 1955 football season and began to attract favorable publicity. Following a 21-0 victory over Northwestern University at Tulane Stadium, newspaper reporter Jack Fiser wrote, "There's an underrated center and linebacker name of Jim Carmody who bugged out a lot of eyes in the Northwestern game. This Holy Cross alumnus ranged all over the field to unjoint Wildcat ball carriers." He added, "In the line center Jim Carmody stood out like a lighthouse. He was all over the premises throughout and

Tulane Offense — 1955

made two score-saving tackles….when there was no body else to bring them down." Carmody played a major role in head coach Andy Pilney's leading Tulane to its first winning season since 1950 as the Green Wave finished at 5-4-1, defeating VMI (in the first night game in the history of Tulane Stadium) Northwestern, Georgia, Auburn (the Auburn victory considered to be a major upset), and Alabama, and tying LSU but losing to Texas, Mississippi State, Ole Miss, and Vanderbilt.

Carmody graduated from Tulane on schedule on May 28, 1956, earning a bachelor of arts degree in history. He had compiled the highest academic average on the football team. He decided on a career of coaching football and was eager to get started along that career path. He also knew that men his age were being drafted every day. Rather than waiting to be drafted, Carmody discussed his options with the draft board and inquired if he could enlist early so he could begin his coaching career earlier. On June 26, 1956, he enlisted in the U.S. Army for two years.

Jim and Noonie
Tulane Graduation, 1956

Jim and Mother
Tulane Graduation, 1956

3

Armed Services - First Coaching Job

When Jim graduated from Tulane in 1956 with a degree in history, he entered what some pundits call the "real world" and had to make a decision on what he would be doing in the next phase of his life. He had many options. The events taking place in America at that time and his personal interests played a major role in his decision-making.

He landed squarely in a changing America and an American South that was led by President Dwight D. Eisenhower, who had just been elected to a second term. The economy allowed American families to dream of employment, wealth, leisure time with the family. The mid-1950s saw development of antibiotics to treat various diseases — rheumatic fever, pneumonia, tuberculosis; Jonas Salk developed the polio vaccine, essentially eliminating this dreaded disease. Television was introduced into our culture, and the first National Football League game, the Baltimore Colts vs. the New York Giants, was televised. There was no playoff system to determine a national champion in college football, and television was beginning to make a big impact on the sport. Interstate highways flourished, opening America to millions. Rock and Roll, led by Bill Haley and the Comets, Elvis Presley, Fats Domino, and Chubby Checker ignited a revolution among American youth. No day was complete without viewing "American Bandstand." Frank Sinatra was crooning tunes that enthralled female audiences. James Dean and his "Rebel Without a Cause" depicted a youth role model of emotional confusion. Women were becoming independent. But the Cold War, the "Red Scare" and the atomic bomb threatened civilization. The Russians launched Sputnik 1, opening outer space to the world. The civil rights era had begun with the

Supreme Court Brown vs. Board of Education decision, the Montgomery bus boycott, the integration of Central High School in Little Rock, and the emergence of civil rights leader the Rev. Dr. Martin Luther King. Fighting in the Korean War, described by author David Halberstam as "The Coldest Winter," had stopped, but conscription, or the American draft system, had not.

This was the exciting world and America that existed at the time of Jim's graduation from Tulane. He had many options to consider. With his degree in history in hand, Jim could pursue a career in that discipline. However, as much as he enjoyed history and continues to enjoy reading histories, he never viewed himself as a historian. Because of his father's interest in journalism and his own experiences as a journalist for the Copiah-Lincoln student newspaper, he had a strong interest in journalism and at one time considered a career in journalism. However, he never pursued that career. He also gave considerable thought to going to law school. He asked himself which of all these options he liked best, and he thought about his love of football and coaching. His football eligibility expired, but his love of the game did not. So he decided he wanted to pursue a career in coaching football. He thought of football as not just a game but as a model for life: discipline, teamwork, hard work, respect, etc. He played for men he respected highly, men such as Lou Brownson and Andy Pilney, and he knew he could make an impact on the lives of his players just as his had been affected by his coaches. Once he decided on his future career he wanted to start the pursuit of coaching as soon as possible. However, despite the country's being "at peace" during the period of 1956-58, the Selective Service Draft system was still in effect. Carmody knew he would be drafted soon and would have to serve in the armed forces, but he did not know when his number would be called. He decided he could begin his coaching career sooner if he enlisted and served his time in the military rather than just waiting to be drafted.

Carmody made the decision to enlist right then and serve his two years so he would be discharged in August of 1958 and could begin his coaching career the following football season. He graduated from Tulane on May 28, 1956, and less than a month later, on June 26, 1956, signed up for a two-year enlistment in the U.S. Army. The period of 1956-58 represented an ideal time to fulfill one's military obligation while the U.S. Army was in a relatively safe, war-free period between the Korean and the Vietnam wars, although the Vietnam War was just getting started.

Service in the U.S. Army — Korea

Right after enlisting he was assigned to Ft. Hood, Texas, for basic training and to take several aptitude tests. He was assigned to the Signal Corps as a Teletype operator — presumably because he had previously taken three years of typing — and was assigned the Military Occupation Status Number 723.10 (a number he never forgot). He was then transferred to Ft. Gordon, Georgia — home of the Signal Corps — for his specialty training. In December 1956 his unit was shipped to South Korea, first flying from Georgia to Ft. Lewis, Washington — the embarkation point for Korea and the Far East — and was then shipped to Korea. He recalls spending Christmas aboard the ship and arriving in Inchon, Korea, just before New Year's Day of 1957. He was then transported by truck to Munsan-Ni, about eight miles from the 38th parallel, near Panmunjom and the Joint Security Area, where the 8th Army Support Command (EASCOM) was located. His unit was based in a fenced-in compound in which troops from England, Turkey, and other countries were housed. Their main function was to gather information transmitted from North Korea that was then translated by a cryptographic unit to determine if the messages had any secret codes. The transmissions were mostly propaganda messages.

South Korea had held its presidential election in May 1956, just before Carmody's unit was shipped there. Syngman Rhee emerged victorious as president of South Korea, claiming 70 percent of the popular vote. North Korea's president, Kim Il Sung, attempted to de-Stalinize his country. During this period the South Koreans charged that the Communists of North Korea were preparing for another aggression despite promoting a peaceful policy. Kim Il Sung tried to enhance Communism in the South through psychological warfare rather than through a military process. Carmody's unit was set up to intercept these messages. From the viewpoint of military warfare, this relatively peaceful period of 1956-58 was a good time to serve in Korea. One of Carmody's memories was that he spent most of 1956 without watching football.

Armed Services Coach

In the spring of 1957 the local 8th Army newspaper advertised for coaches for the football teams assembled in the Far East to enhance troop morale. He could have been a player, but he realized this would give him his first coaching opportunity. His application was accepted, and he was transferred to Ascom City. Carmody was assigned to the EASCOM Loggers (nickname for logistics) where players were selected based on experience. The head coach was Lt. Carl Keese, who had played for Southern Arkansas. Since Ascom City was the arrival point for the 8th Army, Keese was able to get lists of everyone assigned so he could determine which arrivals had college football experience. Keese would essentially pull those with experience out of the arriving lines and send them directly to the practice fields. Carmody was one of five coaches assigned to the Loggers. Joining him were PFCs Frank Gagliardi (Gettysburg College), Ray Phillips (who played and coached at Dickinson College), and Bob Ford (Memphis State). Carmody and Ford had played against each other when Tulane played Memphis State in 1954. Fortunately for Jim, his coach-

THREE ZAMA TACKLERS HIT EASCOM BACK CARL NORMAN AFTER 11-YARD GAIN
As Loggers Clinch For East Army Title With 41-6 Win At Seoul

ing duties were on a full-time basis, and he had no other military assignments during the football season.

The staff initially greeted 70 prospects with another 40 expected by the end of the first week. Practice was conducted in sweltering 90-degree heat on fields that had little or no grass and reminded some of Bear Bryant's summer camp at Junction City, Texas, in 1954. The first cut reduced the number of players from 110 to 60 and then to 45. Carmody coached the line. Gagliardi was needed more as a quarterback than as a coach so he was transferred to the team, leaving four coaches. The coaches had converted a barracks to a small coaching office and an equipment room. There were no showers, so after practice players would return to their assigned units to shower.

The season consisted of ten games against other Army units. Some of the Logger players were running back Carl Norman (West Virginia), tackle Jack Kelder (Western Michigan), center Ed Kleist (Penn State), and running back Gayle Dick (Louisiana Tech). Most of the games attracted standing-room-only crowds. Carmody's coaching debut was successful as the Loggers won their first game 46-7. It was played on September 7, and the team emerged as one of the more powerful teams in the 11-team 8th Army Grid League.

SEASON RESULTS OF THE GAME SCHEDULE WERE:			
EASCOM	47	21st Infantry Regiment 7th Division Gimlets	6
EASCOM	41	34th Infantry Regiment Dragons	6
EASCOM	33	19th Infantry Regiment Chicks	12
EASCOM	31	3rd Infantry Bulldogs	13
EASCOM	26	I Corps Bullseyes	7
EASCOM	39	31st Infantry Bearcats	0
EASCOM	52	1st Cavalry Division Buccaneers	0
EASCOM	14	24th Division Artillery Redskins	37
EASCOM	66	17th Infantry Buffaloes	0
EASCOM	37	34th Infantry Bruisers	0

Winning the league title set up an All Far East Army Championship game against Camp Zama, Japan. The title game was played in perfect football weather in Seoul, South Korea, and was watched by 10,000 fans and by Syngman Rhee, the first president of the Republic of Korea. The game was called The Rice Bowl. EASCOM trounced the Camp Zama Ramblers 41-6, delighting President Rhee, who enjoyed Korea's defeating his lifelong enemy, Japan, in anything. Penalty flags were flying — it was a heavily penalized

SYNGMAN RHEE, REPUBLIC OF KOREA PRESIDENT, WATCHES GAME
Right Is Lt. Gen. Arthur G. Trudeau, I Corps (Gp.) Commander

game (340 total yards of penalties with the Loggers getting 150 of those penalty yards). EASCOM was led by the passing of coach-turned-player Frank Gagliardi. Carmody had the defensive line ready to play — the service newspaper, The Pacific Stars and Stripes, said that penalties plagued the Zama Ramblers, but "what stymied Zama most was an aggressive Logger forward wall which refused to let the vaunted Rambler ground attack get into high gear."

This set up the Far East Inter Service Championship game, also in Seoul and referred to as The Kimchi Bowl, against Johnson Air Force Base on December 1. However, the Loggers' winning streak came to an end as the Johnson AFB Vanguards beat EASCOM 30-10 to win the Far East Inter Service Championship. This introduction to coaching immediately stamped Carmody as a defensive coaching expert, holding all teams to 13 or fewer points — except for the 24th Division Artillery Redskins. Over the 12-game season the Loggers scored 437 points while giving up only 117 points. The season's successes gave Carmody confidence that he had indeed made the right decision to pursue a coaching career.

Rather than return to Munsan-Ni at the end of the football season, Carmody joined a basketball team EASCOM had put together. The team consisted almost entirely of Logger football players and was coached by Bob Ford, one of the Logger football coaches. The team, called the Ascom Rams, finished the season with a 16-8 record. Carmody had accrued sufficient unused leave so that his enlistment came to an end in April 1958, and he was honorably discharged two months ahead of schedule. Now Carmody could aggressively pursue his coaching goals.

Assistant Coach at Holy Cross

Coach Lou Brownson retired as Holy Cross head coach in 1956, and the Tigers immediately went into a tailspin having "two drastic seasons" in a row. The Tigers hired Jesuit's Ken Tarzetti to coach the 1957 team. Tarzetti then left Holy Cross to return to Jesuit when Blue Jay coach Eddie Toribio passed away. Tarzetti's brother-in-law, John Kalbacher, was an assistant on Tarzetti's staff at Holy Cross and moved up to the head coaching job when Tarzetti left. A long-standing duel between the two brothers-in-law had its beginning. Kalbacher was putting his coaching staff together when Carmody's brother-in-law, Vince "Pepe" Gonzalez, heard about an opening at Holy Cross and recommended his brother-in-law, Jim Carmody, fresh from a two-year stint in Korea, for the job. Gonzalez, who played for Holy Cross with Carmody and then played halfback for LSU, married Carmody's sister, Elizabeth, and was coaching high school in Baton Rouge. It did not hurt that the Holy Cross principal remembered Carmody from his high school days. Kalbacher hired Carmody shortly after they met, in time for the 1958 season. Jim spent most of the summer of 1958 meeting with Kalbacher, often at his home, to review the offensive and defensive game plans the Tigers would be using.

Carmody had secured his first paid coaching job and signed his first contract with Holy Cross on May 13, effective September, 1958-June, 1959. He was paid $4,000 to coach the defensive line and teach civics and serve as assistant track coach. Jim coached at Holy Cross for three years from 1958-60. Holy Cross went 7-1-2 in 1958, 7-3 in 1959, and fell somewhat to 5-5 in 1960. As successful as his teams were, Carmody is still irritated by the fact that Holy Cross lost to Jesuit all three years he coached, while as a player Holy Cross never lost to the Blue Jays. This explains his dislike for Jesuit to this day. When asked if he would have accepted an offer from Jesuit had it offered him his first paid high school coaching job, he answered emphatically, "No way!"

Kalbacher coached Holy Cross for 17 seasons, from 1958 until 1975, and ranks fifth among the Top 10 Catholic League Head Coaches by victories. Lou Brownson ranks tenth on that list. After his three years as a high school coach Carmody was ready to move into the college coaching ranks.

4

FAMILY LIFE

To understand Jim Carmody the coach, one has to understand Jim Carmody the family man, the husband, the father, for one is simply an extension of the other. Dedication, commitment, respect, discipline, loyalty and, yes, love are qualities and traits that apply to both his coaching profession and his family life.

Jim's sister, Elizabeth, attended St. Joseph Academy in New Orleans, and one of her best friends was a classmate, Earlyn Regouffre, whose mother, Beryl Lynn, was born in Thibodaux, Louisiana — right in the heart of Cajun country. Earlyn's father was born in New Orleans. Her given name was a contraction of her father and mother's names. Earlyn was nicknamed "Noonie" by her family (Noonie in Cajun refers to a baby pacifier but is also a nickname name given to the "most wanted child" in the family). She is still called Noonie to this date. Noonie was very close to her Thibodaux family — a large group that consisted of her parents and her grandparents, Alphonal and Louise. Noonie had two brothers.

Noonie grew up in the mid-town area of New Orleans near the Fairgrounds Race Track and went to both St. Rose and St. Leo The Great grammar schools. She then went to St. Joseph Academy where she met and became friends with Jim's sister, Elizabeth. When Jim was playing at Copiah-Lincoln Community College, his sister would often go watch him play. Noonie went along. Elizabeth introduced Jim to Noonie, and they started dating. Noonie and another friend, Barbara, would often go to Pontchartrain Beach Amusement Park and lay out on the beach, getting suntans. One day a man who worked for the park (it is tempting to speculate that the man could possibly have been Harry Batt, Jr., president of Pontchartrain Beach Amusement Park, or one of his sons who were known to be active promoters of beauty contests) talked the girls into entering beauty contests put on at the park. The girls liked the idea, and Noonie entered many beauty contests in New Orleans, finishing second in her first Junior Miss New Orleans contest, then winning the title in her second attempt. She then entered the Miss New Orleans contest finishing second in her first attempt and winning the title in her next. In 1957 she was named both Miss New Orleans and Miss Louisiana. Her relationship with Jim became more serious, reminding one of the lyrics to the

Noonie — Miss Audubon 1956
with George Douglass, Audubon Park Superintendent

song of the same name: "You've got to be a football hero to get along with the beautiful girls." — very apropos. Noonie graduated from high school in 1956 — the same year Jim graduated from Tulane. Jim and Noonie were married on January 2, 1960, (Jim fittingly remembers it was the day after the LSU-Ole Miss rematch in the Sugar Bowl).

Growing up in Jim Carmody's household was not too dissimilar from that of the childhood of writer Pat Conroy and his well-known literary father, the Great Santini, but without the verbal and physical abuse extremes administered by Conroy's father, Lt. Col. Bull Meechum. Discipline was the

Noonie — Miss Louisiana 1957
(Carmody Family Collection)

key to this relationship. Eldest son, Steve, likens his father to legendary football coach Vince Lombardi: "strong disciplinarian and demanding, a father who expected only your very best, but sensitive and caring in how he handled your faults and setbacks." Whatever the comparison, Noonie and Jim raised a highly close-knit family.

Being the wife of a football coach can be very demanding. Coaching kept Jim away from home a considerable amount of time, and Noonie ran the house, wrote the checks, paid the bills, etc. She says she and Jim have moved sixteen times, and each time she engineered the move. She said if her grand-

Noonie — Miss Louisiana 1957, Cover of Dixie Magazine
(Carmody Family Collection)

children ever chose coaching as a career and decided to get married she would encourage the wife-to-be to be a very independent person. But coaches' wives tend to be a very close-knit group, and many of Noonie's best friends are wives of fellow coaches.

Jim and Noonie had four "oak trees" as they referred to their sons (each of the four was 6'4" or taller). Steve, who was born at Ochsner Hospital in New Orleans in 1960; Brian, who was born in 1962 also at Ochsner; Keith, who was born in Lexington, Kentucky, in 1964; and Chris, who was born in Starkville in 1965. All were good athletes, and all have turned out to be highly successful. Steve and Keith both played for their father at Southern Mississippi. Steve lettered at center from 1980-83, and Keith lettered at center from 1985-86. Steve is a partner in the law firm of Brunini, Grantham, Grower and Hewes in Jackson, Mississippi, and following his final season at Southern in 1983 was named to the second team of the All-South Independent team and was invited to play in the East-West Shrine and Senior Bowl games. He was an Academic All-American, a Rhodes scholar finalist and won a NCAA National Merit Scholarship. He signed as a free agent with Denver of the NFL but decided to attend law school at Southern Methodist University. Brian was in the home construction business and now sells real estate in the Jackson area. Keith is in the home remodeling business in Jackson, and Chris is an inspector with Willis Engineering in Grenada, Mississippi.

Jim and Noonie are the grandparents of six grandchildren, all of whom are excellent athletes. Steve's son Connor played tight end and wide receiver (breaking the string of Carmody centers) for Jackson Academy and won the state championship in the discus, and his daughter, Mackenzie, was an excellent track, softball, and basketball player, also at Jackson Academy. Keith's son, Chase, played (not surprisingly) center at Southwest Community College and Delta State University. He is the only Carmody grandchild to pursue a career in coaching. Chase graduated from the Law School at Ole Miss and passed the Mississippi bar examination, but instead of practicing law he has chosen a coaching career and is currently the defensive coordinator and defensive line coach at Pearl High School in Pearl, Mississippi. Keith's daughter, Caitlin, played softball for Madison Central, and his youngest daughter,

Mary Blair, runs track and plays basketball at Germantown High School in Madison. Chris' daughter, Caroline, plays soccer at Grenada. No doubt that athletics runs deep in the Carmody bloodline.

The author has known Chase since he was ten years old or so. When taking Jim and Chase to their automobiles following an Ole Miss football game I asked Chase what he would like to be one day. To my amazement he said he wanted to be a marine biologist. I was stunned with that unusual reply from a ten-year-old and, therefore, was surprised when he chose a career in coaching football over a career in the law. In one sense, Jim is a mentor for Chase — when asked.

Raising four active sons made the Carmody household an often-raucous place. Brian tells the following stories:

"I always used to laugh when players would tell me how tough and hard he was. There are many stories about lessons he used to teach us growing up and the methods he used to demonstrate his point — almost always by example. There are numerous stories but one of my favorites was his lesson on hard work. One day in Oxford he came home in a borrowed truck with the bed full of old railroad crossties. He had promised Mother he would build her a dedicated rose bed, one we could not destroy. I would say our ages at the time were 13, 12, 10, and 9. These were not the old light rotten crossties, but heavy ones weighing about 200 pounds each. He parked at the street, and we slaved to unload the truck one crosstie by one, with three of us on one end, and Dad and I on the other. Why he didn't drive the truck closer to the bed I have no idea. After moving all the crossties we thought we were done, but oh no. We had to move the ties around and place them in the exact position to be marked for cutting to assure a perfect fit. So, one by one we moved them again and prepared for cutting. Dad came out with a big hacksaw and a hand saw. He was taking his turn as well, but when he tired, he would put the saw in one of our hands. At this time it was down to just Steve and I as helpers. I think we had cut through about 5 or 6 of the ties, and seeing the futile process, Steve says to Dad, 'You know our neighbors the Threadgills have a chain saw we can probably borrow, if you will let me go ask them.'" The look he got is one of those you never forget, and in a very stern voice he replied, "No, son, that's the easy way to do it. Life isn't always easy, and you must appreciate the meaning of hard work." And back to sawing we went.

"And there was the time when he was coaching at North Carolina, and we were probably 10, 9, 7, and 6 years old. After an afternoon of playing in the neighborhood and one of us getting into a fight, we returned home. I think it was Keith who got his butt whipped by an older kid in the neighborhood. He came home crying and all and told Dad what had happened. Dad immediately summoned all of us, and the interrogation began. We got the long talk that evening and a butt whipping to go with it about taking up for and backing up your brothers. That never happened again, and if you fought one of us, you had better be prepared to fight all four if you happened to get the better of the first one. Just another life lesson."

"There are numerous summertime stories because that is the only time we ever saw him. Several stories of the time we were at North Carolina come to mind, like the BB gun incident; the dump truck load of cow manure in our back yard; hours of meticulous yard work required (twig story, grass cutting perfectionist, etc.); the time we got caught smoking as kids (he made us eat a cigarette); the backing-out-of-the-driveway-and-running-over-the-mailbox story; Dad playing barber and cutting all of our hair with electric clippers when we were all very young because he refused to pay the $6 each for haircuts for the four of us."

Brian went on to tell about playing golf with his dad and his blue collar group at the old USM golf course (he had a membership to the country club but would not play there) "taught me more about people than anything. The man was a tight wad to the extreme... he always put his wallet and change on his closet shelf (which was organized in military fashion with two-finger spacing between the hangers), and he knew to the penny how much he left there. I took a quarter one time, which was a mistake."

Brian recalled a summer vacation in 1973 when Nasty was at UNC. "We didn't get to vacation very often, but this summer was special. Wrightsville Beach, North Carolina, here we come! Dad somehow hooked us up with a beach house just a couple of blocks from the beach. What a glorious week. For us, anyway. Kids everywhere to play with, and especially right next door to our cottage. We became friends quickly (the kids that is). After the first day, Dad realized who was next door to us. It was Coach Lou Holtz and his family. Coach Holtz was at the time the head coach of North Carolina State, a bitter rival of The University of North Carolina (UNC). Coach Lou was probably my entertainment for the week, even more than his beautiful daughter Lou Ann, who I was also smitten with. Coach Lou was the life of the party, telling us stories and doing card tricks inside his family's cabin. My brothers and I had a blast with the family. I think we spent more time in Lou's house than we did at the beach. Dad would have to send someone over to get us after dark because he wouldn't step foot on the property occupied by the enemy. I am sure at some time they spoke to each other, but I don't recall that happening. I think someone set him up!"

Another Brian recollection: "When we went home after church we immediately had to hang up all of our church clothes, make our beds, pass inspection, and then we could eat lunch. There wasn't any of this laying-around-watching-TV-all-afternoon stuff. If he caught you hanging around inside, he would find meticulous chores for you to do. He had a famous saying that remains embedded in our minds: 'If you ain't got nothing to do, I can find something for you to do.'"

Jim tells the story about a BB gun incident that took place when he was coaching at North Carolina. "It was dark when I got home so it must have been during the football season. Noonie talked to me about a problem that had taken place at the house. We lived close to our neighbor, with just a driveway dividing the houses, and one of the boys had fired a BB gun in the back yard. The pellet went through an upstairs window at the neighbor's house and broke the window. Our neighbor was a music teacher at the university, a really proper family. The neighbor told Jim later that he and his young son were upstairs around 7 or 8 o'clock saying their goodnight prayers, the son in bed and the father on his knees when, boom, the window broke. The neighbor said, 'Sniper!' He pulled his son from the bed to the floor, and they crawled along the floor to the steps, and when he got to the steps he called out 'Call the police; there's a sniper here!' The police came, but in the meantime, since they were told there is a sniper involved, they called the FBI. So FBI agents arrive and check out the driveway, found no one there, and they did not know exactly where the shot came from. The back yards of the Carmodys and their neighbor sloped steeply down into a ravine and a wooded area between the next street over and us. So the FBI is back there with flashlights, searching for a sniper. One of the FBI guys falls into the ravine. That did not go over too well; the guy has his suit on and all that. So they finally did what they should have done to begin with and checked the hole in the windowpane. They went upstairs into the kid's room and saw just a small hole and said, 'This was probably a BB gun. They asked the neighbor, 'Who lives next door. They came knocking on the Carmodys' door and started asking questions, and they started grilling the kids, one by one. They took the kids into a room one at a time. Of course there's this guy sitting there with his wet suit on, and he's pissed off. They know by now a sniper is not involved. One of the boys fessed up, and they all deny today who is the one. I think it was Brian, but I am not sure. All of this has taken place before I got home, and the FBI is gone; the Chapel Hill police are gone, and Noonie is steaming. She is livid; she told Jim, 'Did you know the FBI was just here?' Nothing came of it except to this day nobody will tell who shot the gun. They all blame it on Brian, but Brian denies it. But he would not say who it was. It was Stephen's gun that he bought with money he made on his paper route and kept it under his bed between the mattress and the springs because I always told them they could not have a BB gun. Somebody got the gun out and shot that guy's window out. I still don't know who shot the gun. Maybe one of them will confess one day. On top of all that, one day Chris got into the neighbor's car parked in the driveway near the sloping back yard and released the brake, and the car rolled down that sloping back yard into the ravine. Eventually, the boys ran that neighbor off."

In Keith's "confession," he today tells a version of the BB gun story that is slightly different than his dad's: "In North Carolina Steve had purchased a BB gun without the knowledge of our parents. He had it hid above his ceiling in his bedroom. One night I decided I wanted to shoot it so I took it outside and aimed at a neighbor's upstairs bedroom window. I pulled the trigger and thought I didn't hit anything, so I shot again. The lights in that window

Carmody Family, circa 1978
L-R Steve, Jim, Brian, Chris, Noonie, Keith (Carmody family Collection)

went out, and I went inside. About ten or fifteen minutes later a bunch of police and FBI agents were in our back yard trying to determine where the 'sniper' took the shot. The neighbor was a professor at UNC and was from Russia, and he had called the police and FBI saying that a sniper was trying to assassinate him. The police and Mom questioned Steve and Brian about the incident, and they said that they did not shoot a gun at the window. Just as the police were fixing to leave, my mother came and asked me if I had shot the BB gun at the window, and I told her it was me. She wanted to know why I didn't say anything. My reply was, 'You never asked me if I knew anything.'

Can't remember what kind of punishment I received for that one. I think Steve had gotten in more trouble than I did."

Keith tells more stories about growing up with Big Nasty. Like the cigarettes story: "Steve and Brian had taken some cigarettes out of Mom's purse, and I followed them down to the ditch behind our house, where they smoked them. They tried to get me to smoke one, and I refused and went back to the house and told my mom what they were doing; she was not happy. When Dad got home he took all three of us to the back of the house and made each of us eat a cigarette. I asked him why I had to [since] I didn't smoke anything, and he said, 'You were with them.'"

Or the story about pine trees: "When we lived in Oxford we had a house that had a bunch of pine trees in the front yard. When we did something to get in trouble, Dad would sometimes make us go outside and pick up every little twig in the yard, and you better not miss one. I think that came from his army days of cleaning a bathroom floor with a toothbrush."

Or about staying out late: "In high school he always knew when you stayed out a little bit too late because he would come and wake you up at 7 a.m. to cut the grass and say, 'If you're going to hoot with the owls at night, you better be ready to soar with the eagles in morning.'"

Youngest son Chris had a few stories about the way Jim gave the boys life lessons: "One time in NC this guy comes to our home and told Dad it was unfair, that the Carmody boys were picking on his sons. Dad said, 'Well, let the boys fight it out, and let's settle this thing.' The guy went home and brought back his sons and some boxing gloves. Steve and Brian fought the guy's two boys, whipped them soundly, and they had no more problems."

Chris said he was 15 years old and had just gotten his driver's license, so he and a buddy picked up some beer and drove around. They parked to sip some beer, but a cop caught them and brought them home. When Carmody got home Noonie told him what happened, but Jim did not say anything. "He didn't talk about what happened to me that day, but at 6 o'clock the next morning he woke me up, told me to take a shower, and put on some good clothes. No hint at what was coming next. When I got dressed Dad drove me down to the end of the main drag in Hattiesburg, Hardy Street, and told me to get out of the car and then told me do not come home until I got a job. I could not believe my dad would just drive off and leave me there. I pulled myself together and started down the street. No luck. I called Mom and told her no jobs were available: 'Come get me.' Mom told me that Dad was serious; don't come home until you get a job. I really started looking harder but had no success. Halfway down Hardy Street I called Mom again and said, 'Nobody's hiring, come get me.'"

Noonie told him to go see Mr. Buckley, who ran a Captain John's Seafood place.

Chris recalled, "I found Mr. Buckley and asked for a job. Buckley said it just so happened that he needed a busboy. I began work immediately and have worked every day of my life since then."

Chris went on. "I remember being in Buffalo and going to the Buffalo Bills' practices. When practice was over I went into the locker room and saw Conrad Dobler, an offensive guard. Dobler said to me, 'You must be CC's boy.'"

He asked him why he called his dad CC, and Dobler told him that it meant "college coach."

Chris continued, "But I also remember how humble Dad could be, in addition to being so tough. When he got the USM head-coaching job, they gave him a white Cadillac. Dad had been driving an old Ford LTD, so this was quite a step up. But Dad gave Mom the Cadillac and continued to drive that old LTD.

"When I was 15 years old I asked Dad if I could go to Mardi Gras in New Orleans. Dad gave me permission but told me to stay on the right side of the street. A buddy and I went down to join the party on Bourbon Street. We sat on a police barricade, drinking beer. The police told us to get off the barricade and keep moving. My buddy gave the policeman a hard time, refusing to get off the barricade. The police arrested both of us and took us to jail. I was finally able to make a phone call to my grandmother and asked her to come get me out of jail. Mr. Warren Doussan came to get me out and told me that everything was going to be okay, not to worry. Knowing Dad, I kept worrying what he was going to do to me, and Mr. Doussan again told me not to worry, everything would be okay. I asked how he could keep saying that knowing my dad. Doussan told me, 'Don't worry; your dad was young once, and he will understand.'"

5

Coaching at the College Level

After his stints at coaching at the armed services level in Korea and the high school level at Holy Cross, Carmody was ready to make the jump to coaching at the college level. Thus his long journey as a head coach, assistant head coach, assistant coach, defensive coordinator, and defensive line coach began at his alma maters, Tulane and Holy Cross.

Tulane University (1961-62)

As Carmody wrapped up his third year at Holy Cross he felt prepared to move into the college coaching ranks. Fortunately, the freshman football-coaching job opened up at Tulane when Joe Blaylock moved up to join Coach Andy Pilney's varsity staff. With Pilney's full support Jim was hired as the freshman coach. Pilney knew Carmody very well since Jim played for Pilney when Jim was at Tulane. Pilney said, "We know Jim will do a good job for us. He is familiar with our system, is well respected by our coaches and also by the coaches of this area, and has a warm, sincere personality, which is so vital to our recruiting." Jim was eager to make the jump to the college ranks — he and Noonie had just had their first child, Steve.

Jim's freshmen had a good season, but the varsity did not, finishing 2-8 in 1961. Pilney's eight-year career as the head coach of the Green Wave came to an end. Not only had the Greenies been shut out five times in 1961 but also their final game of the season ended in a 62-0 loss to LSU. A group of alumni calling themselves "Friends of Tulane" held a meeting just prior to the LSU game. The meeting was attended by an estimated four hundred angry alumni and fans who made several recommendations designed to restore Tulane to its days of glory. The number one recommendation was to hire a new head coach. Tulane President Herbert Longenecker met with leaders of this group at the end of the season, and Pilney resigned on November 26 — the day after the overwhelming loss to LSU. Pilney's career record at Tulane was 25-49-6. Stunning upset victories against Auburn in 1955, Ole Miss in 1956, and Navy in the 1958 Oyster Bowl in Norfolk, Virginia, were not enough to overcome his overall record. The de-emphasis of football at Tulane had taken another victim.

Tulane turned to one of its own to restore the program. Former Tulane All-American lineman Tommy O'Boyle, an assistant to Andy Pilney in 1961, was promoted to head football coach for the 1962 season. O'Boyle played on the 1939 Tulane team that finished the regular season unbeaten and lost a 14-13 decision to Texas A&M in the Sugar Bowl. O'Boyle had a successful career as head coach at Southwest Missouri State University from 1947-48, compiling a 16-4-1 record. And he had coached at Kansas State, Duke, and Miami.

When O'Boyle was hired, Tulane President Herbert Longenecker said the new coach would be free to name his own assistants. O'Boyle ended up firing the entire 1961 coaching staff — all except Jim Carmody, who was retained as the freshman coach. O'Boyle said, "I have selected Jim as our freshman coach for several reasons. I believe that fundamentals are the most important thing a freshman coach can teach his team, and Jim was great at this. His boys are well conditioned and soundly disciplined. Jim has an enthusiastic approach to his job as well as his recruiting duties. I feel that he will be one of my very valuable assistants, not just as a coach but also in recruiting. A freshman coach is not just a football coach, but he must be a father and a good listener to these young men. I was favorably impressed with the job Carmody did. I welcome his enthusiastic response to my request to stay and help accomplish the tremendous job that lies ahead of us."

When Tulane's freshmen played the LSU freshmen, Tulane was out-manned and out-gunned, yet Carmody attracted the praise of a New Orleans sports writer, who wrote, "Carmody has imagination, a flair for the different and the courage to try something new when the odds are eyebrow-high against him. Carmody knew his Baby Billow was outgunned and outmanned by the Tigertown Terrors. But he devised a little system he called his 'Alley-Oop' offense. 'Really nothing much to it,' Carmody said modestly the day after the game. 'It was just something I thought I'd use to confuse 'em for a minute. It was not much, but I wanted them to have something to think about.'" The sportswriter continued, "O'Boyle made a smart move by keeping Alley Oop on his staff. Maybe he can put up something to keep the enemy guessing next fall. With the murderous schedule, O'Boyle can use all the help he can muster."

Taking a shot at Andy Pilney soon after he was hired, O'Boyle was quoted as saying, "A man should never let himself get in position to get beat 62-0." These were words O'Boyle would come to regret. His 1962 team posted a 0-10 record, the first Green Wave squad to go winless since the 1910 team finished 0-7. Tulane was outscored 293-76. In 1965 Tulane went 2-8, giving O'Boyle a career record at Tulane of 6-33-1. In the final game of O'Boyle's Tulane coaching career, LSU defeated Tulane 62-0!

University of Kentucky (1963)

After the 1962 season Carmody thought it was time to make a change. His entire college football experience was at Tulane and Co-Lin, first as a player and then at Tulane as a coach. It was time to expand his experiences. He wanted to learn a new system and meet new coaches. He had always been impressed with the system Bear Bryant put into place, and he wanted to be associated with someone who knew that system, knew how to recruit, how to practice effectively, how to make out offensive and defensive game plans. His old Army coaching buddy, Bob Ford, was an assistant on Charlie Bradshaw's staff at the University of Kentucky.

Bradshaw had been named head coach at Kentucky in 1962 after serving as an assistant coach on Bear Bryant's staff at Alabama that won the 1961 national championship. Bradshaw coached the Kentucky team known as the "Thin Thirty," so called because of the 88 players he inherited, only 30 survived the rigorous Bradshaw program — reminiscent of Bear Bryant's Junction City Camp. Bradshaw played at Kentucky and began his career as an assistant there under Bryant. He coached with Bryant at Alabama for three years before accepting the Kentucky position. If anyone knew the Bryant system, it was Charlie Bradshaw.

Bob Ford played center and end for Memphis State and received a bachelor's degree in 1955 and a master's degree in 1956 while helping coach the Memphis State freshman team. He entered the U.S. Army in 1956 and was stationed in Korea, where he and Carmody coached the 8th Army football team. Ford knew the head basketball coach at Memphis State, Eugene Lambert, and when Lambert left Memphis in the fall of 1956 to take over the Alabama basketball program, Ford asked Lambert to introduce him to Bear Bryant. Ford wanted to be a graduate assistant, and when he and Bryant met, Bear offered to help Ford out. Ford worked with the team's centers and linebackers and scouted future Alabama opponents. Bryant then gave Ford a paid position for the 1959 and 1960 seasons, when he became familiar with another assistant coach, Charlie Bradshaw. Ford then joined the University of Georgia football staff at a salary three times greater than what he was making at Alabama. After one year at Georgia, Bradshaw offered Ford the defensive coordinator position on his new staff at Kentucky. Ford introduced Carmody to Bradshaw at a coaching conference, and Carmody was offered a position on Bradshaw's staff as freshman coach and assistant coach. Ford and Carmo-

1963 The University of Kentucky coaching staff — Jim Carmody 3rd from left
(Carmody (Family Collection)

dy remained lifetime friends.

Carmody's 1963 freshman team went undefeated (playing four freshman games) and beat Tennessee 70-0 in the final game. Carmody said, "We had a helluva team." On the weekend Kentucky traveled to Nashville to play a winless, and seemingly hapless, Vanderbilt team, Carmody's freshmen had a Monday game. He approached Bradshaw and asked that since if his freshmen, who were scheduled to play on Monday, could stay home and prepare for their game. Bradshaw said that should be no problem. Carmody listened to the game and was discouraged that the Wildcats played so poorly. He was embarrassed that the team was held to a scoreless tie. On Sunday morning, Carmody went to 7 o'clock Mass as he usually did and then went to the dining hall. No one was there. Jim asked the housemother where everybody was, and she said, "Coach, they are at practice. They started practice at 5:00 am." Carmody asked what time the team got back from Nashville. The housemother said, "Coach, it must have been 1 or 2 o'clock. I don't think many of the players went to sleep."

Carmody jumped back into his car and drove to the practice field, changed clothes, and went to the field. It appeared to be pure mayhem — coaches and players yelling and screaming, and he approached Bradshaw. "Coach I didn't know anything about this."

Bradshaw said, "Hell, it was not your f****** fault. You didn't have anything to do with it. It was the players' and coaches' fault."

Carmody recalled that it was hot, despite being November weather, and the early morning practice was brutal, players lying all over the field, coaches tackling players. Carmody remembers it was more like a street fight than anything else. "I've seen everything now," he thought.

Adolph Rupp

Carmody enjoys telling Coach Adolph Rupp stories from the time he spent at Kentucky. One of the highlights of Carmody's one-year stay at Kentucky was being assigned an office in Memorial Coliseum next door to legendary Kentucky basketball coach Adolph Rupp's office. Rupp, considered one of the greatest college basketball coaches of all time, played for the legendary

Phog Allen (assisting Allen at that time was his former coach and inventor of the game of basketball, James Naismith) at the University of Kansas. In his 41-year head basketball coaching career (1930-72), Rupp is still ranked sixth in total wins, with a total of 876 victories in spite of expanded schedules and post-season playoffs that have taken place in today's modern game. For example, entering the 2015-16 season, career coaching leader Mike Krzyzewski has compiled 150 more victories than coach Rupp but has coached in nearly 300 more games. Rupp has a .822 winning percentage compared to Krzyzewski's .766 winning percentage. Rupp is a legend in the game, and Carmody felt in awe at having an office next door to The Baron's office.

Rupp's longtime assistant coach, Harry Lancaster, had an office right across the hall from Rupp and Carmody. Lancaster was an assistant basketball coach and freshman basketball coach for Rupp for 22 years and doubled as Kentucky's head baseball coach for 16 seasons over a two-stint period (1947 and 1951-65). He served as Kentucky's athletic director from 1969 until 1975, and thus was Rupp's boss from 1969 to Rupp's retirement in 1972. The Lancaster Aquatic Center at the University of Kentucky is named in his honor.

The desk in Carmody's office was right against the wall to Rupp's office, so he could not help but hear Rupp talking. One day, after the end of the 1963 football season, Carmody could hear Rupp talking loudly with a prospect who was in for a visit while Lancaster paced nervously in his office waiting for the prospect to come out. Carmody could hear Rupp say, "So, son, we are offering you a scholarship, and I want you to come here to play for the University of Kentucky."

The recruit said, "Well, Coach I really appreciate it. I really like Kentucky, but I am not ready to make a decision at this time."

Coach Rupp said, "Well, by God, it's time you made a decision." (Coach Rupp said by God a lot.)

Rupp said, "We need to know something."

The recruit said, "Well, Coach, I have some more visits to make, and I am contemplating some other schools, but right now I really like Kentucky the best, but I am not in a position to make a commitment."

Rupp said, "Son, I cannot believe that I am giving you a opportunity to play for the greatest coach in America, on the greatest basketball team in America, with the greatest prestige of any school playing basketball in America, and you are standing there telling me well, by God, I am not ready to make a decision."

Rupp then called across the hall and said, "Harry, come get this guy."

The recruit was Wes Unseld, who would have been the first black player for Rupp. Unseld went to Louisville, was an All-American, and then had a great NBA career, where he made the NBA Hall of Fame. Rupp did not sign a black player until he signed Tom Payne in 1971. Payne became the first African-American to play basketball for Kentucky.

Carmody told other Rupp stories. Right across the street from the coliseum was a place called "The Huddle." One day Rupp stuck his head in Carmody's office and said, "Young Fella (for some reason Rupp always called Carmody "Young Fella" — Carmody said, "Here I was, 30 years old, and he was calling me 'Young Fella.'" — "would you like to go across to the Huddle with Harry and I and have some chili?"

Carmody could not pass up an offer like this and said, "Yes, sir."

As they were walking down the hall in the coliseum, the threesome ran into the Kentucky swimming coach.

Coach Rupp said "Coach, congratulations on your season."

The swimming coach said, "Coach, I appreciate that, but you know we didn't win a meet."

Rupp said, "Well, by God, nobody drowned."

On another occasion Carmody was walking to his car in the crowded parking lot. Parking was always tight. He saw Coach Rupp in his characteristic brown suit, kneeling on the ground and working on a tire. Carmody thought he had a flat tire, but he saw that Rupp was not fixing the tire, he was letting air out of the tire. About that time this guy comes walking up to the car — it was his car. He asked, "What are you doing, sir?"

Coach Rupp looked at the guy and said, "Is this your goddam car?"

"Yes, sir," was the reply.

Rupp said, "Well, by God, what do you do?"

The guy said, "I am an English professor here."

Rupp said, "No damn wonder all my players are flunking English; you can't even damn read. Look, it says R-U-P-P right on the parking spot. By God, what are you doing parking in my spot?"

The professor answered, "Well, Coach, there was no place else to park."

Rupp replied, "That is not a good reason. Well, by God, I am going to let it all out."

Rupp continued to let the air out, and the professor pleaded, "Please, Coach, don't do that. I am going to have to change the tire."

Rupp said, "That's the damn idea. You're going to have to change this tire, huh? I am getting hot and sweaty. By God, I'm going to let it all out." And he did.

Another day Carmody asked Rupp if he could watch a practice. Carmody knew that Rupp conducted great practices that strongly emphasized basketball fundamentals and overall discipline, stressing individual instructions, but that he always conducted practice behind closed doors. Carmody felt he could learn a lot about coaching football just watching Rupp's team practice basketball. Carmody asked Rupp if he could watch a practice one day. Rupp answered, "Well, by God, we are going to start at such and such a time. You can come for the first ten minutes."

Rupp always held closed practices, so Carmody thought this was a big deal. Carmody decided to watch one practice, standing in the bleachers behind a goal — the only non-player or non-coach there. He was convinced that Rupp knew he was there. He observed a drill during which no coaches or players spoke.

Jim said, "The players just passed balls from one to the other, making layups. The only sound was that of the balls slapping the players' hands, the swish of the nets and feet squeaking on the court. It was very eerie. It was very precision-like, not a mistake made during the full-speed drills.

Rupp never said anything to him, but Jim said, "I bet he knew I was only there for ten minutes. The only people other than players who were out there were me and him and Harry."

Carmody recognized a few players like Pat Riley, Cotton Nash, and Larry Conley. Carmody learned much in that ten-minute period that he could apply to football, especially about precision and the fact that a coach can be effective without yelling at the players. "It was a good teaching lesson, and I was trying to learn everything I could."

It was an eventful year for Carmody. His third son, Keith, was born in Lexington. Carmody recalls having lunch at a diner in Florence, Kentucky, on November 23, 1963, when news about the Kennedy assassination came over the television. The revelation that the assassin, Lee Harvey Oswald, had a New Orleans connection — that he attended the same high school, Warren Easton, that Jim's lifelong friend Bruce Howe had also attended — made the assassination much too personal. He also remembers after dinner at home watching the Ed Sullivan show on February 9, 1964, when the Beatles made their U.S. initial appearance. Carmody said to Noonie, "This is the end of civilization as we know it. This country will never be the same. And he was right.

Fortunately, Carmody learned much about the Bryant system but not the entire system as modified by Bradshaw, who carried Bryant's tough conditioning and discipline building program too far. Bradshaw, in the book The Thin Thirty, by Shannon Ragland, is accused of coaching brutal, abusive, brainwashing football when he first arrived at Kentucky. But Carmody said that he learned more football in the one year under Bradshaw than he did in the previous six years of coaching in Korea, Holy Cross, and Tulane. Jim thought a lot of Bradshaw as an individual, a teacher, a leader, and a coach.

Mississippi State (1964-66)

Carmody had the opportunity to become a full-time defensive line coach at an SEC school when Mississippi State head coach Paul Davis offered him the position of defensive line coach. Carmody recalls also receiving a pay raise in the amount of $1,400 as an additional motivating factor. Also, Starkville was a lot closer to New Orleans than Lexington. Carmody had met Davis a few times and liked him. Davis played football (center and fullback), basketball (guard), and baseball (first base) at Ole Miss in the 1940s and, like so many others, served in the armed forces during World War II. He served nearly three years in the military including seven months in the European and Rhineland campaigns, and he was awarded a Purple Heart. Following his military service he came back to Ole Miss in 1946 and played for Ole Miss Coach Red Drew. Davis was named head football coach at Mississippi State from 1962-66 after serving as an assistant coach there in 1960 and 1961. Although his overall record there was a disappointing 20-38-2, his 1963 team defeated North Carolina State on a frozen field in bitter cold temperatures in the Liberty Bowl, which at that time was played in Philadelphia, Pennsylvania, at John F. Kennedy Stadium. Davis was named U.P.I. SEC Coach of the Year. In 1966 State finished with a 2-8 record and Davis was dismissed.

When Carmody first arrived at State he met Billy Tohill, who told him a bizarre story about the 1962 season. Tohill had played fullback for Mississippi State, stayed on the staff as a graduate assistant and then had become a full-time assistant, coaching running backs. Coach Davis wanted Tohill to "walk on" the University of Florida football team. At the time the NCAA

Coaching Staff 1964 — Coach Paul Davis (front Row 3rd from left), Carmody (back row far left), Billy Tohill (back row, 2nd from right), David "Dog" Owens (back row, 4th from right) (Carmody Family Collection)

regulations regarding walk-ons was quite lax — anyone could walk on to a team with any coach's permission. Regulations are much tougher these days. For example, walk-ons now are required to submit transcripts, must pick up a walk-on/practice compliance review form from the head coach, complete it, and have the head coach sign the form. The student must be also be registered with the NCAA Initial Eligibility Clearinghouse and meet with the athletic trainer and show proof of a recent physical exam to gain medical clearance and to show proof of insurance. When all the paperwork has been completed, the compliance office will determine if the student is eligible to practice with the team, and a memo will be sent to the coach informing him or her of the decision. Back then you could just walk on.

Tohill was stunned — he had already played fullback for Mississippi State during the 1958-60 seasons and obviously had no eligibility left. Besides, he told Davis he had not played football in a good while and was not in playing shape. Davis told him, "You're in good shape, Billy. You can make it." Davis had the idea that if Tohill could walk on the Gator team, he could learn a lot about Florida's game plan against MSU since the two teams would meet early in the 1962 season. Davis thought that since Tohill had played offense for MSU, Florida would put him on the scout team offense, and he would be able to learn Florida's defensive schemes since they would be running MSU-type defenses getting ready to play the Bulldogs. Davis told Tohill to telephone him every day and give him a report. Tohill finally agreed and went to the Florida coach's office (Ray Graves was the head coach at the time), told them that he had played high school football, had gone into the service for two or three years, and asked if he could walk on. He was told to check out his equipment, and at the first of the two-a-day practices they told him to play fullback. Since he had not played for several years, he took a beating. Tohill called Davis after the first morning practice and said, "Yeah, Coach, they are running the 50 scheme and getting ready to put in what we do on the option."

Davis told him, "That's great, Billy, really great. Call me this afternoon and tell me what else has happened."

After the second practice Tohill told Davis they were doing the same thing.

The next day, after morning practice Tohill told Davis, "Coach, I need to come home — they switched me to defense. They put me at nose guard. Coach, I never played down in the line; I can't do this."

Davis was delighted since now Tohill could observe Florida's offensive game plan against MSU. Davis told Tohill to stay there and do the best he could.

Tohill called Davis after practice and asked if he could come home. Davis said, "Billy, we've been through all this. I told you what you had to do. Do you want to continue coaching here?"

"But coach, my arms and hands are hurting," said Tohill.

Davis told him to get more equipment.

Tohill stayed, nonetheless, and the next day called Davis and told him now his nose was all cut up, that his helmet was coming down and cutting his nose.

Tohill stayed all through the two-a-day practices. Davis told him that after the last practice before school starts to get his clothes and pack his car late at night and come on back but not to tell anybody — to make it look like another walk-on quit. When Tohill got back to Starkville hardly anybody recognized him. He was all cut up; his nose was cut; there were scrapes on his chin, and arms were bruised. He looked like hell, like he had been to Corregidor. Davis's ploy did not work, however. Florida defeated MSU 19-9 in the season opener in Jackson.

A graduate assistant at MSU recalls the Friday afternoon workout before the game. When he went into the MSU locker room, he saw that game programs had been set out for the Saturday game. He knew about Tohill's travels to Florida and was worried that Tohill's photograph would show up among the MSU coaching staff, and sure enough it was. The assistant then thought that game programs would possibly be placed in the visiting team's locker room, and he was afraid a Florida player or coach would recognize Tohill's photograph as a Florida "walk-on." He went to the visiting team locker room, and saw a large number of programs ready for distribution. The assistant confiscated all the game programs before the Florida team arrived and put them in the trunk of his car so that Tohill's secret would be kept.

Tohill left MSU in 1965 to become an assistant at Tulane for five years before joining the TCU staff in 1971 under head coach, Jim Pittman. When Pittman died midway through the 1971, season Tohill became head coach. Not a bad career for a walk-on!

Coming off an excellent 1963 season, Bulldog staff and fans were disappointed that their record fell to 4-6. The season began on a sour note as MSU dropped its season opener at Texas Tech 21-7. Then came two heartbreaking losses to Florida, 16-13 in Jackson, and 14-13 to Tennessee in Memphis. They bounced back to put together a three-game winning streak, beating Tulane, Southern Mississippi, and Houston in Starkville. The season was comprised of three game streaks as State lost its next three games to Alabama in Jackson and then to Auburn and LSU on the road.

As disappointed as State was, the season ended on a strong note as State ended a 17-game winless streak against Ole Miss, beating the Rebels 20-17 in Oxford before a crowd of 30,000 in cold weather with a brisk 10-knot wind out of the north. The game was nationally televised on NBC-TV. Ole Miss was coming off a winning but disappointing season themselves at 5-4-1, while State came into the game sporting a 3-6 record. Ole Miss had recorded four 10-win seasons in the past five years under Johnny Vaught and had not lost to State since 1947. In a classic defensive struggle, the Rebels jumped off to a 3-0 lead, but State replied with two Justin Canale field goals, the second coming on the final play before halftime. Both Vaught and Davis thought that the last-second Canale field goal before halftime was the big play of the game. MSU then scored on a 17-yard pass to take a 13-3 lead — the Bulldogs had not scored that many points against Ole Miss in 12 years. With five minutes left in the game the Rebels cut the lead to 13-10 and were driving for the lead when Carmody's defense intercepted a Jimmy Weatherly pass and returned it to the Ole Miss 6-yard line. State's great running back, Hoyle Granger, then scored to give MSU a ten-point lead. The Rebels would not quit and drove the ball 80 yards to cut the lead to 20-17 with 1:29 to go. State got the ensuing kickoff and held on to win the game 20-17. A newspaper reporter wrote, "It was tremendous line play of the Bulldog defenders that told the final story."

This was the first game Vaught lost to Mississippi State in the rivalry. Paul Davis said, "We were past due." State fans and students were so excited that MSU President Dean W. Colvard declared the following Monday as a university holiday and cancelled all classes.

Carmody recalled, "Man, that was a big deal back then. The game was on national TV and Vaught had just dominated State. It was such a big deal the president cancelled classes the following Monday. I remember that."

Photo left -right: Carmody, MSU head coach Paul Davis and defensive ends coach Vic Spooner (MSU Sports Collection)

The 1965 season, despite an excellent 4-0 start, was equally disappointing. The Bulldogs won their opener against Houston and then travelled to Gainesville to take on the No. 8 nationally ranked Florida Gators, who were led by their great quarterback Steve Spurrier. MSU upset Spurrier and the Gators 18-13. State rallied from a 13-6 halftime deficit but jumped ahead and held on, thanks to a gutty defensive effort in the closing moments.

Florida drove to the State 10-yard line, where it faced a game-deciding fourth-and-two situation. Spurrier, who completed 17 passes in 36 attempts for 211 yards and one touchdown, then overthrew a receiver in the end zone. Paul Davis said, "This is the second biggest win that any State team I've coached has achieved, the top one being last year's win over Ole Miss... our defense deserves credit for holding Spurrier down as well as we did."

Then State defeated Tampa and then whipped Southern Mississippi 27-9. State was 4-0 and off and running. The State defense yielded only 29 points in those first four games. Then the roof fell in as State lost their final six games with the State defense yielding 143 points in those games. The season ended when Ole Miss gained revenge for its 1964 loss by shutting out State 21-0.

If the 1965 season could be called disappointing, then the 1966 season was a disaster. State opened the season, losing to Georgia and Florida, then coming back to win the next two against Richmond and Southern Mississippi, but then losing their next five games (Houston, Florida State, Alabama, Auburn, and LSU). The Bulldogs lost the Egg Bowl to Ole Miss 24-0 to finish the year at 2-8. The shutout loss to rival Ole Miss was unacceptable to the administration, and Davis was dismissed along with most of his coaching staff. The only good news for Carmody that season was that his Army coaching buddy, Bob Ford, had joined Davis' staff at the start of the season, and they got to work together once again — even if for only one season.

Carmody said as bad as the season was there were some funny moments. Two of the State coaches, Leonard McCullough and Dave "Dog" Owens, were friends of comedian Jerry Clower, who was from Yazoo City and had played football at MSU. Carmody shared an office with McCullough. Every time Clower was in Starkville he would drop by to see his friends. Carmody says, "If you thought Clower was funny, you should have heard McCullough and Owens. Owens would mispronounce almost everything, slaughtering the English language. That season we were under the gun. But Owens would come down the hall saying, 'Top of the morning, laddies. Put a smile on your face and a song in your heart!'"

One day he walked past Carmody not saying anything. Carmody said, "Wait, Coach. Why don't you have a smile on your face and a song in your heart?"

Owens said, "Not if you had seen what I just saw coming across campus. I saw our head football coach hanging in jeopardy.'"

Carmody said that a few weeks after the season was over the coaches were sitting around wondering what was going to happen to them. Coach Davis came in and said they would find out something later, that the Board of the Athletic Council was having a meeting. A little later Davis called them back in and said he had some good news. "We're okay — we got salary approval with only one dissenting vote."

Owens said, "Coachman (his nickname for Davis), I want to know who that descending s.o.b. was. I am not doing this much longer, and when I get out of it I am going to go back and knock the s*** out of him." But the whole coaching staff was not retained.

Carmody coached several Mississippi State stars who later played in the NFL, including Hoyle Granger, D.D. Lewis, Tom Neville, and Justin Canale.

M.Ed. Degree in Education and Counseling

During the early part of his coaching career, Carmody was advised by Dick Corrado to pursue a graduate degree. Corrado was an assistant basketball coach at Holy Cross and was himself working on a master's degree. At the time, Carmody was an assistant coach at Holy Cross, and Corrado told him, "You never know when you might need this. You could be coaching at the high school level and need this degree to become the principal at that high school — or something similar."

So when he was at Holy Cross he began taking courses at Tulane. He continued taking courses, usually one course in the spring and one course in the summer, at Tulane, the University of Kentucky, and Mississippi State University. He needed to get permission for an extension in the time period between starting a degree and completing all prerequisites since he moved around so much. He was granted that extension by Tulane and received his master's of education degree in 1965 — seven years or so after beginning his graduate career. He persisted, and he succeeded. But Carmody added, "You know, I never used any of that degree. I worked my tail off to get that degree and never used it."

UNC (1967-73)

Bill Dooley, a Mississippi State graduate, was coaching with his brother Vince at Georgia. When Davis got fired at MSU Dooley was offered the head-coaching job. Bill had been an assistant on Paul Davis' staff, and whoever was offered the job would face the same problems at State that confronted Davis. Bill was also offered the head job at the University of North Carolina, so he had to choose. The thought of going back home to State was tempting. Vince called Bill into his office and asked, "Do you think you are a better coach than Paul Davis?"

Bill said, "No."

Vince said, "Well if I were you, I'd get myself up to North Carolina and start building me a new family." The next day Bill took the UNC job.

MSU hired Charlie Shira as head coach and fired him in 1972. Dooley was head coach at UNC until 1977. A newspaper reporter wrote that Dooley had implemented at UNC the same tactics Vince employed at Georgia with great success: "commando conditioning, brutish blocking, running, and tackling. Hard-nosed, hard running, winning football."

Bill Dooley inherited a woeful Tar Heel program. The team mentality was not dedicated to football. UNC finished the 1966 season with a 2-8 record under head coach Jim Hickey. Hickey left Dooley an "empty barn," making the rebuilding program difficult. But he brought in fresh assistant coaches like Carmody as defensive line coach, Bobby Collins as the head offensive coach, Jimmy Vickers as the offensive line coach, Vic Spooner as tight ends coach, and Lee Hayley as the head defensive coach. Many of these had Mississippi State backgrounds and six members of the staff had SEC experience. Dooley was faced with the problem of finding out which of the returning players on the 1966 team really wanted to play. Many returnees were considered to be fraternity party boys. This was similar to the situations faced by Bear Bryant at Texas A&M and Charlie Bradshaw at Kentucky. Bryant developed his "Junction City" approach — an approach also adopted by Bradshaw.

An Internet columnist, Bob Lee, who blogs for SaidWhatMedia.com, posted a blog about "Carolina's Junction Boys," stating that football at UNC was more like a social scene than a football game. "Fans got drunk and had a good time. Any disappointment at the game could be forgotten at the frat parties that night." UNC fans had no illusions of "competing on a national level" in football. Lee writes about the approach Dooley took to UNC football and called that approach "Carolina's Junction Boys." The players Dooley inherited did not place playing football as a high priority, and Dooley let everyone returning know that he needed to free up scholarships in order to recruit "his type of players."

Dooley showed great patience, hired an excellent coaching staff with a lot of SEC experience, and employed the same tactics his brother Vince had used to build the Georgia program. Bob Lee says the coaches Dooley brought in was a collection of unique personalities — and most of them were certifiable "psychos," the exception being Jim Carmody, whom he described as being "of a species and mental condition still unclassified… much darker than 'psycho.'" He went on to say that only one other coach, Vic Spooner — who coached with Carmody at Mississippi State — was "the only one who could communicate with Carmody."

Bill Dooley flanked by his UNC coaching staff in 1967. Carmody far right.
(Photo Carmody Family Collection)

Lee goes on to describe what he calls "a Mat Room." He claims, "The floor was covered wall to wall with old beat-up worn out gymnastic mats. These were dirty old 'horsehair' mats; pound them and dirt and dust puffed out. The thermostat for the room was set on 'sauna.' The players were herded into the Mat Room after 45-60 minutes of intense outside running and agility drills under the constant shrieking of Carmody and company. With players lining the walls, forming the boundaries of a pit… a 'cockfight' was essentially what happened. Pairs of players were called out to 'go at' each other. The rule was simple if unorthodox: if you pinned your opponent, you were allowed to rejoin the 'spectators.' If you were pinned, another gridiron gladiator was called out to pummel you again…the players were worked into a hysterical frenzy, adding audio to the video of the heat and dust and edge-of-sanity atmosphere…. No deference was given to position. Quarterbacks fought defensive tackles… kickers fought linebackers… et al… and the 'referees' were the coaches screaming obscenities and demeaning the manhood of one and all…. There were about 80 boys in ill-fitting gray sweat suits, who had lived and played together for two and three years, being compelled to beat the crap out of each other in a survival of the fittest…. The matches were designed to persuade one or both to quit the team. Friends, roommates, even a pair of twin brothers were pitted against each other. It only lasted four to six weeks, shorter for some." Lee does give warning that there "may be a few inaccuracies" in his account, but says, "Be assured you're not likely to ever read a better eye witness account of what happened."

Dooley's approach achieved its purpose. The UNC program began to steadily improve from a 2-8 record in 1967 to 3-7 in 1968 to 5-5 in 1969 to 8-4 in 1970 to 9-3 in 1971 and peaking at 11-1 in 1972. Improving on the previous season record for five consecutive years was an amazing feat, a feat accomplished probably for the first time in college football.

The 1967 season opened on a depressing note as UNC lost its first five games before defeating Maryland and then lost their next three games before ending the season with a victory at Duke. The 1968 Tar Heels showed slight improvement with three victories, but two of these were against SEC teams (Vanderbilt and Florida). The1969 season was a break-even 5-5 season that included close losses to rivals North Carolina State and Duke, and the Tar Heels were headed for a breakout season in 1970 when they went 8-4 and went to the Peach Bowl — UNC's first bowl appearance in some time — but lost to Arizona State. They improved again in 1971 to a 9-3 record and won an appearance in the Gator Bowl in Jacksonville, Florida, losing 7-3 to Georgia and Bill Dooley's brother Vince. UNC continued their amazing stretch of improved seasons in 1972 going 11-1 and beating Texas Tech in the Sun Bowl held in El Paso, Texas. UNC ended the season ranked #12 in the nation. The Tar Heels won consecutive ACC championships in 1971 and 1972. Dooley was named ACC Coach of the Year in 1971.

The improvement streak came to an end in the 1973 season when injuries decimated the team, and the Tar Heels fell to 8-4. Carmody admitted that he had been around a while but had never seen so many key injuries hit a team. On the other hand, he noted that the 22 players who started on the season opener on offense and defense in 1972 also started the final game of the season. He said he had never seen a team so injury-free before.

One of the key players Carmody coached while at UNC was Ken Huff. Born in Hutchinson, Kansas, Huff was recruited as a defensive tackle but was switched to offensive guard where he made All-ACC and Consensus All-American in 1974. Huff was a first-round draft pick (third overall) by the NFL Baltimore Colts. Huff enjoyed an eleven-year NFL career with Baltimore and the Washington Redskins and was selected for membership in the North Carolina Sports Hall of Fame.

Following the disappointing 1974 season, Carmody decided to leave UNC for Ole Miss. He had developed strong friendships with and respect for Bill Dooley and Bobby Collins and the coaching staff. He thought Dooley was a real innovator in recruiting techniques and organization. He made it clear that he was reluctant to move on, but his career goal was always to be a head coach of a major program, and he felt that the move to Ole Miss would help him achieve this goal. He had in December 1973 applied for the head coaching job at the University of Southwestern Louisiana. The long list of applicants had been narrowed to two candidates: Carmody and Augie Tammariello, an assistant coach at Colorado.

Carmody said, not meaning to demean UNC or the ACC, "He's a fine coach, and he got the job, but I still feel my chances would have been better had I been in the SEC or another stronger conference."

Carmody's reputation as a strong recruiter was among the best in the profession. At UNC he was assigned the recruiting area of Virginia, an area untapped previously by UNC. He recruited All-American guard Ron Rusnak and All-ACC tackle Robert Pratt from the area of Richmond, Virginia, and signed 14 of the 16 prospects from central Virginia who were offered scholarships by UNC. But going to a stronger conference was not the only reason Carmody felt a move was best for himself and his family. Carmody, a staunch conservative, had a difficult time accepting the "hippie" atmosphere of Chapel Hill during the 1970s. Chapel Hill is considered to be a very liberal college town. The Vietnam War protests and open use of marijuana on a wide-scale basis caused Carmody concern about raising his children, now of high school and junior high school age, in an atmosphere that liberal.

He was particularly incensed when folk singer Joan Baez refused to perform in concert at a university auditorium as long as the American flag was allowed to be hung in the concert hall. The flag was taken down, and Baez performed. Carmody also remembered the time students staged a concert and used the football stadium and field for an overnight sleep after the concert He said that several days and weeks after the concert, the football field grounds crews noticed the field sprouting a new grass — marijuana from the seeds the students spilled. Finally. Oxford, Mississippi, was much closer to his hometown of New Orleans than was Chapel Hill. When Ole Miss head coach Ken Cooper offered Carmody the job of leading the Rebel defense, the choice was obvious, and the family packed for Oxford.

Ole Miss (1974-77)

Johnny Vaught put Ole Miss on the football map. In the 24 years he served as head coach, his teams were virtually unbeatable in Oxford, going 57-6-2 in games at Hemingway Stadium. During the period of 1952 to 1964 Ole Miss was 33-0-1 at home. It is not surprising that the stadium has been renamed Vaught-Hemingway Stadium. The Rebels played in 15 consecutive bowl games during the period of 1957-71 and 18 bowl games overall. He coached 26 first-team All Americans during his 24-year coaching tenure. But Vaught retired in 1970 because of heart problems, and he was succeeded by one of his players, Billy Kinard (who was hired by his brother Bruiser Kinard, who was named athletic director that same year). Kinard was head coach through the 1971 and 1972 seasons and compiled a winning record, but he was replaced after the third game of the 1973 season following a 17-13 loss to Memphis State in Jackson. The "Sunday Night Purge" following that Memphis State loss resulted in the firings of both Kinard brothers as Vaught returned as both head coach and athletic director. In a stirring return to the field against Southern Miss the following week, a game the Rebels won by 41-0. The crowd welcomed Vaught back, and as he strode to the 50-yard line the applause got louder and louder. When he reached mid-field the Rebel band struck up "Happy Days are Here Again." It looked as if they truly were. Ole Miss won four of its next seven games, and at the end of the season Vaught retired from head coaching a second time but remained as athletic director. He hired his replacement, Ken Cooper, who had been an assistant coach at Ole Miss since 1971. Vaught's record as head coach when he retired was an amazing 190-61-12.

1974 (3-8)

When Carmody was still at UNC, Cooper called Bill Dooley to ask permission to talk to Carmody about joining his new staff at Ole Miss. Cooper had spoken with Bobby Proctor, who had coached with Carmody at Mississippi State, and asked for recommendations. Proctor recommended Carmody. Jim had never met Cooper but relied on Proctor's assessment of the Ole Miss situation. Carmody had wanted to get an SEC job to strengthen his resume for when a head coaching opportunity presented itself. By the time he joined Cooper's staff, spring practice had ended. Carmody made his coaching debut that fall at Ole Miss by having his defense shut out Missouri 10-0. The Rebels then lost to Memphis State 15-7 but bounced back to defeat Southern Miss 20-14 to go to 2-1. However, Ole Miss lost its next seven games to Alabama (35-21), Georgia (49-0), South Carolina (10-7), Vanderbilt (24-14),

LSU (24-0), Tennessee (29-17) and Mississippi State (31-13) before defeating Tulane 26-10 to end Ken Cooper's (and Jim Carmody's) first season at Ole Miss with a 3-8 record.

1975 (6-5)

The Rebels got off to a slow start in the 1975 season, losing their first three games to Baylor (20-10), Texas A&M (7-0) and Tulane (14-3). The defense was playing well enough, but the offense scored only 13 points in those first three games. The Rebels beat Southern Mississippi 24-8 but then lost to powerful Alabama 32-6 before pulling off a big upset against Georgia 28-13 in Oxford. Georgia came into that game nationally ranked. After losing to South Carolina 35-29 in Jackson, the Rebels won four straight games, including victories over rivals LSU (17-13) and Mississippi State (13-7) to end the season with a winning record, Cooper's only winning season in his tenure as head coach at Ole Miss. The Rebels finished the season 5-1 in the SEC. Carmody's influence on the defense began to show. The 1975 defense yielded 80 fewer points than the 1974 squad had.

1976 (5-6)

Among the great football victories of Carmody's coaching career, the Alabama game in Jackson, Mississippi, on September 11, 1976, stands out. The week before playing Alabama, Ole Miss lost a lackluster game to Memphis State. Ole Miss bounced back by defeating Bear Bryant and the Alabama Crimson Tide 10-7. Alabama was a heavy 14-point favorite. A birthday cake had been delivered to the Alabama dressing room to celebrate Coach Bear Bryant's 63rd birthday after the game. Carmody's Rebel defense stuffed Alabama's offense. Carmody said, "Their wishbone is not like Florida's or Oklahoma's because Alabama will throw on you when they see eight- and nine-man fronts."

Bryant himself was not optimistic, "The Tide offense so far isn't capable yet of challenging the Rebel defense."

Going into the game Carmody said that there were two things the Rebels had to do to beat 'Bama. "We were primarily concerned with stuffing their belly series and their option," he said.

Of course, Alabama also passed, ran draw plays, and ran sweeps, but they beat people with their belly series and option plays. Carmody had the defense spend three practice days working on Alabama's two favorite plays. It worked.

Carmody said, "We took away their bread-and-butter stuff."

The Rebels held the usually powerful Alabama wishbone offense to less than 250 yards. Ole Miss placekicker Hoppy Langley kicked a fourth-quarter field goal to win the game. The game marked the first Ole Miss victory over Alabama in the state of Mississippi. The fate of Bryant's birthday cake is unknown.

Alabama took on Southern Methodist University the following week in Birmingham. SMU defensive coach, Bobby Cope, called Carmody to congratulate him on the Ole Miss defensive effort against 'Bama the previous Saturday and asked him for advice about how to stop 'Bama that he could pass on to head coach, Ron Meyer.

Jim said, "Here's what you have to do…" and reviewed the Rebels' defensive game plan against Alabama.

Having a game plan does not guarantee success — success requires execution of that plan. On the Sunday after Ole Miss beat Tulane 34-7 in Oxford, Carmody read the scores of other games played that Saturday. He found the Alabama score — 'Bama beat SMU 56-3. The game plan did not take into account Bear Bryant's anger after getting beaten by Ole Miss.

The Rebels were nationally ranked #17 going into the Southern Mississippi game that they won 28-0. Following a disappointing 10-0 loss to Auburn, the Rebels took on #4 ranked Georgia in Oxford and won 21-17. Then the Rebels faced a scheduling quirk in which they played five straight games outside of Oxford to end the season. After losing on the road to South Carolina, they defeated Vanderbilt in Nashville and then seemingly collapsed, losing to LSU 45-0, Tennessee 32-6, and Mississippi State 28-11. After yielding only 75 points in its first eight games and leading the SEC in defense after its first six games, the Rebels gave up 115 points in their final three. Carmody said he had a difficult time keeping the defense from losing heart after the offense's lack of productivity. Whatever the reason, the Rebels ended up with a losing season after a promising start.

Ken Cooper had coached without having offensive and defensive coordinators, as such. Carmody was offered the position of defensive coordinator at the University of Kansas by coach Bud Moore and was tempted to accept that offer since having a coordinator title would help him in his pursuit of a head-coaching job. He told Cooper about the offer, and Cooper decided to name him as defensive coordinator and defensive line coach.

1977 (5-6)

The 1977 season opened with a 7-0 victory over Memphis State in Jackson followed by a 34-13 loss to Alabama in Birmingham. But the 1977 season was marked by the momentous victory over eventual national champion Notre Dame in Jackson (See Chapter 6) only to get upset by Southern Mississippi 27-19 the following week and losing the next week at Auburn 21-15 to go 2-3. Pressure began to mount from Rebel alumni. The Rebels lost a heartbreaker to Georgia 14-13 on the road before coming back to beat South Carolina at home, 17-10.

After that game South Carolina Coach Jim Carlen said, "Their defensive line played aggressively. Their inside five (the middle guard, two tackles, and two linebackers) just ate our offensive line's lunch."

The Rebels beat Vanderbilt 26-14 and Tennessee 43-14 down the stretch but lost key games to LSU (28-21) and Mississippi State (18-14). It was probably the Egg Bowl defeat that cost Coach Ken Cooper and his staff their jobs.

Second Quarter

OVERLEAF PHOTOGRAPH
"Second Quarter"

Carmody carried off the field after USM upset
of Alabama at Tuscaloosa in 1982
Steve Carmody #51
(Carmody Family Collecton)

6

BESTING THE NATIONAL CHAMPIONS - UM 20 ND 13

Sometimes football games are not won only by coaches or players — sometimes the meteorologists play an important role in the outcome of a game. If there is truth in that, then certainly the outcome of the Ole Miss-Notre Dame game on September 17, 1977, was determined by the Weather Channel and by clever rescheduling of the time of the kickoff on the part of Ole Miss athletics.

Sports Illustrated magazine predicted that Notre Dame would win the 1977 national championship, and the Fighting Irish were well on their way to proving them right. They opened that season against the Pittsburgh Panthers on the road. The Panthers were the defending 1976 national champs under Johnny Majors and were now coached by future Ole Miss nemesis Jackie Sherrill. Notre Dame was ranked third by the Associated Press behind the preseason favorite, University of Oklahoma Sooners, while the defending champs were ranked seventh. Notre Dame beat Pittsburgh 19-9 and was on its way. They then traveled to Jackson, Mississippi, to take on the Ole Miss Rebels, who had split their first two games, beating Memphis State in Jackson 7-3 and losing to Alabama in Birmingham the next week, 34-13. Not surprisingly, the Fighting Irish were heavy 21-point favorites. But the Ole Miss fans were not concerned and felt they had a good chance of an upset. When the team busses pulled into Jackson the Friday night before the game, Rebel fans held a big pep rally at Highland Village. Rebel fans were fired up.

On April 5, 2012, Rick Cleveland, sports editor of the Jackson *Clarion-Ledger,* wrote a memorable and brilliant article titled "25 Years Later, Win Over Powerhouse Notre Dame Still a Defining Ole Miss Moment." Much of the following accounts of this game were taken from that article, available on ClarionLedger.com.

Ole Miss running backs coach, Jack Carlisle, told Cleveland that he felt Ole Miss was not even in the same class as Notre Dame talent-wise or size-wise and feared total embarrassment. His feelings only got worse when the Irish took the field for their pre-game warm-ups. More than one Ole Miss fan wondered why this game was even scheduled. Maybe that's why athletic director Johnny Vaught and the weatherman gave Ole Miss the break it need-ed several weeks earlier — Vaught had gotten the kickoff, changed from a night game to a day game. Vaught told Ole Miss Head Coach Ken Cooper of this important change in the time of the kickoff, and Cooper announced the change in the kickoff time at a coaches' meeting. The coaches welcomed the news. The weatherman cooperated. Although the official high temperature was recorded at 87°F (most fans and players swore it was hotter than that. Unofficial estimates placed the high temperature at 86°, 88°, and 93°), a high average relative humidity at 82%, and only a slight 6 mph breeze. Using the National Weather Service heat index charts, one would calculate a heat index

Ole Miss defense vs. Notre Dame, 1977, in Jackson
(Carmody Family Collection)

at game time of between 106° and 110°F. In addition, the NWS stated that "exposure to full sunshine can increase heat index values by up to 15 degrees."

It would not be unreasonable to estimate that at kickoff the heat index was near 120°. Veterans Memorial Stadium in Jackson was like a steam bath. (The author was at this game and would agree with the estimate of a heat index of 120°). Writer Willie Morris often referred to Notre Dame athletes as "those pale-skinned Yankee boys" who were not acclimated to the heat. To make matters worse for the Irish, the weather in South Bend for the previous two weeks was unseasonably cool and rainy.

When Notre Dame came onto the field for pre-game warm-ups, Ole Miss offensive assistant coach, Jack Carlisle, was impressed with the size of the Notre Dame players. "They were so big I thought the field was going to tilt their way… they were huge. They made our players look puny."

Carmody recalled how hot it was and noted in the pregame warm-ups that Notre Dame players were wearing heavy jerseys more conducive to playing games up north. He had a hunch the Irish would regret wearing those jerseys before the game was over.

Detail: Kitchens (#53) Detail: Charlie Cage (#95)

Forty years after that memorable game, quarterback Tim Ellis — the offensive hero of the game — recalled that at pregame, "We came out fully dressed, and they came out fully dressed, and I remember looking around, and about 10 minutes after they had been on the field, they went back into the locker room and took their jerseys and shoulder pads off and came back in T-shirts."

The Irish had to try to adjust to the heat as the game went on. They did not. Ellis and the coaches felt that if Ole Miss could hang around and get a break or two, they might just have a chance to win it. And they did.

Junior Ole Miss quarterback Bobby Garner earned the starting job when offensive coordinator Jimmy Vickers installed the option veer offense. Garner felt honored but not awed at the thought of bringing the Rebels up to the line against heavily favored Notre Dame and knew the Irish would be a difficult opponent but said ,"If we can do a good job early, I think we will be all right."

Notre Dame fans and alumni in the Jackson area did their best to help their team by renting five big fans (Ole Miss was not about to provide the Irish with any cooling equipment) and bringing over 300 pounds of ice to the sidelines. Notre Dame realized that they were indeed in hostile territory, surrounded by 48,200 Rebel fans waving their Confederate flags, the band playing "Dixie," and on top of that the crushing heat.

Both teams were in the middle of quarterback controversies. Notre Dame head coach, Dan Devine, was faced with a three-quarterback race among Rusty Lisch, senior Gary Forystek, and Joe Montana bringing up the rear. Montana showed flashes of excellence as a sophomore in 1975 after leading Notre Dame to comeback victories against North Carolina and Air Force and appeared to be the early favorite for the starting position as a sophomore in 1976. But he was plagued with injuries, having suffered a shoulder injury that forced him to miss the entire 1976 season. Rusty Lisch was now the starting quarterback. As the number three quarterback Montana would not play in the Ole Miss game — contrary to the claims of a large number of fans who swear they saw Ole Miss beat Notre Dame and Joe Montana. However, Devine pulled Montana off the bench the next week against Purdue, and he led the Irish to a 31-24 victory. Of course, Montana went on to become one of the greatest quarterbacks in the history of professional football.

Ole Miss head coach, Ken Cooper, was faced with a different situation. The fight for the starting Ole Miss quarterback position was a battle between Bobby Garner and Tim Ellis. Garner was known as an option quarterback better suited to Cooper's and Jimmy Vickers' offense. Ellis brazenly wore legendary Archie Manning's number 18, and at one time in his career was thought to be the Rebels' starter. His reputation as a passer was not particularly suited for Cooper's switch to the veer offense. The Rebels had a third quarterback, Roy Coleman, who would become the first black quarterback to play at Ole Miss. In 1976 he was the first black high school quarterback to be offered a football scholarship at Ole Miss. As a sophomore Coleman played wide receiver, and he caught a key 52-yard pass in the Notre Dame game. He was switched to quarterback in his junior season.

Carlisle told Rick Cleveland: "Jim Carmody's defensive plan was masterful. His players knew just what to do."

Jim noticed that one of the key plays Notre Dame used quite effectively was the counter play. On this play the Irish normally did not block the trailing defensive tackle since they felt he lacked the speed to catch up to the ball carrier running away from him. Carmody thought, and was proven correct, that Charlie Cage possessed the speed to do so. Carmody characteristically deflected credit to the Rebel defenders, particularly Brian Moreland, who came off the bench, and defensive tackle Charlie Cage. Cage, from Natchez, made 17 tackles and consistently chased down Irish runners in their own backfield. Moreland was in on 12 tackles, recovered two fumbles, and intercepted a pass.

Carmody said, "Charlie Cage might have had the best game of any defensive lineman I ever coached. Rick added, "Which is saying a lot."

Brian Moreland was just all over the field making plays." Moreland was named *Sports Illustrated*'s national defensive player of the week.

Hoppy Langley kicked a 29-yard first-quarter field goal, and the Rebels jumped ahead after the first quarter. Each team scored a touchdown in the second quarter, and Ole Miss led at halftime 10-7. The key play on the Rebel touchdown drive occurred when Garner completed a pass to Roy Coleman that resulted in a 52-yard gain, setting up a scoring pass to James Storey with only 32 seconds left in the half. Neither team scored in the third quarter, but Notre Dame's Dan Reeve kicked two fourth-quarter field goals to push the Irish ahead 13-10 with just less than five minutes left in the game. Both teams, especially Notre Dame, were feeling the effects of the heat. Quarterback Bobby Garner particularly suffered from the heat and became dehydrated. Jimmy Vickers was the offensive coordinator and called the plays from the press box. Vickers felt that the time for a quarterback switch was at hand and transmitted that suggestion to Carlisle, who then passed it along to Cooper.

According to Cleveland, Cooper said that Ole Miss needed to go with their best throwing quarterback, who, of course, was Tim Ellis. Ellis had been on the bench up to that point and was fresh. Ellis was not expected to lead Ole Miss that day, or even play.

Ellis recalled, "I remember Coach Carmody coming up to me and telling me I was going to play. We had just punted to them. He said, 'When we get the ball back, get ready because you're going in.' I said, 'Are you sure? Have you cleared that with Coach Cooper?' He said, 'It doesn't matter; you're going in.' I said, 'Okay, let's do it."

In all likelihood Vickers passed the suggestion to switch QBs to Carlisle, who passed that on to Cooper, who passed it on to Carmody, who found Ellis on the bench.

Ellis continued, "I had an idea I might be going in, but you don't know what's going on in the minds of the coaches." Ellis said he had been running the two-minute offense in practice. "When I went into the huddle, I just told the guys that this was it; this was our chance to make a big mark on Ole Miss football."

Ole Miss had the ball on its own 20-yard line when Ellis entered the game. The heat was taking its toll on the Fighting Irish. "You could see them wilt as the game went on," Ellis said. "By the time I got in the game, they were throwing up on themselves."

Ellis felt fresh and does not recall being nervous when he entered the game. Ole Miss smartly put some fresh people in the game at the skill positions. Ellis' first pass was incomplete, but on the next play he hit his tight end,

Curtis Weathers, for 10 yards and a new set of downs. Cooper sent in a play with fullback L.Q. Smith. Carlisle called that decision "a stroke of genius."

Knowing that the Irish would be expecting sideline passes to stop the clock, Cooper called a play for Smith to fake a route to the sidelines and then go long down the middle. Ellis spotted him and threw to Smith, threading the ball between two defenders. Smith caught the ball at the Ole Miss 40 and ran all the way to the Notre Dame 22. Notre Dame's All-American lineman, Ross Browner, caught Smith from behind to save a touchdown. This was the only pass Smith ever caught during his Ole Miss career.

Fullback James Storey picked up 12 yards with a hard run up the middle down to the 10-yard line. Jimmy Vickers said, "We had to run the ball inside. You can't beat them just by passing or with the outside running game." Ole Miss rushed for 157 yards while holding the Irish to 147 yards.

Cleveland credits Cooper with another great call — a so-called "flood pass" or, in the Ole Miss vernacular, "8-86 flood pick" — a rollout pass to the running back on the right, who was supposed to be Roger Gordon, whom Carlisle had sent into the game because of his pass-catching ability. The play called for Ellis to roll to his right and pass to Gordon with the wide receiver setting up a block. The backs, Gordon and Storey were split and were supposed to switch positions before the snap. However, for some reason, Storey did not switch the side he lined up on with Gordon, and Ellis ended up completing a wobbly pass to Storey, who was all alone. In one of the more memorable plays in Ole Miss football history, Storey caught the pass and dashed into the end zone to give Ole Miss a 17-13 lead. Ellis was in the game for only nine plays but was a hero nonetheless.

Devine thought the ball was tipped by Irish tackle Bob Gollo, who Devine thought might have a chance at an interception with an open field ahead of him. But Gollo denied touching the ball, and Ellis would claim that the pass was not deflected or tipped and modestly said, "It was just a lousy throw."

Storey could not see whether the ball was deflected since he initially had his back to the ball. After the game Storey said, "I could not see if it was deflected. I reached back and caught it, and the next thing I knew I was at the

1, and then I was over." Notre Dame fumbled following the ensuing kickoff, and the Rebels recovered. With just 1:39 remaining, Langley kicked his second field goal of the game, a 27-yarder, and Ole Miss had one of the most historic victories in its rich history.

Ole Miss finished with 351 yards in total offense and held Notre Dame to 271 total yards. The heat had taken its toll — Ross Browner had only four solo tackles and three assists — but it was Carmody's defense that made the difference. *Clarion-Ledger* sports reporter John Adams wrote, "Take away Jim Browner's (ND defensive back) interception at the Ole Miss 26-yard line and a couple of fumble recoveries on the Rebels' side of the field in the second half, and Notre Dame might never have scored against an aroused Ole Miss defense."

Ellis recalled the atmosphere of Ole Miss tailgating forty years ago and the physical training of the Rebel quarterbacks. "We didn't do much back then except stand around in the weight room. We had spring conditioning time under Coach Carmody. It was called the 45-minute drill, and it was really 45 minutes of hell he put us through." That conditioning paid off months later in the Jackson heat.

Notre Dame went on to win its remaining nine games, defeated the Texas Longhorns in the Cotton Bowl, and was named national champions for 1977. In 1977 Notre Dame averaged 35 points a game, but Carmody's defense had done its job holding the Irish to just one touchdown and two field goals. The 13 points they scored against Carmody's defense were the fewest points they scored in their 12 games that year.

Ellis said, "I don't think this game would have become anything to what it's become historically if they hadn't won the national championship. If they had gone on and lost another game or two and finished out of the national championship slot, it's nowhere near the legacy game it's turned out to be historically for Ole Miss." The nine-play stretch earned Ellis the offensive player of the game award, but Jim Carmody's defense and the heat were the stars of the game.

Notre Dame Coach Dan Devine made no excuses about the heat being a factor. He pointed out that the heat was the same on both sides of the field.

Fighting Irish players were gracious, although still somewhat arrogant, despite being hit hard by the defeat. Notre Dame tight end Ken McAfee said, "We don't make excuses here. If you lose, you lose. There's always a game next week. This doesn't destroy our hopes for a national championship whatsoever. In fact, a loss like this can be a motivating factor." He then added, prophetically, "So many top teams play each other this year that I don't think anyone is going to go undefeated. If we had to lose, I'm glad we lost early." Notre Dame indeed went on to win the national championship.

After the game the author went down to the locker room area to congratulate Carmody on the big victory. Carmody told me, "Borne, I didn't know we were that good." Turns out they were not.

Clarion-Ledger reporter Tom Patterson recalled, "On a blackboard in the Ole Miss dressing room after the game was a sign which proclaimed 'Remember Southern.'" Turns out the Rebels didn't. Inexplicably, Ole Miss lost its next three games to USM, 27-19, at Auburn, 21-15, and at Georgia, 14-13, before coming back to beat South Carolina and Vanderbilt. A bone-crushing loss to LSU, 28-21, came after the Rebels built a 21-0 halftime lead and uncharacteristically blew that lead. In that contest, Steve Ensminger led the Tiger comeback by throwing two touchdown passes and running for two more, scoring the final touchdown with less than a minute to go after a Willie Teal interception. Ole Miss bounced back to crush Tennessee in Knoxville, 43-14, but ended the season with an 18-14 loss to Mississippi State in Starkville. It was probably the latter defeat that cost Ken Cooper his job as the Rebels, after defeating the eventual national champions, ended the promising season with a 5-6 record.

This victory would be ranked among the greatest Ole Miss victories in its history. It is amazing that the game is recalled with as much fervor as it is even to this day. As time goes by, the number of fans claiming they were there seems to increase. In fact, today one would guess that over 200,000 people were at that game. What is more difficult to accept is the fact that Ken Cooper and his coaching staff that managed to pull off this magnificent upset would be dismissed at season's end — another reminder of the axiom "It's not what you did yesterday that counts, but what have you done lately."

Carmody and sons at USM 1982, Keith (#91) and Steve (#51).
(Carmody Family Collection)

7

BEYOND OLE MISS - ON TO USM

The Ken Cooper era at Ole Miss was over following the 1977 season. Ole Miss was upset by Southern Mississippi the week following its milestone upset of Notre Dame and finished with a losing record after losing five of its last eight games, which included losses to LSU and Mississippi State. Ole Miss led LSU 21-0 at halftime but lost the game 28-21, while Mississippi State secured an 18-14 win after the Rebels had taken an early 14-0 lead. In both games the offense got off to a fast start and then bogged down. Ken Cooper was fired at the end of the season. Ironically, Notre Dame's Dan Devine was named national coach of the year and was later elected to the National Football Foundation College Football Hall of Fame.

Leaving Ole Miss

Cooper resigned under pressure on November 30, 1977. Texas Tech head coach, Steve Sloan, immediately expressed interest in the position.

Influential Ole Miss alumni were not content with Cooper's four-year record of 19-25 that included only one winning season (1975) — not counting the two Mississippi State forfeits in 1976 and 1977 because of NCAA infractions — and no bowl appearances. These alums knew, based on their involvement in the "Billy Kinard coup" in 1973, that they could apply sufficient pressure on the university administration, particularly Chancellor Porter Fortune, to cause change in athletic matters. The handwriting was on the wall, and Carmody and the other assistants realized the inevitable — when a head coach is fired, eight to ten assistants are indirectly fired with him.

Cooper, line coach at Ole Miss under Johnny Vaught, was hired on January 17, 1974, following the controversial Billy Kinard era that ended with Johnny Vaught's making an emotional return to lead the Rebels. Vaught retired from coaching in 1973 to assume full-time duties as athletic director Vaught's successor was expected to match or possibly surpass the Vaught record (15 consecutive bowl games, 185-58-12 over 24 seasons and a 5-3 mark in 1973 when he returned). The pressure of the Ole Miss job of following Johnny Vaught was felt by Billy Kinard and then by Ken Cooper and was thus considered to be one of the toughest coaching jobs in the country.

The search for a new coach in 1974 apparently boiled down to a choice of Cooper, who played at the University of Georgia and who had served as an assistant at Georgia from 1962 through 1970 when he was hired at Ole Miss, or Bill Pace, former Vanderbilt head coach and at the time an assistant at Georgia Tech. Pace apparently pulled out of the race to accept a position on the University of Georgia staff.

Four years later, Cooper, 40, stepped down almost two weeks after the university had announced that it would retain him for next season despite alumni discontent over his 19-25 record. His coaching victory over Notre Dame was quickly forgotten. The Rebels dropped three straight games (USM, Auburn, and Georgia), and Cooper was under heavy fire. However, Carmody's Rebel defense rose to the occasion, and Ole Miss beat South Carolina 17-10 in Oxford. The South Carolina win was an emotional victory for Cooper. When a reporter asked him after the game if the victory eased some of the pressure he was under, Cooper testily replied, "If anybody wants to talk about the game or anything about that, then we will, but I said all I want to say about the other [game] two weeks ago."

At the end of the game the Ole Miss M-Club alumni chapter issued a statement that said, "We are in support of the chancellor, the athletic committee, the athletic director, the football team, Coach Cooper, and his staff." But, following a victory over Vanderbilt, Ole Miss lost to LSU, beat Tennessee and lost its final game of the season to Mississippi State, 18-14. Cooper lost his last two games against State and actually lost 3 out of the 4 games between Ole Miss and MSU, although State had to forfeit two of their victories because of NCAA violations.

Cooper finished 1-3 each against rivals LSU and MSU, a sequence of losses unacceptable to Rebel fans who were accustomed to winning under Vaught. Especially irritating to Rebel fans was Cooper going 1-3 against MSU head coach Bob Tyler, who was an assistant under Coach Vaught and was thought in the late 1960s to be the favorite to eventually replace Vaught at Ole Miss. Losing 45-0 to LSU in 1976 and blowing a 21-0 lead to LSU to lose 28-21 in 1977 in addition to the poor record against MSU did nothing but stir the critics. Cooper then resigned under pressure. (Ironically, Tyler stepped down at MSU following the 1978 season).

Ole Miss assistant athletic director, Warner Alford, had expressed an interest in Texas Tech head coach, Steve Sloan, shortly after Cooper announced his resignation. Sloan had an impeccable image as a head coach at both Vanderbilt and Texas Tech and had been rumored as the successor to Bear Bryant at Alabama.

Shortly before Cooper's resignation, sources reported that university officials were seeking authority from the state college board to buy up the remaining two years of his contract, which called for about $31,400 per year. Looking back at coaches' salaries, one can easily conclude that college football has sold its soul to the television dollars. The current Ole Miss coach, some forty years later, is paid almost $5 million a year or almost $14,000 per day. Television sets kickoff times, even team uniforms — but that is another story for another day.

But in the announcement of Cooper's resignation, no mention was made of the disposition of Cooper's contract. Nor was there any mention of an earlier report that Cooper might be named as assistant athletic director. Chancellor Fortune said, "I have not pressured Coach Cooper to resign; I certainly have not fired him." He added, "Coach Cooper has displayed dignity and character in triumph and adversity."

Carmody wanted to join the new coaching staff and remain at Ole Miss. He and his family were very comfortable in Oxford. The four boys were heavily involved in the local school system, and Jim and Noonie made many friends in the Oxford community. While all of the other assistants on the Cooper staff left Oxford in pursuit of jobs elsewhere, Carmody continued to recruit for the Rebels, taking many trips to the Gulf Coast and New Orleans. Carmody saw the inevitable coming when Sloan brought four of his Texas Tech assistants to the press conference at which he announced his hiring at Ole Miss. Sloan signed for a salary of $75,000 a year (more than doubling Ken Cooper's salary) along with a $100,000 signing bonus. Sloan was hoping to bring Bill Parcells, who had coached the defense at Texas Tech, as his defensive coordinator, but when Parcells chose to go to the pros, Sloan asked his former Alabama roommate, Paul Crane, to come to Ole Miss as defensive coordinator rather than retain Carmody. Carmody was later told he would not be retained. Sloan's eventual undoing as coach at Ole Miss (he never had a winning season there, finishing with a 20-34 record) was his leaky defenses. Many Ole Miss faithful felt that had Sloan selected Carmody as his defensive coordinator, his record at Ole Miss would have been a winning experience.

Part of the camaraderie Carmody felt in Oxford came from Friday "seminars" at the upstairs bar of a local restaurant, The Gumbo Company. On most Fridays a diverse group, constantly changing, of local businessmen, professors (including the author), lawyers and, of course, writers, met to solve the problems of the day and enjoy a glass or two of beer. The Friday after Carmody was informed that he would not be retained, he showed up at the "seminar" very upset. But he soon calmed down and faced reality.

He began his job-hunting search and soon was offered a position with his old friend, Bill Dooley. In 1977 Dooley had left the University of North Carolina to take the position of athletic director and head coach at Virginia Tech. When Dooley learned that Carmody was no longer on the staff at Ole Miss he offered him a position of assistant coach at Virginia Tech. Carmody joined Dooley in Blacksburg, but three weeks later he received an offer from his long-time friend Bobby Collins to become assist head coach and defensive coordinator at the University of Southern Mississippi. Collins was named USM head coach in 1975 and went 7-4, 2-9, and 6-6 in his first three seasons (but Mississippi State had to forfeit its victories over USM in 1975 and 1976, making Collins's official record 8-3 and 3-8 those two years.) Carmody found the offer too tempting to resist. Dooley understood Jim's situation, and Carmody accepted the USM offer. He and the family moved to Hattiesburg.

With Carmody as the defensive coordinator Collins then enjoyed winning seasons each of his last four years at USM.

USM (1978-81)

A series of events was initiated at USM following the end of the 1973 season. Roland Dale, an assistant coach at Ole Miss for 12 years under Johnny Vaught following a three-year stint as line coach at USM and serving as head coach at Southeastern Louisiana for two years, was named athletic director at USM, succeeding Reed Green, who had served as USM's athletic director for 25 years. Dale had accepted the head coaching position at USM in 1968 but changed his mind. Coach Bear Underwood resigned effective at the end of the 1974 calendar year. Although he had compiled a losing record of 31-32-2 in six seasons, Underwood felt he had improved the quality of the program but that it was time for a change in leadership. Three weeks later Dale and USM President Aubrey Lucas announced the hiring of Bobby Collins, offensive coordinator and assistant head coach at North Carolina. Collins and Carmody had served together on Bill Dooley's staff from 1967 to 1974. In 1974 Carmody went to Ole Miss, and then Collins went to USM. Collins then hired Carmody in 1978. It is interesting to note how the careers of Dale, Collins, Dooley, and Carmody overlapped through those years.

The Nasty Bunch and Big Nasty

Soon after Carmody took over the USM defense his influence began to be felt. His constant motivation began to have its effect. The defense developed a swagger, a persona. They considered themselves "Nasty" and began to call themselves "The Nasty Bunch" — both with Carmody's encouragement. The defense bestowed the title "Big Nasty" on their leader. There are several versions of how this process took place. Carmody recalls several players coming to him saying they wanted to call themselves "The Nasty Bunch." Carmody told them, "You can call yourselves what you want, but make sure you can back it up."

One of the most credible accounts is given by one of the defensive players, defensive end Rhett Whitley. Whitley played for USM from 1977 to

1981 and is a member of the original "Nasty Bunch." Here is his version:

"This is how I recall 'The Nasty Bunch' starting. I don't remember who we were playing, but it was a home game. It was the first play of a game in the 1978 season, and I was starting as a redshirt freshman. I was a bucked-toothed, knobby-kneed, freckled-faced Alabama and Auburn reject from Bluff Park, Alabama. Coach Bear Bryant said, 'We don't need you, Rhett Whitley,' in a letter that I still have to this day. Maybe that was part of the Nasty Bunch being nasty; at least, I know it was motivation for me.

"Big Nasty" — Coach Jim Carmody. (From "Rock Solid")

"Back to that home game at USM. Nose guard Thad Dillard always got nervous before a game and lost his stomach. On this day, it rested on the football before the center came to snap the ball to the QB. We were all laughing at Thad as he did it, but history took place that day, when that center said, 'You are NASTY.' We loved it and in practice it stuck, as we started calling ourselves the Nasty Bunch and our fearless leader, Coach Carmody, Big Nasty.

"That is the way I remember it starting, but you know, after so many licks to the head, these stories probably got more embellished as the older we got, but who cares? I have two brothers who played football. Chuck Whitley, a Hoover High School coach with tons of championships, and my brother Ryan Whitley, who played at Auburn then transferred to USM as a center.

"The next story has two versions I am aware of, and I believe you can get this out of the Memphis paper from a 1978 sports page. It goes like this: the opponent's quarterback was rounding my end, and Ron Brown or Cliff Lewis and I all did a nose dive to hit him, as he was diving in the dirt to miss our hit. Cliff and I pick him up after the play, and the QB said, 'This is just a game,' we replied, 'This is not a game; it is war.' I believe the paper said, 'This is not a game; it is life.' Either way, we made our point.

"And it wasn't a game to us. We were out to prove we were number one in the country. USM hadn't been to a bowl game since 1956. We were, according to Coach Carmody, Big Nasty, the leftovers, the Ole Miss, Miss State, Alabama, Auburn, Georgia rejects. Every day in practice he reminded us of that. It was not subtle. We took that statement seriously, and we had something to prove to those that did not pick us.

"We played Alabama three times while I was there. We lost 2 and tied 1. But I had the privilege to play in the East West All-Star game in 1982. I had always told my mom I would play for the 'Bear' one day. She said, 'You will.' Well, he coached that game and told me, 'I never should have let you out of Alabama.' I owe those words from Coach Bryant to Coach Carmody.

"Coach Jim Carmody used war-type analogies to keep us revved up and nasty. Although we didn't win all our games, we certainly made a name for ourselves on the gridiron. I use to tell Coach Carmody, if he called us at midnight to get on our uniforms, go to the top of the stadium, spread out your arms like wings, and you will fly to the ground, unhurt, we would have done it. We believed in him. If he said it, we just did it. His game plan was faultless. I always felt sorry for the offense, because our preparation was so intense, I felt like we had prepared so well that we knew what plays they were going to run better than they did. We watched so much film, and Coach Carmody had us so well prepared we would not lose. We were the Nasty Bunch. People feared us. Our own scout team feared us. I lost a tooth at the Ole Miss game one year and left it out on purpose because it made me look nastier!

"Coach Carmody used psychology against the offense. If the Nasty Bunch was on the field at the end of a quarter, no matter how tired we were, we would get down in our stance and sprint by the offense, go to the new line of scrimmage sometimes 90 yards away, and Coach said, 'Do not let them see you breathing hard, or tired.' They freaked out as we ran by them screaming like a bunch of wild animals.

"Coach also told us, 'You never take yourself out of the game; we will tell you when you are hurt. Don't show pain, ever.'"

Rhett Whitley was named second team All-South Independent in 1981 and was one of the captains of that 1981 team. He was elected to the USM Football Hall of Fame in 2010.

Carmody earned the nickname "Big Nasty." "That nickname was given to me by the defensive line at USM. They were called 'The Nasty Bunch' and, since I was their leader, they just started calling me Big Nasty. I would like to think that it doesn't reflect my personality. People that hear that sometimes don't understand where it came from."

Rick Cleveland quotes Carmody about the Nasty Bunch in his Jackson *Clarion-Ledger* article on Carmody's selection for the Mississippi Sports Hall of Fame: "That was the players' idea. Hanford Dixon, J.J. Stewart, and Cliff Lewis all came to me with the idea and I told them it was okay with me, but they better live up to it. Call yourselves whatever you want as long as you live up to it. Over the years, I really believe they did."

1978 (7-4)

The schedule makers certainly did not favor USM as the Eagles opened the season with four straight road games. Carmody's Nasty Bunch showed up in the season opener against the Richmond Spiders at Richmond. USM, despite a disappointing offensive showing, won 10-7, and the Nasty Bunch held the Spiders to only 153 yards total offense. USM defeated Arkansas State in Little Rock 21-6 with another fine defensive showing. The defense finally weakened in Cincinnati as the Bearcats won 26-14.

UM 16 — USM 13

The fourth game of the season, on September 30, 1978 had been marked on Carmody's calendar since he joined the USM staff. — USM vs. Ole Miss. Carmody was still angry at the way his last season ended at Ole Miss, and he fired up the Nasty Bunch. As expected, the game was a defensive struggle, and with less than four minutes to be played, Ole Miss kicked a field goal to tie the score at 13-13. USM then started what was hoped to be a game-winning drive. With one and a half minutes left in the game, USM drove to the Ole Miss 22-yard line. Facing a third-and-one situation USM quarterback Dane McDaniel rolled out to his left, and it appeared he had room to run for a first down, but he spotted a receiver downfield and decided to lob a pass over the head of the Ole Miss defensive back, Jon Fabris. Fabris, 6'4" tall, leaped up and intercepted the pass and raced down the sideline toward the USM goal line. However, a USM player, defensive end James Hale, came off the Eagle bench to tackle Fabris at the USM 36 yard-line. Ole Miss coaches reacted vigorously, but the officials had seen what happened. The officials decided that Hale had assisted in tackling Fabris and was not the primary tackler and penalized USM 15 yards rather than award a touchdown. From the 21-yard line Ole Miss ran the clock down with three straight running plays by Leon Perry to the Southern 12, and Hoppy Langley kicked a field goal with only 16 seconds left in the game to give Ole Miss the win, 16-13.

Perhaps the only explanation for Hale's over-enthusiasm was that he got too fired up about the Nasty Bunch defense. After the game a teary-eyed Hale said, "Yeah, I did it. It was a stupid thing to do. I don't know why I did it."

Carmody was reluctant to criticize Hale because he said that when Fabris ran by the USM bench he was tempted to tackle him himself!

Fabris said, "I thought I had a chance to go all the way. I picked up some good blocks, and I had an open field. Then I looked up, and there was somebody in front of me. I don't know if it was the guy who was supposed to come off the bench or not. It all happened so fast."

A fight broke out on the field between the two teams after the game. Steve Sloan stated the obvious, "We were lucky to win. That's about all you can say."

The incident brought back memories of the 1954 Cotton Bowl game when Rice running back, Dickie Moegel, took off on a 95-yard scamper down the right sideline in front of the Alabama bench. Alabama fullback Tommy Lewis left the bench, without his helmet, and tackled Moegel around the Alabama 40-yard line. Rice was awarded a touchdown on the play. Lewis later apologized to Moegel, and Rice and offered only a simple explanation: "I'm just too full of Alabama." Perhaps James Hale was "too full" of the Nasty Bunch and Southern Mississippi.

Carmody recruited Fabris for Ole Miss during his recent stint there.

Although the loss was a devastating one, there was some brightness for the future as running back Sammy Winder, one of the all-time great USM running backs, made his debut.

USM bounced back from the crushing Ole Miss loss to win three straight games, defeating Mississippi State 22-17, East Carolina 17-16 in Hattiesburg, and Memphis State 13-10 in Memphis. The Nasty Bunch defense stood out in these three games. Then the Golden Eagles faced always-powerful Florida State in Hattiesburg. The Nasty Bunch could not hold back the Seminoles and lost 38-16. In perhaps the most disappointing game of the 1978 season, USM traveled to Denton, Texas, to face North Texas State. The Eagles came out flat and played uninspired football to lose 25-12. However, the USM ship straightened itself out, and they won the final two games of the season at home, defeating Bowling Green 38-21 and crushing the Louisville Cardinals 37-3. The Nasty Bunch ended the season on a high note, limiting the Cardinals to only 132 total yards and keeping them from scoring a touchdown. With a final 7-4 record USM expected to receive an invite to a bowl game, but no bids were received.

1979 (6-4-1)

The Eagles entered the 1979 season on an optimistic note, coming off a successful 7-4 season in 1978. Although the season was not as successful as anticipated, the year was highlighted by the late-season debut of a freshman quarterback, Reggie Collier, who would go on to be not only among the best quarterbacks in Golden Eagles' history but one of the best in the country. USM opened the season in Tallahassee against Florida State and started the fourth quarter with a 14-3 lead. But the USM punting game caused an Eagle collapse. In the fourth quarter, the Eagles, relying on a freshman punter, Bruce Thompson, were forced to punt. The Seminoles blocked the punt and subsequently scored, narrowing the lead to 14-9. On the following possession USM was again forced to punt. This time Florida State returned the punt 65 yards for a touchdown to go ahead 15-14. They successfully converted a two-point conversion and held on to win 17-14. Carmody's Nasty Bunch defense did their job, but the kicking game could not do its job. The Eagles returned to friendly Roberts Stadium to face the Cincinnati Bearcats and sufficiently regrouped to win 24-6. Once again The Nasty Bunch played well, holding Cincinnati to less than 200 yards on offense and picking off two passes.

The 1-1 Eagles then made their annual trek to Auburn to play their nemesis, the Auburn Tigers. Auburn prevailed in a run-away, 31-9. The Nasty Bunch defense inexplicably allowed Auburn to almost score at will, but most of the blame fell on an inefficient offense that was forced into a passing game. Next up on the schedule was Ole Miss in Jackson. Carmody had been waiting for this game after the way he felt he was treated by Ole Miss when Ken Cooper was fired and after last season's stinging loss to the Rebels when Ole Miss kicked a late field goal to win 16-13. The 1979 game was played in Jackson, and USM got off to a sizzling start, taking the opening kickoff and scoring after an 11-play, 80-yard drive. The Ole Miss team never recovered. Bobby Collins made a radical decision to install the I-formation, and the offense clicked, running the Rebels into submission. Later in the first quarter, quarterback Dane McDaniel threw a 63-yard touchdown pass to tight end Marvin Harvey to give USM a 14-point lead before the first break. USM then rubbed the Rebels' nose in the dirt a little bit by recovering an onside kick. Bobby Collins reportedly promised his team they would go for an onside kick if they were up two touchdowns, and the promise was motivation enough. He kept his promise, angering the Ole Miss fans even more. The Rebels regrouped and forced a USM punt, but the punt was fumbled, and USM recovered on the Rebel 10-yard line. The Golden Eagles quickly scored and took a 21-0 lead into halftime. USM added to the lead in the second half, scoring two touchdowns (one set up by another Ole Miss fumble) and a field goal, and allowing only one Ole Miss score, to win 38-8. I met Carmody after the game at the USM bus, and he was irate. "I can't believe they scored," he complained.

Sloan, on the other hand was gracious as usual and stated the obvious: "We just got beat very soundly."

The following week was a historical one for the Eagles — their first appearance on national television — a delayed telecast on ESPN. USM took advantage of the national exposure opportunity and impressively defeated North Texas State 30-10. The following week Tulane paid a visit to Roberts Stadium to play what was to become one of its rivalry games. With the two schools located just over 100 miles apart, one would have thought that they'd have played each other before 1979. Yet this was to be the first time they met in football. The two teams began what became known as "The Battle for the Bell." They played annually until 2006 when conference affiliations brought the series to a temporary end.

When the series came to an end on an annual basis, USM held a 21-7 series lead. However, Tulane won the first meeting in an exciting game, 20-19. Tulane scored on a 67-yard scoring drive with forty-four seconds to go to take the lead — thanks in large measure to two pass interference calls against the Eagles. On the ensuing kickoff, tailback Ricky Floyd lateralled to Marvin Harvey, who raced to the Tulane 10. However, the Eagles were assessed a controversial clipping penalty, and the ball was brought out to the 30-yard line. Out of timeouts and with the clock running down, McDaniel completed a short pass, and USM rushed to get its field goal team on the field. The 41-yard game-winning field goal attempt barely missed, and the Green Wave won, 20-19. As the home crowd sat stunned at the outcome, the officials sprinted for their cars!

The Nasty Bunch then shut out Memphis State 22-0 (the first shutout for USM at Roberts Stadium) and then held Mississippi State to a single touchdown as USM won 21-7. Against Memphis The Nasty Bunch picked off four Tiger passes and recovered three fumbles. The USM record stood at 5-3 when the Eagles traveled to Louisville. The game turned into a defensive struggle with The Nasty Bunch again playing well, holding the Cardinals to less than 200 yards total offense. However, the USM offense committed seven turnovers, and the game ended in a 10-10 tie. The Eagles then travelled almost 900 miles to Bowling Green, Ohio, to take on the Bowling Green Falcons. This was the third straight road game for Southern, and this seemed to affect The Nasty Bunch, who could not keep up its defensive streak and yielded nearly 500 yards of total offense to the Falcons. The game seesawed back and forth, and USM led 27-24 with about five minutes remaining in the game. But Bowling Green scored with just over a minute to play, and McDaniel was intercepted after the kickoff. The Eagles lost 31-27.

Arkansas State of the Southland Conference paid a visit to Hattiesburg for the season finale. Once again defenses prevailed as The Nasty Bunch regained its form. The game was scoreless after three quarters. But USM built up a 14-0 lead in the fourth quarter, and when Arkansas State scored with just over 20 seconds left, the Eagles held on for a 14-6 victory. But perhaps even more significant than the score was the debut of USM quarterback Reggie Collier. Collier replaced McDaniel in the second quarter and quickly gave an indication of great things to come, both running and passing. USM had entered a new dimension in its quest for national recognition.

1980 (9-3)

USM entered the season determined to win the "Mississippi Championship" once again. In 1977 the Eagles beat both Ole Miss and Mississippi State; in 1978 USM lost to Ole Miss but beat MSU. In 1979 USM beat both Ole Miss and State, and the Eagles were looking forward to extending that winning streak. Clearly, USM was dominating the in-state series. They would sweep Ole Miss and MSU again in 1980. Ole Miss decided to drop

USM from its schedule in 1981 while Mississippi State continued the series to their regret as Southern won 7-6 in 1981 and won again in 1982, 20-14. Ole Miss and USM resumed the series in 1982 with Ole Miss beating USM 28-19. USM beat both Ole Miss and Mississippi State again in 1983. State finally beat USM in 1984, but the Rebels lost to USM 13-10 in 1984. Ole Miss decided to drop USM from its schedule following the 1984 game after losing six of the past eight games, while Mississippi State dropped USM from its schedule in 1990 after losing 10 of the past 14 games. USM clearly dominated the state in the late 1970s and 1980s.

USM got off to a sizzling start at 6-0 in 1980 to begin one of its best seasons in its history. As a result the Eagles earned their first Top Twenty national ranking. By beating both Ole Miss and Mississippi State they were considered the champions of Mississippi. However, they were far from being the champions of Alabama, as Alabama and Auburn both defeated USM soundly (42-7 and 31-0, respectively). But now, In addition to the continuing solid defense of The Nasty Bunch, The Golden Eagles now had the offensive power of sophomore quarterback Reggie Collier to go along with the solid rushing game provided by junior walk-on Sammy Winder.

USM opened the season on the road against the Tulane Green Wave in the Superdome in New Orleans. They were determined to avenge the 20-19 defeat they suffered to the Greenies in 1979. The game was televised by ABC-TV and attracted almost 45,000 fans. The season was almost ruined when Tulane jumped out to a 14-0. Then The Nasty Bunch woke up and shut the Wave down the rest of the game. USM slowly got back into the game by scoring twice to knot the score at 14-14. Then with 30 seconds left in the game, placekicker Winston Walker made a 36-yard field goal to win the game. Walker made up for missing the game-winning field goal at the buzzer in the 1979 loss to Tulane. USM was off and running following the 17-14 victory.

Following an open week, Louisiana Tech came to Hattiesburg, and USM put on a complete game victory, winning 38-11, with Winder running for two touchdowns and Collier passing for two more. In addition, The Nasty Bunch held the Bulldogs' offense to just over 200 total yards. The Eagles hit the road again, this time traveling to Greenville, South Carolina, to face East Carolina. Once again both the offense, led by Winder and Collier, and The Nasty Bunch defense excelled as USM won their third straight game, 35-7. Winder ran for three touchdowns, and Nasty Bunch defensive end Rhett Whitley blocked a Pirates punt that was picked up by defensive end Robert Phillips and returned for a touchdown. The Nasty Bunch held yet another opponent to less than 200 yards total offense. The next game featured Southern against its archrival Ole Miss Rebels in Jackson. The Eagles were expecting the Rebels to be fired up to atone for last year's drubbing by USM and, indeed, the game was tight. Ole Miss jumped out to a 14-0 lead, scoring in each the first and second quarters, but the Eagles tied up the score at halftime behind a short touchdown run by Winder and a 62-yard pass from Collier to Don Horn. Sammy Winder gave the Eagles the lead in the third quarter with one of the most memorable runs in USM history, although the run was for only 11 yards. At the 5-yard line Winder high jumped, or hurdled, over a Rebel defender and landed in the end zone. The play is remembered by USM fans as "The Dive." Winder scored again in the fourth quarter to give Southern a seemingly insurmountable 28-14 lead. Yet the Rebels, behind quarterback John Fourcade, would not quit and soon closed the gap to 28-22. Winder fumbled trying to run out the clock, and Ole Miss recovered. The Rebels drove to the USM 8-yard line and were looking to take the lead and the win, but the Nasty Bunch's defensive end, George "Too Tall" Tillman, sacked Fourcade three straight times to end the threat. Carmody is quoted in Rock Solid as saying after the game, "We had been rushing three and dropping eight, but you can do that just so much. Sooner or later that guy (Fourcade) is going to scramble around and hurt you. We didn't feel we could blitz when we went into the game, but we had to gamble." Once again, The Nasty Bunch held an opponent to just over 200 yards total offense.

The 4-0 Eagles then traveled to Starkville to play the 4-1 Mississippi State Bulldogs. It was Mississippi State's homecoming game. USM jumped out to a 21-0 lead. The Nasty Bunch defense had shut down the Bulldogs. MSU scored on a 62-yard run in the third quarter only to be countered by a USM 67-yard run by Mike Woodward. MSU's George Wonsley then scored on a

53-yard run, but once again USM answered as Collier took off on a 53-yard jaunt, and USM ultimately emerged with a 42-14 victory. The Eagles had indeed swept their in-state rivals again. MSU would later score one of their biggest victories in their history by beating Bear Bryant 6-3 when the Tide was ranked No. 1 in the nation.

During the game Carmody's son Steve had snapped on a punt and charged downfield to cover the punt. He got blindsided by a MSU blocker and took a wicked lick to the temple, knocking him to the turf. Steve slowly got up and walked off the field. After the game the Eagles were celebrating their big victory, cheering and hollering. Nasty looked in a corner and saw the USM trainer, Dr. Harrington, shining a penlight in Steve's eyes. Carmody asked Harrington, "What's going on, Doc?"

Harrington said, "Steve took a pretty good lick in the temple, and he is having trouble focusing his eyes." Carmody said Harrington was a master of the malaprop, even better than Yogi Berra. Harrington continued, "I'm looking in his eyes to see if he may have a detached rectum."

Carmody laughed and told Doc, "You're probably right because he did get his ass knocked off."

USM ran its record to 6-0 the following week, returning home for the first time in three weeks to shut out Arkansas State, 35-0. The offense and The Nasty Bunch once again jelled, with the offense producing almost 500 yards in total offense while the defense held the Indians to less than 30 yards of total offense — 24 yards rushing and -5 yards passing. ASU made one first down, and that on a penalty. The Golden Eagles were ranked No. 20 in the nation.

The Alabama game in Tuscaloosa drew attention because both teams entered the contest with 6-0 records. Alabama was ranked No. 1 in the country. USM had an opportunity to showcase its program. It was a bad time for the Eagles' offense and The Nasty Bunch to take a week off. The Crimson Tide embarrassed USM 42-7, forcing the Eagles to fumble three times. USM regrouped to defeat the lowly Lamar Cardinals 36-10 to set up a meaningful contest the following week at Auburn. The 7-1 Eagles appeared to have a chance against the 4-4 Auburn Tigers, but once again the offense and defense had poor games at the same time and Auburn easily defeated USM 31-0.

While USM dominated the state of Mississippi, they did not appear to be competitive in the state of Alabama.

Assisted by a three-touchdown game by Sammy Winder, the Eagles managed to bounce back against the visiting Richmond Spiders. The Eagles prevailed 33-12 to go 8-2 for the season and still be in line for a major bowl game. Following the Richmond game USM received a bid from the Independence Bowl to play McNeese State, champions of the Southland Conference, and Roland Dale accepted the bid. This would be the first bowl appearance for the Eagles since the 1957 Tangerine Bowl against West Texas A&M under legendary USM coach Pie Vann. However, the Eagles had one more game to play against the visiting Louisville Cardinals in Hattiesburg. The Cardinals had a lackluster season and came into the game with a 4-6 record. In a miserable rainstorm Louisville beat USM 6-3, and the Eagles ended their season on a disappointing note to earn a 8-3 record most teams would have been happy to experience.

The Independence Bowl was held in Shreveport, Louisiana, on December 13. USM was 0-4 in bowl games coming into the Independence Bowl. Their opponent was the Southland Conference champion, the McNeese Cowboys. McNeese coach, Ernie Duplechin, led the Cowboys to a 10-1 record, losing only to Northwestern State. McNeese State had been to the Independence Bowl twice before, defeating Tulsa in 1976 and losing to Syracuse in the 1979.

USM coach Bobby Collins said that both teams relied on speed and quickness and that McNeese's quarterback, Stephen Starring, was one of the fastest quarterbacks anywhere.

USM defensive end Rhett Whitley summed up Coach Carmody's game plan: "Their running backs have a lot of quickness getting to the line. Their quarterback likes to keep the ball. We feel like if we can stop the quarterback, we can stop the major part of their offense."

Before an announced crowd of 42,600 the Eagles jumped out to a 3-0 lead on a Winston Walker 36-yard field goal. A 14-yard run by fullback Clemon Terrell increased the lead to 10-0. McNeese State closed the gap to 10-7 at halftime when Starring completed a 42-yard pass to set up a Mc-

Neese touchdown. In the third quarter the Cowboys went ahead 14-10 after driving 80 yards. Still behind with time running out, USM had the ball with fourth down. Rather than going for the first down Collins decided to punt to McNeese and hope The Nasty Bunch could force a turnover. That's exactly what happened: with 2:24 left in the game The Nasty Bunch forced McNeese fullback Gerald Polaski to fumble, and USM linebacker Ron Brown recovered at the Cowboys 7-yard line. The offense managed to get down to only the Cowboy 1-yard line. On fourth down Collier faked a handoff to Sammy Winder up the middle. He dove over the line, attracting Cowboys' defenders. Collier then sprinted down the left side of the line on an option, which drew the remaining defenders to him. Collier then pitched out at the last second to fullback Michael Woodard, who had gone in motion. With 1:17 remaining in the game, Woodward circled left end to score one of the few touchdowns of his career.

The Eagles went up 16-14, and The Nasty Bunch held McNeese when nose guard Jerald Baylis sacked the quarterback, and cornerback Hanford Dixon recovered a McNeese St. fumble. The Eagles won 16-14.

According to Rock Solid, after the game Woodward explained the option play. "The play was a zip sweep where I started in motion to the right and then came back to the left for the pitch. Because Reggie waited until the last minute to pitch the ball, it sucked the defense up. First they went after Sammy going over the top, then they almost had Reggie, then when Reggie pitched the ball to me, nobody was around. I just took off for the goal line."

Collier claimed that the game against McNeese was the hardest-hitting game he ever played in. Defenseman Jerald Baylis was named co-Most Valuable Player (along with McNeese quarterback Stephen Starring). But that honor could have easily gone to the whole Nasty Bunch, who recovered four McNeese fumbles and picked off a McNeese pass. The Golden Eagles won their first bowl game in almost 25 years, despite McNeese State's having a statistical advantage. Collier was later inducted into the Independence Bowl Hall of Honor.

Carmody was content following the bowl game. He and the team had a successful season. His Nasty Bunch defense finished third in the nation in pass defense and tenth in the nation in overall defense. But a subsequent invitation to explore opportunities in professional football would mark yet another turn in his career and move him closer to fulfilling his dream of becoming a college football head coach.

8

RECRUITING

Recruiting is the heart and soul of any athletic program, especially college football. The process can represent the best and the worst of the sport — it can be a challenge to convince, legitimately, a young person of the values of a given school and athletic program, or it can become a cesspool of illegal enticements. College recruiters have been accused of treating recruits to cars, money, jobs for family members, and providing female "hostesses." However, overeager, wealthy alumni and fans are as likely to violate recruiting rules, thinking they are doing their alma mater a favor by inducing a high school athlete to attend "their" school. College recruiting can be especially competitive, especially in the football and basketball arenas. Contributing to the problem are the sometimes exorbitant salaries paid to successful coaches and athletic administrators. The temptation to walk the edge in recruiting a prospect with a questionable background in order to protect, and even increase, that salary is real. Television income has been a major factor in driving the process.

The current NCAA Recruiting Manual contains approximately 500 pages of rules and regulations and principles of conduct for intercollegiate athletics. Although the NCAA always had the authority to ban an institution from competing in a particular sport, the NCAA adopted the so-called "death penalty" for athletic programs that are repeat violators, e.g., a school found guilty of a second violation resulting in probation within five years of being placed on NCAA probation in the same sport or another sport could be barred from competing in that sport for one or two seasons. This penalty has been imposed five times, perhaps the most notable being the Southern Methodist University football program in 1987. Others include the University of Kentucky basketball program for the 1952-53 season (tainting the career of legendary Coach Adolph Rupp) and the University of Southwestern Louisiana basketball program for the 1973-74 and 1974-75 seasons. Although university Division I football and basketball programs are the most visible, the death penalty has also been applied to Division II (men's soccer at Morehouse College) and Division III (men's tennis at MacMurray College) programs as well. Currently there are 16 Division I FBS, (Football Bowl Subdivisions) institutions, Football Championship Subdivisions (FCS), Division I non-football, Division II, and Division III institutions on NCAA probation, eight of them for football violations.

In the autumn of 1982 (Carmody's first year as head coach at USM) seventeen major colleges were on NCAA probation, a record, and another thirty-five colleges were under investigation.

When writer Willie Morris published "The Courting of Marcus Dupree" in 1983, it became perhaps the most authoritative examination of college football recruiting. Willie pointed out that adequate enforcement of NCAA recruiting rules has "been complicated by the sweep and complexity of the NCAA rules and procedures themselves, which in some cases appear petty. A college could give a young football player a paid forty-eight hour trip to its campus and a full scholarship, but a cheeseburger away from campus, a T-shirt, a pair of school sneakers, or presumably a package of chewing gum or a novel by Harold Robbins were violations, at least technically." Willie thought that cheating in recruitment occurred more frequently in basketball than in football.

Many famous college coaches, such as Bear Bryant and Darrell Royal, have expressed their intense dislike, even hatred, of recruiting. However, Jim Carmody viewed it as a challenge to out-compete other colleges or schools and was one of a few who seemed to enjoy the process. When Carmody was leaving the University of North Carolina to join the staff at Ole Miss he told a newspaper reporter, "I always enjoyed recruiting. I still do… Recruiting is like a game to me. I get psyched for it."

Carmody's success in recruiting can be summarized in a statement he made while recruiting at Southern Mississippi: "We don't look for players with potential, we want players with production." That formula worked not only at USM but everywhere he coached.

In Mississippi, the competition for quality athletes among the three Division I, predominately white "Big Three" institutions is particularly intense and oftentimes vicious. The Ole Miss-Mississippi State rivalry has been particularly ugly at times for a number of reasons, but since both Ole Miss and Mississippi State are members of the Southeastern Conference, this rivalry is particularly vicious and competitive and appears to be intensifying. It is not uncommon for alumni at one institution to report recruiting violations committed, or supposedly committed, by the rival institution.

Historian David G. Sansing traced the history of the Ole Miss-State rivalry in a report filed to the NCAA in regard to a lawsuit that Mississippi State head coach Jackie Sherill filed against the NCAA. He begins that report by quoting Meridian High School principal, R.D. Harris, who complained in the January 26, 2006, issue of the Jackson *Clarion-Ledger* that "never in his 40 years in Mississippi schools had he seen the State-Ole Miss rivalry sink so low. When it comes to those two recruiting, there's always been a war," he said. "But now it's just at a sad level."

Jackson *Clarion-Ledger* sports writer Rick Cleveland wondered whether the fans hated the other school more than they loved their own.

Sansing quotes Charles Lee, Mississippi State president from 2002-06, as complaining "that the State and Ole Miss rivalry had gotten completely 'out of hand' and blamed the fans and supporters who 'not only want their team to win on the playing field, but... seek to discredit their rivals through the media and through NCAA investigations.'" The mudslinging went, and goes, both ways.

Sansing refers to a 2005 Memphis *Commercial Appeal* article in which sports writer Ron Higgins referred to State and Ole Miss as being "cutthroat cousins." He further noted that State and Ole Miss had not played each other for the SEC championship in more than fifty years and that both teams "had more NCAA probations than ten-win seasons in the past thirty years." Higgins went on, "Every time one of the schools starts stringing together winning seasons, envious fans of the school on the downslope begin digging up dirt to hand over to NCAA investigators."

The almost instantaneous speed of spreading rumors of illegal recruitment tactics via the internet only complicates the problems.

According to Jackson *Clarion-Ledger* Sports Editor Hugh Kellenberger, who wrote in a 2016 article, "Never has the Ole Miss and Mississippi State rivalry been more toxic. It's become mean-spirited, short-sighted and to the detriment of the state as a whole."

Kellenberger claims that the problem has gotten worse in the past five years because "Both programs got good. Really good."

Many fans of either school cannot seem to tolerate the other school's success. Kellenberger attributes this increased vitriol in large part to the social media that he claims is "an absolute cesspool." He attributes this to "the crab mentality — the moment one rises to the top of the barrel, the others will do everything they can to pull him down." Kellenberger is pessimistic that the competition will not get better soon.

The recruiting rivalries of Ole Miss and Mississippi State with Southern Mississippi, while intense, are not as bitter as the Ole Miss-State battles. The primary reason is that both Ole Miss and State have dropped USM from their schedules. Another reason is that State and Ole Miss are members of arguably the strongest football conference in the nation, the Southeastern Conference, and recruiting is even more intense. The Jackson *Clarion-Ledger* annually publishes a list of the top 12 ("Dandy Dozen") high school football prospects in Mississippi. The 2016 list of prospects reflects the intensity of recruiting local talent. Of the 12 players selected, five committed to Ole Miss, three committed to Mississippi State and one committed to Southern Mississippi. Two of the remaining three signed with out-of-state schools, and one signed with a community college in Mississippi.

It was in this atmosphere that Carmody felt recruiting Mississippi athletes was a challenge, a challenge he enjoyed. Having coached and recruited at Southern Mississippi, Mississippi State, and Ole Miss a total of 22 years, perhaps no one understood the challenge of recruiting Mississippi athletes better than Jim Carmody.

The Rebel Flag Issue

Willie Morris wrote, "The competition for high school football players in Mississippi between Mississippi State, Southern Mississippi, and Ole Miss had become suicidal." Under Johnny Vaught, and before integration, Ole Miss used to get the majority of good players in Mississippi.

After integration the three schools began to split these players. Morris wrote, "The rival recruiters from other schools… were telling the black players and their parents that Ole Miss was a slave factory, harkening to the plantation days… The traditional symbols of the older South at the state university were only part of the campaign. This systematic elaboration of the alleged treatment of black students at Ole Miss was relentless and often persuasive."

Ole Miss became an easy target for Southern Mississippi and Mississippi State recruiters because of its Confederate symbols. Over the years Ole Miss worked at changing most of its traditional symbols. Up until 1963 the Ole Miss Marching Band wore Confederate-styled uniforms. These uniforms were changed to uniforms featuring a Confederate flag panel on the chest, and then in 1968 the band switched to more traditional band uniforms. However, traditions such as waving the Confederate Battle Flag, the Colonel Reb mascot, and the band playing "Dixie" remained.

In Dr. David Sansing's sesquicentennial history of Ole Miss, he describes the slow university progress designed to change its national public image. In 1982, the university's first elected black cheerleader, John Hawkins, refused to carry the Confederate flag onto the field as tradition dictated. To worsen matters, the Ku Klux Klan continues to use the Confederate flag as its symbol of racial hatred. Head football coach Steve Sloan, arguing that the Confederate flag made it difficult to recruit black football players, suggested modifying the flag in such a way as to distinguish the Ole Miss flag from the Confederate flag — perhaps by adding the letters "UM" or "Ole Miss" to the flag.

In 1983 Chancellor Porter L. Fortune announced that the university was officially and formally disassociating itself from the Confederate flag and that no university-associated organization would be allowed to display the flag.

In 1991 the University of Mississippi Alumni Association passed a resolution asking football fans, students, and alumni alike to not to bring Confederate flags to football games and other athletic events. The issue was finally resolved in 1997 when the university passed a regulation prohibiting anyone from bringing a stick to athletic events for "safety reasons," thus preventing fans from bringing and waving the Rebel flag. Eventually, the band was prohibited from playing "Dixie," and in 2003 Colonel Reb was removed as the Ole Miss mascot. In 2010, the University of Mississippi announced a ban on the sale of any items bearing the image of Colonel Reb. The most visible images of associating the university with the Confederacy were resolved — but to the continuing displeasure of many students and alumni.

Southern Mississippi and Mississippi State have the luxury of letting Ole Miss continue to fight the Civil War. Most recently, there was a major issue of the Confederate flag's being a part of the state flag of Mississippi. Ole Miss and Southern Mississippi have chosen to not fly the flag on campus anymore, while Mississippi State has chosen to continue to fly the state flag.

The bottom line of the issue of Confederate symbols with regard to athletic recruiting is what effect the symbols had, one way or the other, on the recruiting process. In 1994, a black native of Moss Point, Mississippi, Jack Jackson, said that to him, Ole Miss is the Confederate flag, the song "Dixie," and a direct link to a Deep South past where hatred and racism were once rampant. "The Rebel flag is probably the single most problem a lot of us had," Jackson said.

Around the turn of the century, Ole Miss head football coach, David Cutcliffe, and Rod Barnes, the school's head basketball coach, stuck their necks out and endorsed a new Mississippi flag that was not based on the Confederate flag. They claimed that the fact that the Rebel faithful waved Confederate flags did not help either coach in recruiting, but Cutcliffe also felt it was wrong on a moral level, just as his mother had taught him. The stance was unpopular, and Cutcliffe reportedly received death threats for his opinions.

Former Ole Miss athletic director Warner Alford said, "It's like fighting a ghost." Jim Carmody is in a unique position to make that evaluation since he is the only person to have coached at Ole Miss, Mississippi State, and Southern Mississippi — serving two stints at each of the three major football institutions.

Carmody told newspaper reporter Rick Cleveland, "That's fairly unique, I would say. Two different times at all three schools. I guess it shows I didn't burn any bridges."

He was in the unique position of recruiting football players with the Rebel flag at Ole Miss and recruiting against the Rebel flag at USM and Mississippi State. He, probably more than any coach, knew the effects, if any, the flag had on recruiting. Carmody says that he never signed a player because of the Rebel flag issue, nor did he ever lose a player because of the Rebel flag issue. He says that when he signed a player it was because he outworked other recruiters. Former Ole Miss athletic director Warner Alford backs this statement up saying, "Jim was the hardest working, most organized recruiter" he knew.

During one of our interviews Carmody expressed his feelings about the Rebel flag issue, stating, "Here's my position on the Rebel flag. We never had a Rebel flag in our yard; we never had one on our car, and we never had one in our house. However, I do not feel badly toward people who do have Rebel flags in their yard or on their car. That's their decision. I never have thought much about it. When I look at a Rebel flag, if I see one, I don't think about the Civil War, I just think it's a flag. People say, 'Well, that is a racial sign,' but I don't think of it that way. So the Rebel flag has never been an issue with me. When I was recruiting I never recruited a single black player or talked to his family who asked me about the Rebel flag. Never. That's when I was recruiting for Ole Miss. And when I was recruiting for Southern or Mississippi State I never went into a home, and maybe the player I was recruiting we were competing with Ole Miss, and I never said, 'You know they wave the Rebel flag up there. They're a bunch of racists up there, you don't want your son to go to a school like that.' I never once said anything like that. It never came up, and nobody ever asked me what I thought about the Rebel flag in all the black homes I've been in, hundreds of them throughout this state, nobody ever asked me about the Rebel flag. So I don't have a real feeling one way or the other about it. Did I sign a list saying we should remove it? No, I didn't. If the people who signed the list really believe that, then it's their business. I personally think some of them get caught up in a political situation. The flag is not an excuse for losing a player."

The bottom line is clear, however. In 2015, Ole Miss' football program is devoid of all symbols of the Confederacy; no Rebel flags at football games, no playing of Dixie by the university band, no playing of "From Dixie with Love," no Colonel Rebel mascot. All vestiges of the Confederacy are gone. The result of these actions is more than coincidence. Since 2013 Ole Miss has had one of the top football recruiting classes in the nation.

Recruiting Quality Players

When Steve Sloan was hired to replace Ken Cooper, Carmody felt that since Ole Miss was still paying him, he would continue to recruit. National signing date was not far off, and Sloan came to Carmody and said, "Jim, I need your help." One of the players high on the Ole Miss recruiting chart was Melvin Brown, a highly recruited running back from Biloxi, Mississippi. Sloan, Carmody, and long-time athletic department staff member and UM wide receiver coach Eddie Crawford went to Biloxi to make a recruiting visit to Brown's home. Sloan asked Brown what other schools he was considering, and Brown said, "Alabama."

They had a good visit, but once they were outside Sloan told Carmody not to waste any more time recruiting Brown. "He's going to Alabama," Sloan said. Carmody was not as sure and asked Sloan if he could keep recruiting Brown. Sloan gave in, and Carmody continued his relentless quest to sign him. He asked Sloan if he could stay down there and keep recruiting Brown, and he did.

On National Signing Day Brown signed with Ole Miss and had an excellent career at Ole Miss, initially as a running back his freshman year then as a cornerback his final three years. He was drafted as the tenth pick of the forth round of the NFL draft as a defensive back by the Minnesota Vikings. Another feather in Carmody's recruiting cap. Carmody said he did not have to keep recruiting Brown, after all; he had been fired.

Carmody has been involved in recruiting several great players at every school he has coached, successfully signing some, missing out on others. But not all good players are the result of intensive recruiting. Carmody tells a story of how in 1983 he found a punter for USM. Carmody's son Brian told him one day, "Dad, you ought to look at this guy, Larry Boyd. He is a real good athlete. You look at walk-ons, don't you?"

Carmody told him, "Of course."

Brian said Boyd was also a good baseball player and basketball player. The Eagles were still having spring practice so Carmody called Boyd and invited him out to look the program over.

Turns out Boyd ended up as the number-one punter for USM the following fall.

Boyd told Carmody the story of being in a football locker room for the first time. He had been in baseball and basketball locker rooms before, but they were nothing like the football locker room. Boyd said the defensives guys, The Nasty Bunch, were pounding on the walls, kicking the door hollering, "Let us out! Let us out!"

Boyd had never seen anything like this before so he put his helmet on and sat as far back in his locker as he could. He said, "Get me out of here before these guys kill me!" Boyd turned out to be an excellent punter, averaging 40.5 yards a punt. You never know where you will find good players.

Archie Manning

When Carmody was at Mississippi State, among the areas he recruited was the Mississippi Delta. He knew that there was an outstanding athlete in Drew, Mississippi, named Archie Manning. Carmody recruited him hard because of his overall athletic skills, and he watched Archie play football two or three times for Drew High School. He also watched him play basketball. Although Carmody had the clear impression that Manning favored going to Ole Miss, he continued to recruit him hard. He thought he had a chance to sign him to a Mississippi State scholarship but realized that the reason he felt good about his chances was because Archie's parents were such nice people and were reluctant to hurt anyone's feelings. Carmody visited with

Archie and his parents several times at their home and visited with his high school football coach. Carmody did not watch Manning play baseball, but knew he was considered to be a high draft choice by a major league team.

Carmody thinks Manning was not among the most highly recruited players in the state mainly because of his physical stature. Manning was a tall (6'3"), skinny (about 160 pounds) kid, but Carmody knew he had speed. Apparently only Tulane, Mississippi State, and Ole Miss offered him a football scholarship, and he was, indeed, drafted by major league baseball.

Carmody remembers how fast Manning was. Another skill Archie possessed was a strong arm. Carmody still thinks Archie had a stronger arm than either of his two All-NFL professional football quarterback sons, Peyton and Eli, and was, no question, a better runner. Carmody told Archie that Vaught liked to sign quarterbacks to Ole Miss scholarships and indicated that he would probably sign three or four more this year. Jim was hoping to convince Archie that he would probably be fighting for the quarterback job with seven or eight others, whereas he had a better shot at quarterbacking at Mississippi State.

It turns out that as nice as Archie and his family were to Carmody, the real decision Archie seemingly had to make was between playing college football or professional baseball. Going to college was the deciding factor for Archie's signing with Ole Miss in December 1966 (National Signing Day was set for December at that time rather than the following February as it is today.)

In his autobiography Ole Miss head coach Johnny Vaught wrote, "I wish I could write that I went to Drew and signed Archie myself, but that's not the case. The honor fell to Roy Stinnett, a graduate assistant on the coaching staff at the time."

Carmody never coached against Manning, since by the time Archie enrolled at Ole Miss, Carmody was at North Carolina. The Archie Manning story is perhaps as well known to football fans as any story about any athlete in this country.

Marcus Dupree

The most widely recruited high school football player in the state of Mississippi, and perhaps the nation, in 1981-82 was a talented, almost super-talented, 17-year-old running back from Philadelphia, Mississippi, Marcus Dupree. Dupree was an imposing running back at 6'2" (or 6'3"), weighing 225 lbs. and possessing speed and strength. At times, he was like a man playing with boys. His recruitment was the most intensive in Mississippi high school athletics. Among the "Big Three" Mississippi schools most thought that Southern Mississippi had the inside track, with Ole Miss playing an outsider role, However, when Marcus began his senior year in high school in 1981, the NCAA informed the University of Southern Mississippi that it had begun a preliminary investigation into its athletic department of recruiting violations under Coach Bobby Collins. However, neither the departure of Bobby Collins from USM, the on-going NCAA investigation, nor the appointment of Jim Carmody as head coach had any apparent effect on Marcus Dupree's interest in USM at the time. Most recruiting experts surmised that the two leading schools in Marcus' mind were the University of Texas and the University of Oklahoma, although almost every major college in the country recruited him. Dupree's high school coach said he received more than 100 telephone calls a day about his star running back.

"The Courting of Marcus Dupree" by Willie Morris is perhaps the definitive accounting of college recruiting in general and of Dupree in particular. Most experts who followed his recruitment thought the finalists on Dupree's list were the University of Texas, the University of Oklahoma, UCLA, and Southern Mississippi. Certainly Carmody had the reputation of being a tenacious recruiter, so USM never seemed to be out of the picture.

Morris described Carmody as "an aggressive defensive tactician." Carmody and his offensive coordinator, Keith Daniels, had scheduled an official visit to Dupree's home the day before national signing date. Daniels said after the visit that he and Carmody left the Dupree home with the impression that Southern was in good shape. Willie quotes Carmody as saying, "We feel Marcus is very interested in our school, and we've been very low-keyed in the recruiting of him and remaining there all the time. We've not beaten down his door and constantly called him in any way. We just liked him to know we were around. We tried to impress on him the chance to play in a winning program, to get a quality education, and to be near home where his family and friends can see him play." But Dupree made a verbal commitment to Texas when he visited Austin.

On Marcus Dupree Day on the Sunday before National Signing Day, at the Westside Community Center in Philadelphia, Willie noted that Carmody was sitting next to UCLA head coach, Terry Donahue. He wrote that the two had been chatting amiably. Willie described Carmody as "a rather intense figure whose public countenance was sinewy, lean-spirited and hard-nosed, a man with whom one could not have wished gratuitously to challenge, on whose face seemed to have settled the accumulated fratricides of collegiate football." Willie then described Donahue as wearing "a powder-blue sports jacket and was unexpectedly young; without the sartorial grace, he could have passed for a junior high algebra instructor about whom the matrons of the PTA might have had secret fantasies."

Willie noted that Donahue looked out quizzically at the mixed crowd and he wondered "what might be wafting through his mind in this moment... Was he touched? Intrigued? Baffled? Worried sick about getting his man? A vein of secret recognition seemed to pass across his clean American features, as if he had momentarily divined some fragile regional truth."

Carmody answered that question years later, recalling that their conversation went something like Donahue's asking him, "Jim, do your think we (UCLA) have any chance to get this kid?"

Carmody answered "Nope."

Donahue said, "Well, I am going to fire my recruiting coordinator when I get back. Right now, this weekend. Here I am sitting in Philadelphia, Mississippi, on a Sunday because he told me we had a chance to get this kid. And we've got twenty of the top prospects in California visiting us right now, and I'm still here. Is there any place to get a drink in this town on a Sunday?"

Carmody said, "I'm not sure you can get a drink here anytime, Coach."

Donahue replied, "Can you get a drink in Jackson?"

Carmody said, "Yep, you probably should wait until you get back to Jackson." Willie would have been amused to learn what the Carmody-Donahue "wafting" was actually all about.

On February 10, 1982, National Signing Date, Marcus Dupree surprised nearly everyone by announcing that he was going to the University of Oklahoma and play for Coach Barry Switzer. Most thought he was headed to Texas. Carmody and USM made a spirited but unsuccessful effort to bring him to Hattiesburg.

Dupree had a brief collegiate career and left Oklahoma, where he had garnered second-team All-American honors as a freshman. But he suffered a concussion in his sophomore year after playing five games. Dupree announced that he would be leaving Oklahoma and transferring to either Southern Mississippi or Mississippi State. In fact, he briefly enrolled at USM at mid-term but decided to forgo the remainder of his collegiate eligibility rather than sit out, under NCAA transfer rules, until 1985. The NCAA ruled that since he transferred in the middle of his sophomore season he would not be eligible to play college ball until 1985. Carmody was quoted in the *New York Times* that "Marcus has had difficulty coping with the fact he cannot play college football until 1985 and has talked of the possibility of playing professional football. He is not sure of his plans at this time, but it is obvious he will not be playing football at USM."

Dupree recently claimed on an ESPN 30 for 30 documentary, poorly misnamed "The Best That Never Was," that during the recruiting ordeal, one school offered him $250,000 a year while another offered him an oil well! The schools were not identified. Dupree was described in the documentary as "the biggest, fastest running back in high school history. In college his career ended before it truly began."

Brett Favre

The career of Brett Favre is one of the more interesting stories in college and professional football. Others have published various accounts of his recruitment to USM and his first college game, and many myths have appeared in print. Only one person knows the whole, true story — Jim Carmody.

Favre was from Kiln, Mississippi — located only 70 miles south of Hattiesburg — and his father, Irvin Favre, was the head football coach at North Hancock Central High School. Irvin had played baseball at USM. He ran an option-oriented wishbone offense, and his son, Brett, was the quarterback. Irvin liked the ground game, and Brett had limited opportunities to throw the ball. Yet, he attracted the attention of USM's first-year offensive line coach, Mark McHale, who would bring up Favre's name at every coach's recruiting meeting the fall of 1986. McHale was assigned to recruit the Gulf Coast area, which included Kiln.

McHale told the story of how he recruited Favre in Packer Forum, a Green Bay Packer internet site. McHale's predecessor had compiled a list of potential players in that area — the list did not include Brett Favre. Yet word was out that there was a quarterback at North Hancock Central High School worth looking at. McHale when to the school to look at film, and when he first saw Favre on film he was not impressed, since it appeared that all Favre was doing was handing off the ball. As he was leaving, Brett's father introduced Brett to McHale.

McHale said Brett looked him in the eye and said "Coach, I can play for you."

McHale was impressed with Brett's self-confidence and went back to see him play. He watched Favre throw in pre-game warm-ups, and McHale could tell he had a strong arm. Favre threw some of the hardest and deepest passes McHale says he had ever seen. But Favre threw only four passes in the first half in the game. In the second half Favre scrambled out of pressure and threw a pass that McHale claimed "had flames and smoke coming off it."

Recruiting a quarterback was low on USM's priority list — USM had several returning for the 1987 season including Ailrick Young, David Forbes, and Simmie Carter. And two other quarterbacks made verbal commitments to USM. Carmody needed to be convinced about Favre's talent. McHale has expansively discussed his role in convincing Carmody to recruit Favre.

In a book, *Favre: The Total Package*, it is wrongly stated that "McHale told Southern staff that Favre had a great future playing defensive back at the Division I level. As legend has it, with McHale and Carmody in the stands, Irv really let Brett loose, and Brett attempted six passes that night." The major problem with this story is that Carmody says he never saw Favre play in high school.

While Ole Miss, Mississippi State, LSU, and Florida had shown some interest in Favre, no other universities except perhaps Tulane and Division II Delta State University made him an offer. McHale claims that Brett's dad made up the claim that Delta State had offered him a scholarship only to put pressure on USM to offer his son a scholarship.

The Golden Eagles had three capable quarterbacks on their current roster and had received verbal commitments from two others. If another quarterback was signed, it would have to be with the understanding that he would have to also be able to play other positions, such as defensive back or safety. At a meeting of USM coaches to discuss recruiting, McHale once again pushed for Favre. McHale quotes Carmody as saying, "Mark, can he play another position? If we get him in as a quarterback, and he can't play quarterback, is he athletic enough to play something else?"

McHale says he responded that Favre could play safety, tight end, or linebacker. Then just before signing date, a linebacker from Atlanta who had committed earlier to USM uncommitted late in the recruiting process, thus opening up a scholarship slot. Carmody asked McHale to find out if Favre was still available, and said, "If so, I'd like to put him in that defensive slot that we lost."

McHale telephoned Favre and explained that USM was offering him a scholarship and needed an immediate response. Favre readily agreed, so he was essentially offered a scholarship over the telephone.

Favre was the last recruit USM signed in the spring of 1987. Also in *The Total Package*, a coach who was to follow Carmody at USM relates the following story, which seems to imply that he was involved in the recruitment of Favre when he was not involved in any way: "The story of how Brett was recruited is a great one. Here's a kid from a small school that didn't throw much, and now he's one of the best QBs in the country. It just shows that you can't always judge a player in physical talent alone."

Favre was excited about signing with USM. "When Southern signed me, it was the greatest moment of my life. A few bigger schools showed interest for a while, but Southern Miss really hung in there, particularly coach McHale. I guess some people might have considered me a long shot, but I was just happy to get the opportunity."

As fall practice began Favre asked Carmody for an opportunity to give quarterbacking a try. As quoted in *Favre: Total Package*, Favre admitted, "When I first came here I was depressed. I sat up in the dorm with nothing to look forward to except practice…" Carmody decided to give Favre a try.

After seeing Favre's arm strength first-hand Carmody later told a newspaper reporter, "The first morning, I was standing with my back to his group. I heard this noise, a 'whoosing' sound. I turned around and said, 'What in the world is that?' I coached a long time, and I never heard a ball sound like that."

So he gave Favre a chance to play quarterback, and the rest is history. He was initially listed seventh on the QB depth chart, but injuries took their toll, and he moved up, mainly by attrition, the to third slot, which was important because USM always traveled with three quarterbacks.

Favre said, "I remember looking at the other quarterbacks. I used to envy Ailrick (Young) and David (Forbes). They were somebody. The coaches looked up to them; the rest of the players looked up to them. And I was back there throwing for the scout team." The initial plan for Favre was to redshirt him and get him ready for the 1988 season. It did not take long for Favre, then a 17-year-old freshman, to take over leadership on the field.

Tommy Wilcox and John Fourcade

In 1978, two of the most highly recruited players in the South were quarterback and defensive back Tommy Wilcox and quarterback John Fourcade.

Tommy Wilcox is the son of Fred Wilcox, who was a teammate of Carmody's at Tulane and who played quarterback for the Greenies. Tommy went to Bonnabel High School in Kenner, a suburb of New Orleans, and was highly recruited. Jim and Fred remained close friends over the years. Fred wanted his son to play for Carmody, so Tommy narrowed his college choices to Ole Miss and Alabama. Carmody recruited Wilcox hard. When Fred asked Jim if Sloan had hired him as part of his new staff, Carmody told him that it wasn't likely he would. Fred called Jim, and said he would contact Sloan and tell him that if he hired Jim, his son would go to Ole Miss.

Carmody asked Fred not to do it — that was not the way he did business — "I do not work that way," Jim said.

Tommy ended up at the University of Alabama, where he was signed as a quarterback but switched to defense in order to play right away rather than be a redshirt quarterback. He played cornerback, was a consensus All-American on the 1981 team, and was one of two safeties named to Alabama's Team of the Century.

John Fourcade was a star quarterback for Archbishop Shaw High School in Marrero on the West Bank of New Orleans. He was also highly recruited, and it was obvious that he and Wilcox would not go to the same college football program. Carmody and USM assistant coach Keith Daniels continued recruiting him hard. When Carmody was not hired by Sloan and when Wilcox signed with Alabama, Fourcade was an easy recruit for Sloan, thanks to Carmody's groundwork.

Todd Wade was recruited by Carmody but not coached by Carmody. Wade was an offensive tackle for Ole Miss and was named first-team All-SEC and second-team All-American. Wade was drafted by the Miami Dolphins in the second round and was named to the NFL All-Rookie team. He enjoyed a nine-year professional career with Miami, the Houston Texans, Washington Redskins, and Jacksonville Jaguars.

Other Notable Carmody Recruits

Carmody had recruiting success wherever he coached. While at Southern, other than Brett Favre, among his most notable recruits were these:

Richard Byrd — USM — Jim Hill High School in Jackson, played at USM as a defensive lineman and was a second-round draft pick by the NFL Houston Oilers — played for Houston for five years — one of the leaders of "The Nasty Bunch," Honorable Mention All-American.

Jerald Baylis — USM — from Jackson, Mississippi, nicknamed "The Space Ghost" — played ten years in the Canadian Football League. He was named the CFL Most Outstanding Defensive Player in 1993 and made the CFL All-Star team four times.

Dwayne Massey — USM offensive tackle from Jackson, Mississippi. Lettered at USM. He represented USM at the 1981 Tangerine Bowl in a prime rib-eating contest against a representative from the Missouri team.

When Carmody was at the University of North Carolina, the Tar Heels lacked recruiting success in Virginia. But Carmody considered that a challenge and successfully recruited that area. At UNC his prize recruits were the following:

Ron Rusnak — Grew up in Prince George, Virginia, and played offensive guard for UNC. He was twice named All-ACC. He was a unanimous first-team selection in 1972 to the College Football All-American team.

Robert Pratt — A left tackle from Richmond, Virginia. He was named All-ACC and was an All-American selection. He was drafted by the Baltimore Colts in the third round. Pratt had a twelve-year career in the NFL with Baltimore and was the Seattle Seahawks' NFL Lineman of the Year in 1983.

While at The University of Mississippi he recruited John Fourcade but left Ole Miss before Fourcade's signing date. Among his prized recruits for the Rebels were these players:

Melvin Brown — Recruited as a running back, Brown was switched to defensive back. He was recruited by Carmody but not coached by Carmody. He was drafted by the NFL.

Walker Jones — Recruited by Carmody in 1994, Jones was named permanent captain of the Rebels in his senior year. He served as coordinator of football operations at Ole Miss under Coach David Cutcliffe and served as the head of college sports marketing for Under Armour.

Other Ole Miss notable recruits included Ta'Boris Fisher (wide receiver, Phil Freightman, (safety), Mike Fountain (cornerback), Jon Fabris (defensive back), Chuck Commiskey (center, offensive guard who played for the New Orleans Saints of the NFL).

Among Carmody's most notable recruits at Mississippi State:

Tony James — MSU wide receiver, kickoff and punt return specialist — 1989-92. In 1989 this graduate of Clinton (Mississippi) High School finished first in the SEC and third in the nation in punt returns and first in the SEC and second in the nation in punt return yards. Named to the All-Time Mississippi State football team as special reams kick returner.

Chris Gardner — MSU place kicker from Brandon, Mississippi. Gardner finished his career at MSU ranked No. 8 on the All-Time list of field goals made, and fifth in the SEC in 1992 in field goals made.

Other notable Carmody recruits at MSU included Tommy Morrell (defensive back from Clewiston, Florida (whose dad played as MSU), Andre Bennett (wide receiver, defensive back from Brandon, Mississippi), Frankie Luster (defensive back from Clewiston, Florida), Keo Coleman, (a junior college transfer linebacker from Texas), Nate Williams (a junior college transfer nose guard from Texas).

9

COACHING THE PROS

Southern Mississippi was coming off one of its most successful seasons in 1980, led by the defense of The Nasty Bunch coached by Big Nasty, Jim Carmody. The Eagles finished the regular season at 8-3, a record that included victories over archrivals Ole Miss (28-22) and Mississippi State (42-14). The Eagles received an invitation to the Independence Bowl in Shreveport, Louisiana, and capped off the year with a victory over McNeese State (16-14). Instead of simply being satisfied with this success, Carmody was even more determined to secure his career goal — that of being a head coach. He had compiled an impressive resume, but he thought it could be improved if he had coaching experience in professional football — especially the NFL. He had never previously given much thought to coaching in the NFL, although many colleagues thought that was an ideal job for him in pursuing his head coaching goals. Good fortune lay ahead.

Shortly after the season ended he was sitting in his office when he received a telephone call from the legendary head coach of the Green Bay Packers, Bart Starr. Starr was a legend as the quarterback of two Super Bowl winning Packer teams. He was beloved in Green Bay as their quarterback from 1956 to 1971. After he retired as a player Starr joined the Green Bay coaching staff as quarterback coach. In 1975 he was named head coach. Starr did not enjoy the success in coaching that he had enjoyed as quarterback and after the Packers' 1980 season could claim only one winning season in his first six years. The Packers needed help, especially defensive help. Green Bay went 5-10-1 that year following a 0-4-1 preseason. Among their losses were a 51-21 defeat against the Los Angeles Rams and a 61-7 defeat to the archrival Chicago Bears.

Although Carmody did not know Starr well, apparently Starr was well aware of Jim's defensive coaching abilities. When pro scouts visit a college team's practices and games, they are not only scouting the players, they scout the coaches as well, knowing where the winners are. Still Carmody was surprised by the call. Starr told him the Packers needed defensive line coaching help, that he had heard good things about him, and he invited Jim and Noonie to visit Green Bay for an interview. Jim and Noonie flew up to Green Bay, and Jim interviewed for the defensive line coaching position. The visit went well, but Starr told Carmody that he would feel bad moving the Carmody family to Green Bay since the current coaching staff was under intense pressure and Starr was not certain of his, and his staff's, future. (Starr was indeed replaced after the 1983 season). Carmody told Starr he appreciated his being honest with him. The Packers hired defensive line coach Don Urich from the Washington Redskins. But Jim's hat was in the ring.

A week later Carmody was getting ready for the USM spring conditioning program when he received a telephone call from Buffalo Bills' head coach, Chuck Knox. Knox had an extensive coaching record in the NFL, serving as head coach of the Los Angeles Rams from 1973-77 before becoming head coach of the Bills in 1978. Knox's football philosophy was built around the running game (his teams had the reputation of playing football ten yards at a time) earning him the nickname of "Ground Chuck." He was also a tough-minded coach whose style of football earned him another nickname, "The School of Hard Knox." Knox was on Charlie Bradshaw's "Thin Thirty" staff at the University of Kentucky in 1962 — the year before Carmody joined the Kentucky staff. Knox left Kentucky and took a job with the New York Jets.

Carmody said, "I knew him, but we never had coached together." Jim and Noonie had met Knox at a Sugar Bowl party in New Orleans. The three went out together. Carmody was surprised to get the call from Knox because he had never had a strong interest in coaching in the NFL inasmuch as his goal was to be a head college football coach. But, surprisingly, two weeks in a row he received calls about NFL jobs. He did not think Starr had talked to Knox about him, but he suspected Knox learned that he had talked to Green Bay.

The Bills had a vacant defensive line coach slot open up when previous coach Willie Zapalac left Buffalo to join the staff of Bum Phillips with the New Orleans Saints. Knox told Carmody that he was looking for a college coach steeped in fundamentals, someone who was a student of the game, and someone who was a good teacher, a good technician, and a real motivator. Knox had talked to his star defensive end, Ben Williams from Ole Miss, about Carmody before calling Jim and inviting him up to Buffalo to talk about the job. Williams spent the off-season in Jackson, and Knox asked him what he thought of Carmody, Ben replied, "Well, do you want to be in the playoffs? If so, hire him, and we will be in the playoffs."

Carmody had coached Ben Williams at Ole Miss in 1974 and 1975, and he and "Gentle Ben" had struck up a good friendship off the field.

Williams would recall, "Jim came in at Ole Miss my junior year, and we got better real fast. He was great on techniques and teaching you how to play."

In the fall of 1971, Williams, from Yazoo City, Mississippi, and running back James Reed, from Meridian, Mississippi, became the first two African-Americans offered scholarships to play football for Ole Miss. Williams was recruited by Ole Miss defensive backs coach and former Rebel player, Junie Hovious. Williams was a starter as a freshman and was thus the first black to play football for the Rebels. Hovious was assigned by Johnny Vaught to recruit in an area that included Yazoo City. Vaught did not tell him to specifically recruit a black player, but Hovious had seen Williams play as a sophomore and was highly impressed. Hovious struck up a good relationship with Mrs. Molly Haymer, Williams' grandmother, and he would drop by her house for coffee when he was in Yazoo City. Hovious was convinced that Ben possessed not only the athletic skills to succeed at Ole Miss but also the character to handle the pressure of being the first black player at Ole Miss. Hovious was correct on both counts. The *Oxford Eagle* printed a story regarding the recruitment of Ben Williams and quotes Williams as saying, "I came to Ole Miss because it was a challenge, and I liked a challenge. Also I was recruited by Coach Junie Hovious, and I admired him a lot."

When asked how he would react to the Confederate symbols and "Dixie" being played at Ole Miss Williams said, "How can you be worried about

'Dixie' when you have a six-foot 5,300-pound white boy foaming at the mouth across the line ready to kick in your teeth?... If I play a good game, those white fans are going to stand up and cheer for me." Williams was a pallbearer at Hovious' funeral in 1998.

Reed was redshirted and played the following year. Williams had a great career at Ole Miss and became one of the most popular students on campus. He was voted "Colonel Rebel," the highest honorary position for males on campus — the first black student to be so elected. He was a third-round pick of the Buffalo Bills in the 1976 draft. In 2014 the Ole Miss athletic department honored Williams and Reed by naming the entrance to the Athletics Performance Center the Williams-Reed Football Foyer.

After Carmody interviewed, Knox offered him the job of defensive line coach, and Carmody accepted the offer. Not surprisingly, when Jim interviewed, it was snowing; in fact, Jim said it seemed to snow all the time. The Bills paid him $50,000 a year, a nice raise from the $33,000 he was making as an assistant at USM. At the time he was at USM Carmody was the highest paid college assistant coach in Mississippi since he was also assistant head coach.

He accepted Knox's offer, even though it meant leaving his family in Hattiesburg until the spring term ended in May. He stayed alone in a hotel all through the winter. His son Steve was on the USM football team and needed to stay for spring practice to get ready for the 1981 season, and Jim and Noonie did not want to pull Brian, who was enrolled at USM, from school. Keith and Chris did make the move and enrolled at Orchard Park High School. Noonie said it was getting cold in August, and when the movers finally delivered the patio furniture, she told them that since it would be too cold to use the patio to go ahead and store the patio furniture in the garage.

When Jim told Bobby Collins about this opportunity, Collins was happy for him even though it meant he would lose his defensive coordinator. When Carmody accepted the job of defensive line coach with the Bills, he said, "I never had any real strong aspirations about coaching pro ball until the last two or three years. I felt if I had the opportunity, I'd like to get in, although I was not actually working on it."

When Knox offered him the job with the Bills, he accepted the offer and looked forward to the new opportunity, but he said, "It wasn't any great design or lifelong goal because my family and I loved college coaching all those years."

Although Ben Williams and Carmody had a good relationship, it was not as if they always saw eye to eye. When Carmody arrived at Ole Miss, he moved Williams from his usual defensive tackle position to nose guard, a move that Williams was initially unhappy about. Ben had just made All-SEC as a tackle in 1973, coached by Warner Alford, and was feeling comfortable at that position. But Ben would later admit that the move was good for him, helping him prove he could play another position. (Ben would later be moved to defensive end at Buffalo). The move worked out — Ben made All-SEC in 1974 and 1975 and was a first team All-American in 1975. Ben was co-captain of the 1975 team and was selected to play in the 1976 Senior Bowl, the 1976 Coaches Association All-America Bowl, and the 1975 East-West Shrine Bowl.

Williams had a great ten-year pro career and went to the Pro Bowl in 1983. He is fifth on the list of Buffalo quarterbacks sacks leaders and, like at Ole Miss, he was a fan favorite. In 2014 several Buffalo Bills players from all over the country, mainly defensive players who played with Ben, came to Jackson just to visit Ben and play golf. When the players had a dinner after the golf match many, including Carmody, got up and spoke about him. Ben truly enjoyed the visit from his former teammates and coach. Williams was inducted into the Mississippi Sports Hall of Fame in 1997.

Carmody made an immediate, positive impression on the Bills' defensive linemen. Williams had good things to say about his coach: "He helped me with my fundamentals in college. He was strong on teaching technique; he was real strict on that, and he was a motivator."

Carmody and Williams became lifelong friends. When Williams would see Carmody, he would tease him, saying, "You know coach, I made you the coach you are."

Carmody would reply, "You know what, Ben, before I came to Buffalo you never played in the Pro Bowl. I made you an All-Pro player."

Bills nose tackle Fred Smerlas (a five-time NFL Pro Bowl selection during his 14-year NFL career) said, "He made a good adjustment from working with college kids to the pros. He does a good job. He is very knowledgeable and is a hard worker. He gets along with all the guys well. It's a nice situation. The better we get along, the looser things are. When he first came here, we were all a little tight." Smerlas continued, "It's been a good experience working with him. I had some problems at the beginning of the year with technique when I hurt my leg. We kept talking, and he was good about it. I had never been through something like that, and it was nice to have someone considerate enough to look at all the angles involved. I appreciate what he did. In other respects he helped me out with techniques."

Defensive end Sherman White, who was "a 10-year veteran playing with the gusto of a rookie" said, "He came from a winning tradition down in Mississippi and brought us an enthusiastic approach to football. He emphasized, 'If you work hard, the results will be there.' He came in with some different ideas, which I enjoy myself. He emphasizes pass rush and concentration on getting off the ball quickly, as well as using moves which I think have been effective." White continued, "He's done a great job for the pass rush. For my style of play, quickness and finesse, it's good because I always enjoyed pass rushing. We've improved our sack output over last year by quite a bit, so it's working. I think we've also played the run just as enthusiastically as the pass."

In fact, the 1981 Buffalo defense recorded 47 sacks, breaking the existing record of 33 sacks set in 1980. The team ranked No. 5 in total defense in the NFL that year, ranking third in the NFL after 12 games. But Carmody was not satisfied, saying, "The season is still a long ways from being over. You can talk about how many sacks you have, but you can still fall flat on your face. You can't sit back and say you've had a great year. You have to say the season is just starting, so play with renewed vigor and enthusiasm."

Reporter Dave Rafter wrote, "The players appear to be responding to Carmody. He feels the line's strength lies in its performance as a unit and in not depending on one player as other lines might."

Carmody found no real difference in coaching college football and coaching the pros. His first priority was to just be himself and not try to be someone else. Whether you are coaching high school, college, or the pros, a good coach is a good teacher. If you show these players you are prepared and know what to do, they will listen."

Carmody said he had no problems making the move to coaching in the NFL. The biggest exception was the way he dealt with professional players, some of whom were almost his age. He was more aware that dealing with each of his players required a different approach. "I didn't do any screaming or yelling or getting in anybody's face," he said.

For example, one Monday he was reviewing the previous game film. One of his linemen, Sherman White, had made a mistake, and knowing that White was a sensitive man, Carmody waited until he could meet privately with him to point out the mistake rather than criticize and embarrass him in front of his teammates.

However, Carmody was surprised at how rookie coaches were expected, like the rookie players, to perform in front of the team, singing their alma maters, telling jokes, etc. As a rookie coach Jim had to do the same and was even made to perform a hula dance, wearing a Hawaiian grass hula skirt, for the team.

The snow continued, and the Bills did not have an indoor practice facility. Williams would not let Carmody forget that at one practice Jim thought Knox said, "Go on in," so he began trotting to the locker room. The problem was he was the only one going in. Williams caught up with him and told him that Knox actually said, "Take ten!" The rookie coach took a lot of ribbing about that.

Carmody was given a lot of freedom by defensive coordinator Tom Catlin. Catlin spent 37 years as an NFL coach including stints as defensive coordinator with the Bills from 1978 to 1982 and the Seattle Seahawks from 1983 to 1991. Jim drew up all the front-line blitzes the Bills had. Catlin told the defensive backs' coach he was to draw up all the coverages. Catlin would ask Carmody in a given situation, "What do you want to call?" Carmody would make the call, and Catlin would signal in the defense. Carmody was pleased that he had a lot of decision-making responsibilities.

The Bills started the 1981 season on a high note. They shut out the New

York Jets 31-0 at home in the season opener then defeated the Baltimore Colts 31-3 at Baltimore. The Buffalo defense yielded only one field goal in the first two games. Carmody's professional debut was successful. But the Bills lost the next two games to the Philadelphia Eagles at home and to the Cincinnati Bengals at Cincinnati. They returned home to defeat Baltimore 23-17 and the Miami Dolphins 31-21. They lost a rematch with the Jets in New York 33-14 but then defeated the Denver Broncos in a defensive struggle 9-7, and the Cleveland Browns 22-13 in back-to-back home games. Cleveland Browns' head coach, Sam Rutigliano, was impressed with the Buffalo defense. The Browns went into the game having given up only 13 sacks in their first eight games — among the best in the league — but the Bills' defense sacked the Browns' quarterback six times in that game alone. In the Bills' locker room after the game, quarterback Joe Ferguson told the defense, "I'm glad I'm on your side."

The Bills lost road games to the Dallas Cowboys and St. Louis Cardinals before returning home to defeat the New England Patriots and Washington Redskins. They won their third straight game by beating the San Diego Chargers 28-27 on December 6 at Jack Murphy Stadium. The Bills came back from a 21-14 halftime deficit to score two third-quarter touchdowns while holding San Diego to just a field goal. The fourth quarter was a defensive struggle. The Chargers kicked a 27-yard field goal to cut the Bills' lead to 28-27, and the game ended that way. Although outgained in total yardage by the Chargers, the sixth-ranked Bills' defense forced three big turnovers (one fumble and two interceptions) to help seal the win.

The weather was beautiful in San Diego, with temperatures in the low 60s. Carmody recalled that when the team got home, Buffalo had had another ice storm and snowstorm. When he disembarked from the airplane he went to his car but could not get the key into the iced-over car lock. He had to kick the door hard enough to break the ice to knock the ice from the car. When he finally got into the car, the windshield was iced over, and the wipers were frozen. When he got back out of the car to scrape the ice off the windshield, he thought to himself, "What the hell, we just got back from the most beautiful climate, and here I am fighting my way home through all the ice and snow."

The Bills extended their streak to four straight victories with a 19-10 road win at New England but lost the season-ending game to the Miami Dolphins 16-6 to finish the season with a 10-6 mark. The Bills finished in third place in the AFC East behind the Dolphins and Jets and made the playoffs as a wild card team against the Jets.

The highlight of the season may have come in Game 12 at home against the Patriots when, down 17-13, quarterback Joe Ferguson threw a 36-yard Hail Mary pass to running back Roland Hooks with only 35 seconds remaining as the Bills defeated the Patriots 20-17. The Bills had driven 73 yards in two plays for the win. Most of the Bills' fans had left the stadium, assuming the Bills had lost, but the remaining 25 percent of the crowd was treated to one of the best Bills' victories in their history. This victory turned the Bills' season around, as it was the start of the four-game winning streak at the end of the season.

The Bills traveled to New York where the Jets were playing in their first playoff game since the 1970 merger. In a cold rain the Bills jumped to an early lead as Buffalo linebacker Ervin Parker forced a fumble on the opening kickoff return. The ball was recovered as it rolled on the ground by Buffalo's Charles Romes, who picked up the loose ball and raced into the end zone to give Buffalo a 7-0 lead just 16 seconds into the game. The Jets shook off the shock and drove to the Bills' 30. Jets' quarterback Richard Todd found Wesley Walker wide open in the end zone, but Walker dropped a certain touchdown pass. The Bills then raced to a 24-0 lead with less than ten minutes remaining in the first half. But in the second quarter the Jets began clawing back and were behind 24-10 at halftime. The Bills scored again and, down 31-13, the Jets refused to give in, scoring twice to narrow the score to 31-27 with 3:44 left in the game. The Jets got the ball back in the final minutes, but the Bills' defense rose to the occasion. After a last-minute drive the Jets had a first down on the Bills' 11-yard-line with just 14 seconds left in the game. The Bills' Steve Freeman intercepted a pass on that last drive, presumably effectively ending the game, but the Bills were penalized for defensive holding. An incomplete pass gave the Jets second down with ten seconds left. Todd rolled to his right and passed, but the Bills' Bill Simpson intercepted on the 1-yard line with two seconds left to preserve the Bills victory, only the third playoff win in the team's history and the first since they won back-to-back AFL titles in the 1964 and 1965 seasons. The Bills executed five sacks in the victory.

When the Bills team returned to Buffalo, their plane was met by a crowd estimated to be over 2,000 joyous fans. They were excited about the wild card victory and were there to greet their returning heroes. The police chief was trying to quiet the crowd down before a riot broke out and said, "There was widespread intoxication among the crowd." Two young fans were arrested.

On January 3, 1982, the Bills traveled to Riverfront Stadium in Cincinnati to take on the Bengals. The winner of this game would play the winner of the San Diego-Miami game for the AFC championship. The winner of that game would go to the Super Bowl. Carmody told Noonie, "You know what, just a little over a year ago I was sitting in Hattiesburg after defeating McNeese State in the Independence Bowl, and now here I am only two games away from the Super Bowl. Remember the expression on that TV ad golfer Lee Trevino made when he said, 'Is this a great country, or what?'"

The game was played in a fog with a mild temperature of around 50 degrees. The Bengals jumped off to a 14-0 lead keyed by a 27-yard punt return that led to the first touchdown and the interception of a Bills quarterback Joe Ferguson pass at midfield followed by an eight-play drive. The Bengals led 14-0 before the Bills had made a first down or completed a pass. After another Buffalo punt, the Bengals drove inside the Bills' 10-yard line and threatened to blow the Bills outside the stadium. However, as Carmody philosophized "Never give up," Buffalo's defense put on a goal-line stand and blocked the ensuing field goal attempt.

At the end of the first half Ferguson completed a 54-yard pass to Jerry Butler, and Joe Cribbs scored on a one-yard plunge to bring the Bills to a 14-7 halftime deficit.

At the start of the third quarter Ferguson led the Bills on a 69-yard drive in five plays to set up a 44-yard run by Cribbs to tie the game at 14-14. But a 40-yard kickoff return and an ensuing seven-play, 65-yard drive gave Cincinnati a 21-14 lead.

In a seesaw game the Bills then pulled off a 79-yard scoring drive, scoring on the first play of the fourth quarter to tie the game at 21-21. With eleven minutes left in the game the Bengals scored on a nine-play, 79-yard drive to put the Bengals ahead 28-21.

Once again the Bills responded by driving to the Cincinnati 23-yard line. With 2:58 to play Ferguson completed a fourth-and-three pass to Lou Piccone for an apparent first down at the 14 yard-line, but after the play field judge Don Hakes threw a flag and declared that the 30-second clock expired just before the snap, and the delay-of-the-game penalty wiped out the play. On the subsequent fourth down and 8 yards to go from the 28-yard line, rather than having first and ten from the 14, Ferguson overthrew Roland Hooks, and the pass fell incomplete.

Knox argued the delay of game vigorously with the referees, but Ferguson did not argue the call. What made the situation more difficult to comprehend was that the Bills had called timeout before the fourth-and-three play to discuss their strategy so Ferguson would not have to check off at the line of scrimmage.

After the timeout was over, the 30-second clock started. The Bills were huddled, and two substitutes, Piccone and Ron Jessie, were sent out onto the field. Knox was trying to confuse the Bengals, but it was the Bills who were confused, and they failed to get the play off in time. Ferguson said later, "I think we broke the huddle with 11 seconds left, which is usually enough time to get a play off. There was a lot of crowd noise, and I had to slow up my cadence, but usually you can feel when you are close to running out of time. I didn't sense it this time, nor did anybody else in the huddle."

Knox later explained that the reason for the last-second double substitutions was to prevent the Bengal defense from making any adjustments and to enhance the possibility of completing the fourth-down pass, thus keeping the Bills' drive alive. Had it not been for the delay of the game penalty, Knox's strategy would have succeeded.

After turning the ball over to the Bengals, the Bills' defense forced a punt with less than a minute to play, but the Bills' season ended when Ferguson threw four straight incompletions as time expired, the last being a barely overthrown pass to a diving Roland Hooks at the back of the Bengals' end zone. There would be no overtime; the Bills had shot themselves in the foot and lost 28-21. Super Bowl dreams turned into a nightmare.

Just after the season Knox told his assistants that Buffalo was not sending the coaching staff to Mobile, Alabama, for the Senior Bowl on January 17, 1982, but if anyone wanted to go to the practices and game, they could travel on their own to watch the practices and evaluate the players. Carmody was the only coach to accept the offer, and he drove to Mobile. Just after he left Buffalo he got caught in a snowstorm in Erie, Pennsylvania only 90 miles away and it ended up taking him 2-3 days to get to Mobile. When he drove back to Buffalo before the game was played, he passed through Hattiesburg. Rumors had been floating for some time that Bobby Collins was leaving USM to take the head-coaching job at SMU, but Carmody had not heard anything when he came through Hattiesburg. The day after Carmody returned to Buffalo, he received a call from USM athletic director Roland Dale indicating that Collins was likely to resign, and once the resignation was made official he was going to recommend Carmody for the head coaching job. Dale told Carmody that if Collins did resign he was not going to form a search committee.

"I am going to be a one-man search committee, and I have already talked to USM President Lucas about you and, if the job does open up and you want it, the job is yours."

Carmody said, "Yes, I do want it. I have always wanted to be a head coach."

Collins did indeed resign before the Senior Bowl, and Dale asked Carmody when he could come down to USM.

Carmody said he wanted to let Knox know about the opportunity, and he would come down the next day.

Carmody had a lot of respect for Chuck Knox, "I enjoyed working with Chuck Knox and appreciate the opportunity he gave me. I would think that Chuck Knox is one of the most underrated coaches in the history of the NFL. He had an outstanding record and won every place he was. It was a great year for me and a great opportunity, and I appreciate everything he did for me and my family." (N.B. Knox had been named NFL Coach of the Year three times.)

However, the next day all flights were cancelled because of more snow, so Carmody's trip to Hattiesburg was delayed. Nevertheless, on January 18 Dale announced his intention to offer Carmody the job. On January 19 Carmody officially announced his acceptance of Dale's offer. His lifelong dream had finally come true.

10

HEAD FOOTBALL COACH, USM

After leading the Golden Eagles for seven years, Coach Bobby Collins left USM in January 1982 to become the head football coach at SMU. When Collins resigned he had become the third winningest coach in the history of USM football. Collins, who was earning $62,000 a year at USM, was offered an estimated $100,000 to $250,000 a year at SMU, but he said it was not just the money that led to his joining SMU. The fact that SMU was part of a conference, the Southwest Conference, played a major role in his decision to leave USM. Collins replaced Ron Meyer, who took the head coaching job with the New England Patriots in the NFL.

USM's athletic director Roland Dale wasted no time in putting a search committee together. Dale named himself to be a one-person search, screening, and selection committee. He had seen former assistant coach and defensive coordinator Jim Carmody during the 1978-80 seasons earn his nickname "Big Nasty." Carmody had left USM in 1980 to join the professional ranks as defensive line coach of the NFL Buffalo Bills. At this point in his coaching career, Carmody was generally recognized within the coaching ranks as an aggressive defensive tactician and one of the best defensive coaches in the country. In addition, he had worked with Bobby Collins as an assistant head coach and defensive coordinator through the 1978-1980 seasons. He knew the USM system and the players. They were the ones to give him his nickname Big Nasty and earn themselves their nickname "The Nasty Bunch."

The choice to replace Collins was an easy one and a popular one among Golden Eagles' fans, who had become accustomed to the emergence of USM as one of the strongest defensive teams in the nation.

Willie Morris quoted an unidentified Mississippi football aficionado in his book, *The Courting of Marcus Dupree*, about Carmody: "He knows the territory and the territory knows him."

It did not take Carmody long to decide to leave the position of defensive line coach for the Buffalo Bills and return to Hattiesburg. On January 18, within days after Collins' announcement, Dale announced at a press conference that the university and Carmody had worked out a four-year contract paying him $55,000 a year.

Dale said, "We feel extremely fortunate that coach Carmody accepted the job. He made an impressive contribution to our program during his three years as an assistant coach." He went further to say Carmody was "thoroughly familiar with our operations and with the majority of our players. We look forward to continued progress with him as head coach" and expressed regret at the departure of Collins.

Carmody said he would like to see Collins' staff stay. "I would like to keep all of them; I'd like for all of them to stay, but I realize much of their loyalty is to Bobby, and that's the way it should be," Carmody said.

Meanwhile, Collins was saying almost the same about his staff at SMU. While Collins admitted he was under no obligation to retain any of former Coach Ron Meyer's staff, he said keeping a few assistants would provide continuity in recruiting. He was going to try to take as many of his USM staff as he could persuade to go to SMU with him. "I definitely have an obligation to my staff at USM," Collins said.

Collins and Carmody had long-term connections as coaches and as friends. Collins expressed his pleasure to learn his friend would succeed him. Collins said he and Carmody "coached together for six years at the University of North Carolina (and three years at USM). He's an outstanding person and a tremendous football coach, and he certainly has my best wishes, and I know that he'll do a tremendous job."

Carmody then completed the formation of his first coaching staff at USM, naming Thamas Coleman defensive coordinator and linebackers' coach, Mike DuBose (who later was head Coach at Alabama for four years) as defensive line coach, Ron Cheatham as defensive ends' coach, and Dyer Carlisle coach of the secondary. On the offensive side Keith Daniels was named offensive coordinator, Rick Trickett offensive line coach, Rick Coachys wide receivers' coach, and Jerry Fremin as tight ends' coach.

For Noonie Carmody the burdens of being a coach's wife continued. She had, after all, organized the family move from Hattiesburg to Buffalo less than a year earlier. Now it was time to return to Hattiesburg and create a new home there.

On July 27 USM President Aubrey Lucas announced the good news that USM was joining the Metro Conference, ending years of non-conference alignment. The problem for USM football was that the Metro Conference did not compete in football.

While Carmody achieved his lifelong goal of becoming a head coach at a major football program, the dream was not achieved without a lot of problems surfacing. He was faced with the immediate task of putting his own coaching staff together, knowing the NCAA was conducting an investigation into the Southern football program. Southern had been notified in September 1981 that a preliminary investigation was being conducted by the NCAA to look into rules violations committed by the school. Carmody later said, "I know I'm the first coach to report for work and on the first day have the NCAA show up. My first day — January 10 — the NCAA had a man here on campus." Less than two months after being named head coach, Carmody and USM were notified that the investigation was now official. In June 1982 the NCAA charged USM with 19 rules violations over the previous three-year period.

The response by USM President Aubrey Lucas was to conduct an internal investigation into these charges, so he appointed an attorney who was a member of the university's criminal justice department, James Halsted, and a Hattiesburg lawyer, Eric Lowery, to work with an ad hoc university committee appointed by Lucas. This committee, to the consternation of Lucas, identified three additional violations.

On August 22, 1982, the university appeared before the NCAA in Hyannis Port, Massachusetts, to defend itself against the new total of 22 violations. USM admitted to being guilty to eight of these violations while the NCAA infractions committee dismissed eight other charges, leaving six charges to be decided — or a total of 14 violations.

By the start of the 1982 football season Carmody learned that the program had been found guilty of four major violations (one of unethical conduct by an assistant coach) and three others of illegal recruiting inducements. Of the remaining ten lesser charges, USM was found guilty of two cases involving improper recruiting visits, two cases in which recruits were provided with improper transportation, two cases in which recruits were fed illegally, one case involving excessive off-campus visits, one case of contacting a recruit after that recruit had enrolled elsewhere, one case in which the university had obtained an improper commitment from a recruit, and finally one case in which an assistant coach had attended an athletic banquet outside of dates that were permitted. None of these violations named Carmody of any wrongdoing during his previous three-year stint at USM.

As quoted in *Rock Solid: Southern Miss Football*, by John W. Cox and Gregg Bennett, athletic director Roland Dale made an announcement regarding proposed penalties that the university "felt that (the NCAA's) findings were a little more difficult or tougher than they should be and that Southern Miss had 'asked the committee if they could review the penalty.'" The NCAA, at the request of USM, reviewed the penalties to be invoked but refused to alter the penalties in any way. On October 11 the infractions committee ruled that the penalties stood. President Lucas, athletic director Roland Dale, and Head Football Coach Carmody chose not to appeal the penalties. Lucas, Dale and Carmody accepted the penalties that consisted of no bowl appearances for 1982 or 1983 and no television appearances in 1983 and 1984. Also included in the penalties were the banning of three university representatives from representing university interests in recruiting and banning an unidentified assistant coach from participating in off-campus recruiting activities and not receiving any salary increases during the period of probation.

The official NCAA release stated, "This case involved promises of significant financial benefits to prospective student-athletes who were recruited during the 1979-80, 1980-81, and 1981-82 academic years. The efforts of outside athletic representatives to circumvent NCAA legislation by making these offers and the committee's determination that an assistant football coach was aware of these promises heightened the seriousness of the case."

Carmody entered his first year as head coach with his hands essentially tied by the NCAA restrictions. No bowl games or television appearances for the probation period would place severe restrictions on recruiting. So Carmody's life goal of becoming the head football coach at a major football institution was impeded by the actions of Southern Miss' coaches before him. Carmody's career was dealt a bad hand right out of the starting gate, yet he did not have a horse in the race, having not been named in any irregularity by the NCAA.

Ironically, Carmody's Golden Eagles finished 7-4 in 1982 and 7-4 in 1983 — both years they would have been bowl-eligible. Steve Carmody felt the sting of the probation and recalled that after a week of somber practice he expressed his feelings, which were shared by his teammates: "We went to bowls in 1980 and 1981. We were not in a conference, so the only measuring stick was whether you went to a bowl game. Probation was hard to take, especially since all of the people being accused of wrongdoing were no longer associated with the program."

1982 (7-4)

Jim was unsurprisingly nervous. He had spent nearly 35 years of his life waiting for this opportunity to take full responsibility for his team, his players. His opening opponent was the Northeast Louisiana Indians at home. Despite his previous experiences with USM being on the defensive side of the ball, where he was an expert in evaluating talent, he was pleased that he inherited two very talented offensive players: running back Sam Dejarnette and the brilliant quarterback, Reggie Collins, who was entering his senior year. Carmody would contend that Collier was one of the greatest quarterbacks in the history of the state of Mississippi. Both players stood out against the Indians, with Dejarnette rushing for 171 yards and two touchdowns while Collier rushed for 106 yards and two touchdowns and passed for 240 more yards as USM won their opener, 45-27. Carmody's debut as a head coach was quite successful.

Carmody paid attention to every detail regarding USM's football program and was interested in changing the physical appearance of the Golden Eagles by introducing a new helmet design. He retained the black shell that had become a USM standard, but he changed it to include a one-inch wide white center stripe that was flanked with three-quarter-inch gold stripes. The nickname "Eagles" was block printed in white with white underlining on both sides of the helmet, allowing it to stand out against the black background. The new helmet was a signal to players and fans alike that a different era had begun in USM football.

The Eagles' new block printed helmet design.

The obvious highlight of Carmody's rookie season as a head coach was the upset of Alabama in Tuscaloosa to end Bear Bryant's 57-game winning streak on their home field. On the downside were the NCAA sanctions placed on the USM football program, the 28-19 loss to Ole Miss, Carmody's former employers, in the second game of the season, and a controversial loss to Auburn. USM caught Ole Miss coming off a season-opening victory over Memphis State. The Rebels built up a 28-10 halftime lead and held on to win 28-19, despite solid offensive efforts from Collier and wide receiver Louis Lipps. The loss was a bitter one for Carmody, who returned to Oxford as the USM head coach. This season would be the final season for Sloan at Ole Miss.

USM fell behind Auburn 21-6 at Jordan-Hare Stadium before closing the gap to 21-19. The USM defense held the Auburn great running back, Bo Jackson, to 99 yards rushing. Collier completed a pass to the Auburn 28-yard line with 13 seconds left in the game. The Golden Eagles thought they had plenty of time to stop the clock and set up the game-winning field goal, but Auburn players were slow in setting up, and the officials allowed the clock to run out before USM could stop the clock. USM was out of timeouts.

Carmody was furious. "There were 13 seconds left on the clock when we completed the pass. That's plenty long enough to get the ball out of bounds for a field goal. But the officials let their players lay on ours. I believe the clock should have been stopped as they were doing this."

Steve Carmody felt the same way: "We were in position to kick a field goal at the end of the game. The ball was placed in play. I snapped it to Reggie, and there were two or three Auburn stragglers who had not gotten back to the line of scrimmage. The refs should have called time out since they were slow to line up on purpose. The refs royally screwed us."

The next week, despite Sam Dejarnette's rushing for over 300 yards, the Eagles fell to Florida State, 24-17. FSU's head coach, Bobby Bowden, was determined not to let Collier beat him again, and in containing him the Seminoles allowed Dejarnette to run loose. Steve Carmody recalls, "We just couldn't seem to get it in the end zone that night. We could have packed it in after the FSU loss, but the coaches had a meeting with us and said that we should have faith in them and believe in the system."

USM then put together a six-game winning streak, capping off victories over Memphis State, Mississippi State, Tulane, Louisville, and Louisiana-Lafayette. The team capped the streak off with the great upset victory at Tuscaloosa before running out of gas and losing the season finale to Louisiana Tech.

The Eagles were strong candidates for the Independence Bowl, but with its sanctions, the NCAA had ruled out any possibility of a bowl game.

1983 (7-4)

USM began its second consecutive 7-4 winning season with a blowout of the University of Richmond Spiders, 32-3. Reggie Collier had completed his eligibility after the 1982 season, but his cousin, Robert Ducksworth, took over the helm. The Eagles once again lost to Auburn, this time 24-3. Carmody is quoted in *Rock Solid* as saying, "We have no alibis or excuses. Auburn makes very few mistakes and is very opportunistic. We gave them two touchdowns and a field goal. We can't make very many mistakes and have a chance against them."

The Eagles bounced back with a 28-10 victory over Louisiana Tech in Hattiesburg. USM was down by field goal at halftime, and shortly after the third quarter began Ducksworth suffered a broken nose. He was unable to play the remainder of the third quarter and part of the fourth but returned to the game and threw a 68-yard touchdown pass to his favorite receiver, Louis Lipps. Ducksworth's determination apparently fired up the rest of the Eagles, and USM scored twice more to ice the game.

Carmody exacted a measure of revenge against his former bosses at Ole Miss, defeating the Rebels 27-7 at Vaught-Hemingway Stadium in Oxford. Southern jumped out to a 17-7 halftime lead and turned the game over to The Nasty Bunch. The defense responded. The Rebels advanced into Southern territory four times in the second half, but each drive was repulsed.

After the game Carmody said, "Last year we took a low-key approach to the Ole Miss game. It backfired, and it was my fault. We can't play that way at Southern. Miss… We have to play with a lot of emotion." Carmody tried to downplay his losing return to Ole Miss last year. "We have got to line up and get after folks," Carmody said after the victory.

Southern kept the momentum going by crushing Mississippi State 31-6 in Jackson. Once again the Ducksworth-led offense gave the Eagles a comfortable halftime lead, 17-0, and the Eagles scored twice more in the second half before State could get on the scoreboard. The victory was memorable in many ways since it was USM's seventh straight victory over the Bulldogs, and this win, coupled with the victory over Ole Miss the week before, gave Southern the undisputed state-rivalry championship for the fourth time in seven years. The Eagles were clicking.

USM extended its record to 5-1 with a victory over Memphis State before suffering a disappointing loss to Tulane, 14-7. The Eagles righted the ship by whipping Southwestern Louisiana (Louisiana-Lafayette) 31-3 to run its season record to 6-2 and then defeated the Louisville Cardinals on the road 27-3 — the second of five consecutive wins over Howard Schnellenberger's Cardinals — before falling to Alabama 28-16 in Birmingham. For the second straight year USM's season ended with a home loss, this time a 10-6 defeat to East Carolina in a heavy rain. The Eagles finished its second consecutive final record at 7-4, which would once again have qualified the Eagles for a postseason bowl — but the NCAA penalty was still in effect.

1984 (4-7)

The 1984 season was the only losing season in Carmody's tenure at USM. The season started on an ominous note as the Eagles lost to Georgia in Athens, 26-19 in a game in which USM and Georgia each kicked four field goals. USM bounced back to easily defeat Louisiana Tech 34-0 when The Nasty Bunch defense intercepted four Tech passes. USM problems with Auburn continued as the War Eagles picked up a 35-12 victory at home. Memphis State then won unexpectedly in Memphis 23-13 to drop USM's record to 1-3.

The Eagles' woes continued as they lost two straight to rivals Mississippi State, 27-18, and Tulane, 35-7. But the next week, led by QB Robert Ducksworth, the 1-5 Eagles rallied from a 10-3 Ole Miss half-time lead to pull out a 13-10 victory in Jackson.

Carmody recalled, "It was a real brutal defensive game out there. We were finally able to come up with the big plays we'd been missing all year. We made things happen that haven't happened to us before."

The game was really a USM home game, but somehow Ole Miss arranged to have the shaded press box side of the stadium while tickets were allocated to USM fans to sit on the visitor's side in the sun. Jim would take advantage of every psychological advantage and told his team that their mamas would be sitting in the hot sun while Ole Miss players' mamas would be sitting in the shade and that it was Ole Miss' fault. This pumped up the USM players even more. This game marked the end of the USM-Ole Miss series rivalry as Ole Miss stopped scheduling the Golden Eagles. USM had won six of the last eight games against the Rebels. Mississippi State would stop playing USM in 1990 after losing 10 times in their last 14 games.

USM dropped its next two games to Southwestern Louisiana, 13-7, and Northwestern State, 22-0. Ducksworth was sorely missed in both games due to a deep thigh bruise injury, but USM finished off the season with victories against East Carolina and Louisville.

In what Carmody described as "one of the greatest comebacks in school history — certainly, since I have been associated with the program," USM rallied for a come-from-behind victory against East Carolina on the road to emerge victorious 31-27.

USM was behind by 21 points early in the second quarter and was down at halftime 24-3. Carmody said, "That lead looked insurmountable, particularly considering the way we played defensively in the first quarter. It seemed they would score at will. You looked across our defensive front, and there were only three guys who started the season out there."

But The Nasty Bunch defense recovered and held East Carolina to three points in the second half. With the Pirates ahead 27-10, wide receiver Andrew Mott provided the spark that ignited the comeback by returning an East Carolina punt 66 yards for a touchdown.

With 5:39 left in the third quarter USM trailed 27-17. With 3:03 remaining in the third quarter, quarterback Andrew Anderson scored on a 2-yard run to cap a 74-yard drive, pulling the Eagles to a three-point deficit, 27-24. Mott made a key 36-yard reception from Anderson on a third-and-seven play to give USM a badly needed first down at the Pirates' 20-yard line. Anderson threw a 12-yard touchdown pass with 4:20 left in the game to give the Eagles the comeback win. East Carolina outgained USM by nearly 300 yards, but The Nasty Bunch hung in there and forced six East Carolina turnovers.

After the game Carmody summarized the day's events, "I was real proud of the way those substitute players played in the second half. To fall behind by 21 points and then win shows the character and pride of this football team."

But the worst thing to happen was another NCAA investigation of USM's recruiting practices when a recruit, Don Palmer, claimed, when USM failed to release him from his commitment, that he was illegally recruited (See

Chapter 11).

1985 (7-4)

The 1985 season saw a return to winning USM football, making the 1984 season Carmody's only losing season in his six years at the helm and a low point is his career — except for the looming NCAA-Don Palmer investigation. The season-opening shutout of Louisiana Tech portended a good season. Carmody was optimistic. "Our defense played outstanding, just like our defense of last year, before we were decimated by injuries."

USM played the Bo Jackson-led, top-ranked Auburn team tough at Auburn before bowing 29-18.

Losing QB Robert Ducksworth to a knee injury at the end of the first quarter of a scoreless game did not help (Ducksworth was out for most of the remaining year), but it was the Bo Jackson show that did the Eagles in. Bo ran for 205 yards. At the end of the game Auburn coach Pat Dye told Carmody, "If you don't lose your quarterback, you whip our butts."

In brutal heat in Jackson, Mississippi State beat the Eagles 23-20 to bring the Eagles' record to 1-2.

But USM then put together a five-game winning streak, defeating Northwestern State 14-7, Southwestern Louisiana 38-16, Louisville 42-12, Memphis State 14-7, and shutting out East Carolina 27-0.

Following USM's trouncing of Louisville 42-12, Cardinals coach, Howard Schnellenberger, said after the game, "I've been saying all week if Southern Miss changed jerseys with a Top 20 team, you couldn't tell the difference. I still believe it."

According to John W. Cox author of *Rock Solid*, following the shutout of East Carolina, Carmody was enthusiastic. "It was a good win. We've won five in a row now, eight out of the last ten, and we're very pleased with the way we are playing."

But then the 6-2 Golden Eagles were victims of the Colorado State Rams and a nasty snowstorm to suffer an upset by the 3-6 Rams.

The following week in Tuscaloosa it appeared that Southern had an opportunity to repeat the 1982 upset of Alabama, leading the Tide at the start of the fourth quarter, but 'Bama came back to defeat the Eagles, 24-13. The Eagles hurt themselves with key penalties to offset good field position late in the game.

USM finished the successful season, defeating Tulane 24-6 in Hattiesburg. Although finishing with a winning 7-4 record, no bowl bid was explicitly forthcoming, pointing out the difficulty of an independent, non-conference-aligned team being offered a bowl bid.

1986 (6-5)

The season got off to an ominous start with the death of redshirt freshman running back Eric Sorey on the first day of fall football practice (See Chapter 11). The shock of his death took some time to allow the players to focus on the season. The team played in a lackluster manner against Louisiana-Monroe in the season opener at home but still achieved its seventh consecutive home victory, 28-19.

Carmody carried off the field following USM comeback vs. MSU in 1986.

The team then took on No. 4 nationally ranked Alabama in Birmingham. USM jumped out to an early lead, but the powerful Alabama running game wore down The Nasty Bunch defense.

In the third game of the season against Mississippi State in Jackson, USM was down 24-21 and had the ball on their own 2-yard line with four minutes to play. Offensive tackle Pat Ferrell inspired the team when he challenged them in the huddle, "If there's anybody here who doesn't think we're gonna score and win this game, just leave. Get out of here. We don't need you because we are fixin' to score."

USM Quarterback Andrew Anderson surveyed the 98 yards that separated the Eagles from the winning touchdown and said later, "I was breathing hard and acting strange, but I was in control." The Eagles then launched a 15-play scoring drive with Anderson's running and passing accounting for 77 of the remaining yards, topping it off with a 4-yard scoring run by tailback Shelton Gandy to stun the Bulldogs with only 29 seconds remaining and to win the game 28-24 — one of the most thrilling comebacks in USM history.

Offensive coordinator, Keith Daniels, called every play of the drive. Anderson admitted after the game that when Gandy, a walk-on, scored that he broke down and cried. Daniels was quoted as saying that the drive "brought me to tears… It took some downright courage and character to do what they did out there today." The players carried Carmody off the field on their shoulders.

Carmody recalls looking over the packed stadium and noted that no one left early.

But USM could not sustain the momentum as they lost 16-7 to No. 14-ranked Texas A&M and, in one of their worst performances under Coach Jim Carmody, lost 32-0 to Kentucky at Lexington. They came back to beat Memphis State at home 14-9 at homecoming but then lost on the road to Tulane 35-20 to see their record drop to 3-4.

Bizarre Ending — USM 23, East Carolina 21

In its second amazing comeback of the season, the Eagles beat the East Carolina Pirates 23-21 in Greenville, North Carolina, in one of the most bizarre endings of any football game. Down 21-20 with only eight seconds remaining, USM had the ball on its own 18-yard line. East Carolina had just scored to go ahead and kicked off.

Carmody related, "We told our deep people that whoever caught the kickoff to kneel and call time out. We got the timeout accomplished, and then we went basically to a 'May Day' play."

Quarterback Andrew Anderson threw the ball as far as he could throw it, Hail Mary style. Wide receiver Lyneal Alston made an amazing catch at the Pirate 40-yard line with 4 seconds left, cut to the right sideline, stiff-armed and dragged a defender, and made it to the 10-yard line, where he was tackled.

Carmody said, "And all the time we were hollering for him to lateral the ball, which he finally did." On his way down and, apparently before his knee touched the ground, Alston lateraled the ball to fullback Randolph Brown, who raced into the end zone untouched and with no time remaining on the clock. However, officials ruled that the lateral was an illegal forward pass, resulting in a penalty.

East Carolina was in a quandary. If they took the penalty, the Pirates gave the Eagles a final play since officials ruled that the game could not end on a marked penalty. If they turned down the penalty, they lost the game, so they had no choice but to accept the penalty. East Carolina argued that Alston was actually down before he lateraled, but that argument was rejected.

Carmody said, "They had no choice. And a game can't end on a marked penalty. That gave us the extra play. And, of course, the penalty really helped us because it backed us up for a better angle on the field goal."

The clock had run out, but USM took advantage of the rules, and place kicker Rex Banks kicked a 31-yard field goal to give the Golden Eagles the victory, 23-21.

Total confusion resulted, and the crowd went berserk. Carmody was stunned. He was amazed at the catch Alston made to put the play into effect. "I really thought they intercepted the ball Alston caught. I don't know how Lyneal caught it. They had two or three people up there with us. And all of a sudden Lyneal comes out of there with it."

At the end of the game Pirates fans stormed the field and chased the officials down. Fans hurled debris onto the field. One spectator, Carlton Owens Toombs, came onto the field and attacked the back judge, Dan Blue. Greenville police arrested Toombs. Carmody recalls seeing an official on the ground, presumably Dan Blue, being beaten by fans, but then another official came to his rescue, knocking fans away from him with several effective blows. Bottles and other debris rained on the USM players as they made their way to the locker room.

Carmody gained his composure and said, "Certainly it's a tough way for East Carolina to lose a game, but I thought we played well enough to win. I've never seen a game like this since I've been coaching. I don't know how you could make a more spectacular comeback than that." As the team left the dressing room, Carmody leaned against the wall and told a reporter, "I'm emotionally drained."

Anderson calmly said that Alston's catch was actually a designed play called "May Day." The plan was for the tailback and fullback to trail the wide receivers and tight end down the field. If a receiver catches it, he has the option of pitching the ball back to one of those trailing the play.

East Carolina free safety Ellis Dillahunt said he thought he had just witnessed a crime. "It was like somebody broke into your house and took everything you had."

Two days later the head of the Southern Independent Officials Association admitted that replays showed that the officiating crew should have ruled Alston down before he lateraled, but the ruling could not be reversed.

The 4-4 Eagles then shutout Southwestern Louisiana 17-0, got crushed by Florida State in Tallahassee 49-13, and then beat Louisville 31-16 in the season finale to end the year with its tenth straight home victory and another winning season at 6-5 — but again no bowl bid.

1987 (6-5)

Starting the season with Ailrick Young returning at quarterback, USM was crushed by Alabama in Tuscaloosa, 38-6. A lackluster USM offense struggled against the Crimson Tide defense. USM's quarterbacks were particularly ineffective.

In the second game, playing at home, the Golden Eagles fell behind Mack Brown's Tulane Green Wave at halftime, and the offense again failed to show up. The Green Wave jumped to a 16-10 lead, and Carmody was frustrated once again with ineffective quarterback play and the inability of the offense to move the ball. Before the game Carmody thought to himself that if the offense fell behind Tulane he would put Brett Favre in the game. "The way he performed in August I knew he was going to play, but he was a young freshman. He was 17, and I didn't think a 17-year-old should start against Alabama... I didn't want to put him under that pressure," Carmody said. The week before the Tulane game Carmody added to the offensive game plan some drop-back passes to the veer-option offense especially designed for Favre.

USM was down 16-10 with 5:48 remaining in the third quarter. Neither of USM quarterbacks — Ailrick Young and Simmie Carter — were effective. Carmody then made what turned out to be a brilliant, gutsy decision — he put into the game his freshman quarterback, Brett Favre, who started off fall practice as the seventh-ranked quarterback on the squad. Carmody called the press box and told his offensive coordinator, Jack White, that he was putting Favre in the game.

Carmody later said, "I didn't discuss it with anyone, but I felt like if we didn't get the ball moving against Tulane, I was going to put him into the game."

White was stunned, "I thought we were redshirting him but if you say put him in, he's going to go in."

That was the end of the redshirt idea.

Another story appearing in *The Total Package* was supposedly told by a future USM coach who was not on Carmody's staff at the time: "At halftime of the Tulane game, Coach Carmody asked for recommendations... I told him we needed a spark and that we needed to get Brett in there. I really felt he could get it done."

But in 1987 this coach was actually coaching at Wake Forest. A lot of people want to get credit for the Brett Favre story at Southern Miss, but Carmody alone made the decision to play Favre.

Favre was admittedly recovering from a drinking spree in his dorm the night before, having no reason to suspect he would play against Tulane the next day. Teammate and offensive lineman Chris Ryals tells of playing a drinking game called "Quarters" with Favre in the dormitory and the two of them drinking one and one-half cases of beer. When Favre trotted onto the field, the Southern fans "went wild," USM wide receiver Chris McGee said.

"I heard the crowd yelling and screaming, and I'm trying to figure out what the hell is going on. I thought somebody in the stands got to fighting or something," he said.

Favre was well known to the students since Kiln, Mississippi, was so close to Hattiesburg. Despite not feeling well and playing in the heat, Favre led the Eagles to a 31-24 comeback win, and the Favre legend at USM had begun.

Favre immediately led the Eagles downfield, capping off the drive with a 7-yard scoring pass to put USM ahead, 17-16. But Tulane came back and scored and converted a 2-point extra point to take a 24-17 lead. Favre then led the Eagles to two fourth-quarter touchdowns, the last being a 23-yard scoring pass, and USM came from behind to beat the Green Wave 31-24. Favre was 6-10 passing for 85 yards and two touchdowns and became the starting quarterback for the remainder of the season. He never gave up the starting job during his career at USM. But for the remainder of the 1987 season he often played like an inconsistent 18-year-old freshman.

Favre threw for two touchdowns including the game-winner to McGee. McGee said, "The next thing we know, uncharacteristic of our head coach, we start throwing the football all over the field." Carmody had truly discovered a diamond in the rough.

After a tough loss to Texas A&M, 27-14, in Jackson, USM took out its frustration on the Louisville Cardinals, 65-6, in Louisville. Favre had an excellent game, playing like a senior rather than a true freshman. In five head-to-head matchups Carmody was 5-0 against Howard Schnellenberger after Schnellenberger took over the Louisville program in 1983. But the roller coaster season continued the following week when Florida State came to Hattiesburg and routed the Eagles 61-10 at USM's homecoming.

Carmody said he thought the Seminoles were "the best team we've ever played at Roberts Stadium."

However, Carmody did not appreciate FSU's coach, Bobby Bowden's, decision to score again in the final 15 seconds on a pass play with FSU holding a 54-10 lead.

Florida State finished their season 11-1 and ranked second nationally. The next week, USM was trailing Mississippi State in Jackson at the start of the fourth quarter 14-3 but came back to win the game, 18-14. Playing like a true, inconsistent freshman, Favre was ineffective.

Against Memphis State in Memphis USM squandered a 14-0 lead, and the Tigers came back to tie the score at 14-14. But with just over five minutes to play, USM's Chris Seroka kicked a 43-yard field goal to give USM a 17-14 win and bring its record to 4-3.

Then in a history-making game in Hattiesburg, USM became the first of the state's three major football programs to play a historically black university football team. Roberts Stadium was packed with nearly 34,000 spectators — the event reversed a trend of weak attendance at USM home games. USM won 17-7 in a hard-fought struggle. (See Chapter 11).

But USM could not make another dramatic comeback against Northeast Louisiana, losing to the Indians 34-24.

In a game that has become one of the country's toughest rivalries, East Carolina came back from a 38-20 fourth-quarter-deficit, scoring two touchdowns to almost beat USM. But the Eagles hung on to win 38-34 and guarantee another winning season.

The season ended on several sour notes. USM went on the road to lose at Southwestern Louisiana, 37-30, but still the season ended with another winning record, 6-5. Then, despite Carmody's having a career winning record of 37-29, President Aubrey Lucas forced him to resign, citing low attendance at home games. Carmody's six-year record as head coach was 37-29 and ranked fourth at the time on the USM all-time head coaches' victory totals, behind only legendary Pie Vann (139-59), Reed Green (59-20), and Bobby Collins (48-30).

Carmody did have the opportunity to coach two of his sons, Steve and

Keith, at USM. Steve remembered that his dad "treated me the way he treated everyone else. It was fun to see your dad at work every day. Not everybody gets a chance to do that. I thought he was successful because, No. 1, he was so smart, and No. 2, nobody was going to outwork him. He was always thoroughly prepared."

11

SIGNIFICANT HAPPENINGS AT USM

It would not be surprising if Jim Carmody second-guessed himself on taking the USM head-coaching job. Few new head coaches inherited the problems he did at Southern. In the first three months after accepting the position he was sued by an unsuccessful applicant for an assistant coaching position; one of his players was a suspect in a rape case; the NCAA notified USM that it had officially launched an investigation into rules violations, and severe penalties were imposed for violations that took place under the previous coach.

With the rapid unfolding of the events highlighted above, Big Nasty had to wonder what he had gotten himself into. But Carmody spent his athletic life taking on major challenges, and he took each of these on as if they were competitions.

Other significant events occurred during Carmody's tenure as head coach including the upset of Alabama in Tuscaloosa in 1982 (see Warm-Up), the signing and consequent NCAA probation related to the recruitment of a player in 1984, the death of a player in 1986, and the scheduling of a game between USM and Jackson State in 1987, the first time one of the three major football programs in Mississippi scheduled a game with a historically black college or university.

Jerry Bruner vs. USM

About two weeks after Carmody was named head football coach at USM, he learned a big lesson in dealing with the university administration. His first priority was to assemble a coaching staff before the start of spring practice.

Among those recommended to Carmody by coaching colleagues was veteran offensive line coach Jerry Bruner. Carmody had never met Bruner but based on these recommendations decided to explore hiring him.

On February 2, 1982, Jerry Bruner claimed that Carmody called to offer him the job of offensive line coach — a conversation supposedly overheard by Bruner's wife, Cathy, on a telephone extension — (it is difficult to believe that Carmody would offer an assistant position to a coach he had never met). Bruner played both offense and defense at Florida State in the early 1960s and then began a career as a journeyman line coach. After coaching at the high school level in Florida, Bruner coached at Kansas State, West Virginia, Florida State, LSU, the Canadian Football league, and Marshall University. Most recently, in 1981, he was offensive coordinator at Texas El Paso.

On February 7 Bruner claimed a second telephone call repeated the major points stressed in the February 2 call. Bruner claimed that at this point he withdrew his name from consideration for other football positions. A week later Bruner claimed he flew from El Paso to have dinner with Carmody and to meet USM athletic director Roland Dale. Bruner further claimed that he was given keys to an automobile and an administrative office and contacted Noonie Carmody who, at that time, worked for a local realtor. He then claimed he met USM President Dr. Aubrey Lucas and they had a twenty-minute conversation during his three-day visit to Hattiesburg. Following that meeting Bruner testified that Dale and Lucas had a "two-minute conversation" while Bruner waited outside Lucas' office. Apparently Lucas told Dale to continue the search, that he did not like Bruner's appearance.

Bruner's wife, Cathy, then quit her job in El Paso. A week later Bruner received a telephone call from Roland Dale informing him that he did not have the job and providing no further explanation. After several calls to Carmody were unsuccessful, Carmody apologized and supposedly told Bruner President Lucas said that he did not like his appearance.

Bruner then filed a lawsuit against USM naming Carmody, Dale, Dr. Aubrey Lucas, and the Board of Trustees of Institutions of Higher Learning of the State of Mississippi as defendants. The case was heard by the Circuit Court of the First Judicial District of Hinds County, Mississippi, by Judge

Reuben Anderson.

During the initial trial Carmody and Dale testified that Bruner was only one of several candidates considered for the position of offensive line coach. Carmody denied that he made a formal offer to Bruner during their earlier telephone conversations. However, Carmody supposedly admitted that when Bruner visited USM during the period of February 15-18, he told Bruner he would recommend him for the job, subject to approval by the Board of Trustees of the Institutions of Higher Learning. Dale testified that he told Bruner about other candidates being interviewed but expressed confidence in the ultimate selection of Bruner. On February 17 Bruner testified that Dale told Bruner not to appear on the practice field before the Board of Trustees approved Carmody's recommendation. Bruner testified that this was the first mention of any requirement concerning board approval of his appointment.

Lucas then testified that he had received recommendations from both Carmody and Dale to hire Bruner but that "based at least partially upon Bruner's appearance" asked Dale to look further. Lucas denied that he rejected the recommendation of Carmody and Dale.

During the initial trial the judge granted directed verdicts to the Board of Trustees of State Institutions of Higher Learning, Dr. Aubrey Lucas, and Roland Dale, leaving Carmody as the sole defendant in the suit. Carmody remembers that as the judge was delivering the directed verdicts, he was sitting between Lucas and Dale. He recalls Lucas leaning over and, in a less than convincing voice, trying to assure him that we (obviously meaning the university) are going to try to help him.

Lucas said, "Jim, we are going to try to help you in every way we can in this situation."

But Carmody did not feel reassured. After all, he had recommended Bruner as his offensive line coach to the line of administrators to whom he reported; the recommendation was not accepted, and here he was the only defendant left on trial.

Carmody always followed the chain of command. He made a favorable recommendation to his boss, Roland Dale, who, in turn made the recommendation to President Lucas, and the order came back down the line to continue searching, implying the recommendation had not been approved. The original suit named Carmody, Dale, Dr. Aubrey Lucas, and the Board of Trustees of Institutions of Higher Learning of the State of Mississippi as defendants, and now Carmody was the only one holding the bag — and he was the one who was in favor of hiring Bruner. Can anyone blame him for feeling like a scapegoat? It is ironic that of all of those named in Bruner's lawsuit Carmody was the only person who supported Bruner's hiring and yet he was the only originally-named defendant actually facing the trial.

However, hearing all the facts, the jury returned a verdict in favor of Carmody.

Bruner and his attorneys then appealed the directed verdicts as well as the lower court's denial of his motion for judgment, notwithstanding the verdict. The Supreme Court of Mississippi then unanimously affirmed the lower court's findings. On appeal, The Supreme Court of Mississippi found that the trial judge was correct in directing verdicts in favor of Lucas and Dale on the basis that "there is no evidence in the record to indicate any grounds on which to submit a question to the jury concerning Lucas' liability" and, as Bruner himself testified, Dale had kept him off the practice field awaiting approval of the board, so the finding of a directed verdict was also true for Dale.

The Supreme Court also affirmed the jury's verdict in favor of Carmody, stating that "the jury's verdict was not contrary to the overwhelming weight of credible evidence."

The Supreme Court called this case "a colossal misunderstanding" between Bruner, Jim Carmody, and USM. In especially flowery, non-legal language, the decision stated: "This case concerns a colossal misunderstanding between Jerry Bruner, an unemployed assistant coach, who, languishing in the brown waste of West Texas, viewed Hattiesburg, centrally located between his home in Florida and that of his wife in Louisiana, as a veritable Garden of Eden, and Jim Carmody, then recently appointed head football coach of the Golden Eagles, who was searching for a new offensive line coach."

In reality, this case involved the conclusion President Lucas made following a brief, twenty-minute meeting with Bruner, to not hire him because of his appearance. Imagine using that as a basis of hiring in the climate of today's society.

The Case of Don Horn

If a list was compiled of coaches who showed genuine concern for their players black or white with and regardless of athletic ability, players who had used up their eligibility and could no longer directly contribute to the program, players who were wrongly accused of a crime because of the color of their skin, coaches who believed in the innocence of their player and who would arrange for a pro bono defense of the player, then Jim Carmody would be at the top of that list. The Don Horn (a black ex-Golden Eagle player) story at USM and Coach Carmody's involvement and belief of his innocence is one that writer Willie Morris would be proud of.

Approximately two months after Carmody assumed the head coaching position at USM he was faced with another problem. On March 15, 1982, a 38-year-old Hattiesburg woman reported she had been raped. USM wide receiver Don Horn had been linked with the attack, but it was not until almost a year later that Horn was arrested by Hattiesburg police. The woman was employed as a registered nurse at a dentist's office where Horn was a patient. They also apparently knew each other from her visits to the grocery store where Horn worked. The woman said she was unable to see her attacker's face in an early morning attack because when she awoke a pillow covered her face. Forrest County District Attorney Bud Holmes said, "The victim was bitten on the side of the jaw."

Since Horn was an early suspect, extensive efforts were made by the prosecutor's office to compile evidence, including his dental records, against Horn. As the prosecutor developed his case against Horn, Horn had an excellent redshirt senior season for USM.

Horn heard that he was charged with the crime of rape in February 1983 when he answered a page from Coach Carmody as he was boarding an airplane at the Jackson airport to fly to Detroit to attend a NFL tryout camp. Carmody had attempted to call Horn at his apartment several times that morning before realizing that Horn was on his way to the tryout camp.

Horn, in the company of USM head football coach Jim Carmody and public defender Jolly Matthews, surrendered to Hattiesburg Chief of Detectives Raymond Howell at the Hattiesburg police headquarters on February 17, 1983. Bond was set for the next day.

Carmody said, "We were very shocked. I just left him. We're supportive of him. He's charged, not convicted. He's been here for five years and never was a minute of trouble." Horn was a criminal justice major and had served an internship in the Hattiesburg Police Department.

Teammate Jerald Baylis, who knew Horn well, having attended Callaway High School with him, said, "It is really a surprise. I knew him very well. I would describe him as a nice person, good to be around, a person you can rely on if you need anything. I think this is some sort of mistake."

Holmes said Horn had "voluntarily agreed to submit to blood tests, polygraph tests, and dental tests, and he already had an attorney. Holmes, who was also an agent for several professional athletes, contacted several forensic dental experts, who compared a bite-mark impression from the victim with an impression that Horn had supplied voluntarily. The case was vaguely reminiscent of the famous trial of mass murderer Ted Bundy in Florida three years earlier. Bundy was the first person in the U.S. to be convicted of a capital offense where all of the evidence was circumstantial in nature — all except for a bite mark the perpetrator left on one of the victims. Testimony was given by forensic ondontologist Dr. Richard Souviron comparing Bundy's teeth with bite marks taken from one of the victims. This case was the first in Florida's legal history that relied on bite-mark testimony and, until this Bundy trial, only eighteen states had allowed bite-mark evidence to be admissible in a court of law. Holmes and his staff apparently thought that forensic dentistry was the best way to convict Horn of the rape charge. (Bundy was found guilty and was executed on January 24, 1989).

While Holmes was gathering evidence, Horn had a successful 1982 season, finishing with 22 pass receptions, coming in second behind USM's great receiver Louis Lipps. Horn seemed to have potential to play professional football.

Before filing charges, Holmes, an assistant district attorney, two reporters — one a newspaper reporter for the Hattiesburg American and the other a television reporter from Hattiesburg station WDAM — and one of Horn's criminal justice instructors went to Cincinnati, Ohio, to meet with experts who were attending an American Academy for Forensic Scientists convention. Holmes was concerned that he might be accused of favoritism in this case because of his involvement with other football players.

Three experts, a local forensic dentist, Dr. Michael West, and the district attorney's office sent photographs of the impression taken from the rape victim back and forth and conferred on the telephone on several occasions. A place where all of the experts could meet was chosen to review the evidence. However, one of the experts failed to show up for the meeting, and another expert would not positively identify the bite marks as those of Horn but added that he could not rule out Horn either. Nevertheless, Holmes said that Horn was identified from hair and semen samples as well as blood tests and decided to file the charges against Horn.

Soon after he learned that a warrant for Horn's arrest was issued, USM President Aubrey Lucas scheduled a press conference. Lucas said, "I am shocked, really saddened. I know him personally and consider him a friend. We must all remember a charge does not mean one is guilty." Lucas then added that Horn would be withdrawn from USM until the matter was resolved.

Carmody first knew Horn, a fifth-year senior wide receiver for the Golden Eagles, during his earlier stint as assistant coach and again during his first spring at USM in 1982. Horn had great speed and was a productive player. Carmody was convinced that Horn was innocent and that the sexual liaison with the nurse was completely consensual. When Horn was formally charged in February 1983, Carmody persuaded noted Jackson attorney Sam Wilkins, a USM graduate, to defend his player. Wilkins, like Carmody, was convinced of Horn's innocence and agreed to represent Horn, pro bono.

Carmody was asked why he got involved since Horn had used up his eligibility, and a lot of coaches would have done otherwise for a player who could no longer help the coach or the program.

Carmody replied, "He was one of my players. I would have done the same for any of my players whether they were first-string or fourth-string. I thought that was my job as head football coach — to take care of my players the best that I can. I was not as concerned about his innocence or guilt but only that he was one of my players who needed my help. He was just one of my players."

Because of the local publicity Wilkins was able to obtain a change of venue from Forrest County to Gulfport, Mississippi, in Harrison County. A certificate to transfer the case was filed on December 1, 1983. The trial was held in circuit court in Gulfport, 70 miles from Hattiesburg. The prosecuting attorney was Bud Holmes from Hattiesburg.

Numerous attempts were made to discover the official, final outcome of the trial to no avail. Contact with the lawyers who were involved and are still alive was to no avail. Officials in the Forrest County Circuit Clerk's office in Hattiesburg stated that since the trial had been moved to Gulfport, the Harrison County Circuit Clerk's office would have all the trial papers. Officials in the Harrison County Circuit Clerk's office said that the record would be kept in the Forrest County office. Neither courthouse was able to come up with any documents related to the trial and consistently referred any inquiries to the other courthouse.

Local Gulfport attorney Cy Faneca and his paralegal staff attempted several times without success to obtain trial records. The trial happened over 33 years ago, before computer records were kept, so finding the trial records would be difficult. However, Horn was apparently was freed, whether by a finding of not guilty by the jury, or an acquittal, or some plea arrangement, but Carmody recalls Horn's being found not guilty. Interestingly, no indication other than an item in the 1984 USM annual appears regarding Horn's innocence.

Carmody attended the first day of the trial and recalls being worried about an all-white jury consisting mainly of females. However, Carmody said Wilkins was brilliant and must have convinced the jury of Horn's innocence. It is interesting that no official records related to the trial or the final judgment could be located in either courthouse.

The Horn case revealed much of Carmody's character. The incident occurred in the early 1980s when white Southerners were not as likely to come to the defense of a black accused of raping a white woman. By the time he was formally charged, Horn had used all of his football eligibility, so the only advantage to Carmody in coming to his defense was a belief in the character of his players, former or current, and the need to see that fairness prevailed. As stated earlier, Carmody's involvement in the Horn case was not based totally on his belief that Horn was innocent; rather, Carmody says he reacted as he did because one of "his" players was in trouble, and he was attempting to help him. Since the trial Carmody has not seen Horn or even knows what happened to him after the trial.

Don Palmer Recruitment — NCAA Investigation

Don Palmer, Brandon, Mississippi, football star linebacker, signed a letter of intent with USM on February 8, 1984. He wanted to play for Ole Miss but claimed that his mother pressured him into signing with USM because she had heard of racial prejudice at Ole Miss. Palmer reneged on his agreement with USM and asked that he be released from his commitment. However, Carmody, like many other head coaches, had a policy of not releasing any signee from a national letter of intent to transfer to any school on the USM football schedule. Thus, Palmer was not released. On July 18, upset that his request for release was not granted, Palmer wrote Roland Dale asking again for a release from his commitment (he wanted to go to Ole Miss) and indicated to Dale that he had been illegally recruited by the USM tight ends' coach and was provided illegal recruiting incentives.

Palmer went public with his allegations that the coach made more than the NCAA maximum-allowed three recruiting visits, that he allowed another Southern Miss player to use the assistant's automobile to drive Palmer on the 180-mile round trip to his home, that two boosters drove Palmer's mother to the home of another booster, where the assistant coach and Palmer were waiting. Once they were at the booster's home Palmer claimed the coach gave him a baseball cap and a warm-up suit. He also claimed that the booster gave his mother a ham and that boosters bought three meals for Palmer and his mother — all arranged by the coach and all against NCAA rules.

An NCAA investigator, Ron Watson, working his first case for the NCAA, followed up these allegations by initially talking directly to Palmer to make certain that the allegations were accurate and then went to visit the accused boosters in their homes. Following his meeting with the boosters, who denied the charges, Watson was convinced they were devout, sincere people and that Palmer had "pulled his leg." He thought the boosters were shooting straight and that maybe the kid was just upset that he did not get his way and filed these charges.

Meanwhile, Palmer had been released from his commitment to USM to enroll at Arkansas State University. Three months after the first interview the investigator went back to Palmer and impressed on him the importance of telling the truth. Palmer repeated his allegations, giving Watson almost exactly the same allegations he gave him on his first interrogation. Now Watson thought it would not be easy for Palmer to tell the exact same lies twice and was now convinced that Palmer was telling the truth. Watson went back to the USM campus to interview the accused coach and obtain copies of his telephone and credit card records that appeared to support Palmer's complete story. He also re-interviewed the four boosters, who had obviously attempted to protect the school and the coach in the initial interviews and were concerned that if they had told the truth initially that their friend, the coach, would be fired. Watson felt that the boosters were trying to protect USM as well as a coach with whom they had become quite friendly.

On October 8, 1984, the NCAA notified USM that it was under an official inquiry and listed eleven allegations related to the recruitment of Palmer. Lucas launched an internal investigation into these charges and at a press conference on November 14 admitted that the university investigation supported the NCAA charges. Lucas then announced that he was imposing four charges on the football program: the release of Palmer from his letter of intent, the suspension of the assistant coach and nonrenewal of his contract (thus firing the assistant coach), freezing Carmody's salary for the next year, suspending any discussions relating to the extension of Carmody's contract, and for two years disassociating from the program the alumni and boosters involved. Penalties imposed by the NCAA included placing the team on probation for two years, a public reprimand of USM, censuring the school, and banning the team from appearing on television for the 1985 season. The NCAA then stated that because of the university's rapid response to the initial charges, the television ban and one year probation would be lifted.

When Carmody first learned of Palmer's allegations he met with his assistant and asked him directly if any of the charges were true. Carmody was told that there was no basis to the allegations. When Lucas fired the assistant, Carmody, defending his assistant, pleaded with the university president to reverse his action. Carmody's pleas went unheeded and when Carmody told his assistant that Lucas stood by the decision to fire the coach, rather than the assistant's being grateful for Carmody's intervention, accused Carmody of not completely defending him, essentially throwing Carmody under the bus. The accused coach went on to coach high school on the Gulf Coast before joining the staff at Mississippi State as an assistant coach, where he would again run into problems with the NCAA. He was accused of giving cash and gifts and offering improper benefits to prospective student-athletes and their families.

On December 18, 1985, a newspaper article appeared in which President Lucas was quoted as saying that Carmody and his assistants were in line for a raise but he was not recommending an extension of Carmody's contract. Lucas was further quoted as saying, "Even though we have had to cut our budget recently, we feel it is well deserved and we will somehow find the money" for raises for Carmody and his assistants. Lucas then blamed poor home football attendance as the reason he did not recommend an extension of Carmody's contract, which had two years left.

Eric Sorey — Death August 17, 1986

USM began fall practice on August 17, 1986, in usually hot weather with temperatures in the low to mid-90s. Tragedy occurred on the first day of practice. Carmody historically started off fall practice by having the players run a mile. This fall opening practice was no exception. Redshirt freshman 5-foot-9 inch, 200-pound. running back Eric Sorey, from Campbellton, Florida, suffered leg cramps and collapsed during the first fall practice. Team physician, Dr. Boyd Kellett, and his training staff gave Sorey plenty of Gatorade to keep Sorey from dehydrating — normal procedure. Sorey's condition stabilized, and he had a normal pulse and blood pressure. He sat up and was conversing with the medical staff, saying only that his legs hurt. Kellett gave him a mild muscle relaxant and transferred him in a pick-up truck (no ambulance was on hand as was usually the case back then) to the Southern Mississippi clinic. By mid-afternoon he was transferred to the Methodist Hospital in Hattiesburg. However, on his way to the hospital Sorey went into cardiac arrest. A medical team at the hospital's emergency room worked for more than two hours to revive him without success. He was pronounced dead shortly after 6 p.m. An autopsy showed that four conditions contributed to his death: an inheritable sickle cell trait, a generalized breakdown of muscle cells, the presence of an anemia that caused blood cells to break down, and a slightly enlarged heart with a small left coronary artery. In other words a congenital heart defect complicated by sickle cell anemia. Dr. Kellett said he did not think one could directly blame the heat or exercise for his death. "The heat was not the sole problem. The physical exertion he went through wasn't unusual... He had been running for only six minutes." The team and coaching staff were devastated. Carmody took the entire team to Sorey's funeral and served as one of the pallbearers.

Sorey's mother, Elnora Sorey, filed a wrongful death lawsuit [Sorey v. Kellett, 673 F. Supp.in 1987 (S.D. Miss. 1987)] against Boyd A. Kellett, M.D.; Earnest L. Harrington, R.P.T.; John Doe, Assistant Trainer; Jane Doe, R.N.; Members of the Board of Trustees of Institutions of Higher Learning (William H. Austin, Jr., George T. Watson, Martha H. Gill, Denton Rogers, Jr., Charles C. Jacobs, Jr., Bryce Griffis, Betty A. Williams, John R. Lovelace, M.D., Frank O. Crosthwait, Jr., William A. Hickman, Sidney L. Rushing; Thomas D. Bordeaux, and William M. Jones), Head Football Coach Jim Carmody, and the University of Southern Mississippi.

Those named in the suit sought dismissal based upon governmental immunity. A lower court acting on this matter denied dismissal, and the appellants appealed that ruling. The Fifth Circuit Court of Appeals reversed the lower court's denial of immunity. The Court of Appeals ruled in part:

"We also think that Carmody, the head football coach, is entitled to immunity under Mississippi law. The plaintiff alleged only that Carmody failed in a 'nondelegable duty' to oversee the football program and, in particular, the custody and care of football players. Mississippi courts have held, however, that public officials sued merely because of their general authority over the program or institution that is alleged to have caused injury are entitled to qualified immunity."

The Court of Appeals further ruled:

"For the above reasons, we conclude that qualified immunity under Mississippi law shields appellants from suit in this case. The district court's order denying appellants' motions to dismiss is therefore REVERSED. "

Sadly, just a week later, sophomore University of Alabama defensive tackle Willie Ryles collapsed during a blocking drill. Surgery was performed to relieve pressure that was caused by a ruptured vessel, resulting in the formation of a blood clot on the left side his brain, and he was in a coma for several days. He passed away on August 23. Head coach Ray Perkins said Ryles collapsed after receiving a normal blow to the head. Ryles had experienced headaches before he collapsed but apparently refused to tell team doctors or coaches for fear he would lose his status as a first-team tackle.

Eric Sorey, 1968

12

RESPECT - Making History - USM vs. Jackson State University

The NCAA has classified athletic programs in different ways since 1973. Until 1973 the NCAA classified football programs as Division I (University Division) and Division II (College Division). In 1973 the College Division was split in two and became known as Division II and Division III. In 1978, for football only, Division I universities were divided into Division I-A and Division I-AA. Then in 2006 the NCAA once again changed its classifications, and Divisions I-A and Division I-AA were renamed Division I Football Bowl Subdivision (FBS) and Division I Football Championship Subdivision (FCB) based on the number of football scholarships allowed.

There are eight public universities in Mississippi, seven with football programs (the one exception being the predominately female Mississippi University for Women). There are three Division I FBS programs consisting of the predominately white institutions Mississippi State University, the University of Mississippi, and the University of Southern Mississippi — and three Division 1-FCS universities consisting of the three Historically Black Colleges and Universities (HBCUs) — Alcorn State University, Jackson State University, and Mississippi Valley State University. Delta State University is a Division II football program. While the Division I FBS, Division I FCS, and Division II universities have sporadically played schools in the other divisions in many sports, until 1987 there had not been a football game played between one of the three major predominately white universities with either of the HBCUs or the one Division II university. In 1987 Carmody made a bold effort to have his USM Golden Eagles play the Jackson State Tigers.

On October 31, 1987, USM played Division I-AA, Jackson State University in a truly historical moment in the relationship between sports and society, particularly in the state of Mississippi. The game marked the first time that any of the three predominately white Division I Mississippi institutions played football against a team from a historically black university. Southern Mississippi was also Jackson State's first Division I-A opponent in its history. The game attracted a record attendance of 33,687 fans to Roberts Stadium. But far more important than setting an attendance record, this game had the potential to contribute to enhanced social relations between the HBCUs and the so-called "Big Three" institutions in Mississippi.

Carmody and USM Athletic Director Roland Dale held many meetings to discuss sagging attendance at USM home games, despite the team's winning eleven straight home games over a three-year period, beginning that streak with a 34-25 victory over Louisville in 1984 — a game that attracted only 11,000 fans to Roberts Stadium. The Eagles were averaging fewer than 20,000 fans per game, and the team needed a boost. Dale resigned effective July 1, 1986, Bill McLellan assumed the athletic directorship, and attendance discussions continued.

Then on December 2, 1986, Wichita State University discontinued the football program, opening up a slot in the USM schedule for 1987. Carmody told McLellan he did not have a full solution to the attendance problem but made a radical suggestion: "I know one game that would fill the stadium — if we scheduled Jackson State."

Carmody recalled a suggestion previously made by Jackson *Clarion-Ledger* sports editor Rick Cleveland, who suggested to Dale that USM play Jackson State University, thus marking the first time one of the three major predominately white Mississippi football programs would play a Historically Black College and University in football.

Carmody felt this was the ideal time to act on Cleveland's proposal. Cleveland had several years before proposed that Southern play Jackson State, a Division I-AA-classified program. Cleveland discussed the attendance woes at USM and wrote, "Economically they could not afford not to play." Cleveland was happy the game was finally going to happen. "It's just good for the state," he wrote.

Retired JSU athletic director Walter Reed remembers the scheduling of this historic matchup from the JSU perspective: Roland Dale was the athletic director at USM when this all started. Rick Cleveland, whose dad was S.I.D. at USM. Rick was aware that USM had an attendance problem and proposed in the Jackson *Clarion-Ledger* that if USM wanted to fill its stadium it had better schedule JSU.

When Dale and Reed were attending an NCAA meeting in New Orleans they discussed the scheduling further, and agreed to meet the following morning to finalize the game. However, Dale had to return to Hattiesburg that night, and plans to schedule the game were put on hold. Dale resigned for medical reasons, and the issue was dropped while USM searched for a new athletic director

When Bill McLellan came on board, Dale told him that his first order of business was to finalize the JSU game. McLellan and Reed subsequently met at a Jaguar dealership in Jackson, agreed verbally to the matchup, and scheduled a press conference in Jackson.

Prior to the Jackson meeting, McLellan responded to Carmody's suggestion, saying, "Well, I do know about that. I'll have to run that by Dr. Lucas."

Noting that such a game could present problems, none of the other predominately white Division I schools in Mississippi had seriously considered the idea. The suggestion raised initial concerns on McLellan's part, primarily regarding the issue of safety, but generated great interest among Jackson State fans.

Because of the obvious racial implications, university administrators feared potential trouble, even fights breaking out in the stands. Carmody continued to push for the game, claiming it might be the most publicized game in the history of Mississippi. Carmody assured them that there would be no trouble. "I know there will not be any trouble." He was asked how he could be so sure and he replied, "Because I know the respect Jackson State fans have for head coach W.C. Gorden and the respect JSU fans have for his program."

McLellan convinced USM President Aubrey Lucas of the advantages of such a matchup and began negotiations with JSU athletic director Walter

Reed. The game was scheduled for October 31, 1987 — Halloween day — in Hattiesburg. Gorden, head football coach at JSU since 1977, was not involved in negotiations for this game, but when details of the games were approved by the two athletic directors, Gorden gladly accepted the challenge. Coach Gorden fully understood the historical significance of the matchup, wishing only that the game had been scheduled twenty years earlier when JSU would have been more competitive since the black players would have had no choice but to go to a HBCU.

The next hurdle to be overcome was the date of the game. The key to the scheduling occurred on December 2, 1986, when Wichita State University, who was on USM's schedule for 1987, dropped its football program, opening a slot for the JSU matchup. However, JSU was scheduled to play Alabama State on the date proposed by USM. Reed tried to drop that game to play USM, but the SWAC Conference told them they had to play this conference game.

Earlier, Grambling had dropped a conference game in order to play Oregon State. Reed said that if JSU did not fufilll its conference obligtions, the conference was "getting ready to get in our britches."

JSU and USM found a mutual date they could play, but Alabama State was scheduled to play Fort Valley State on the date Reed proposed for a JSU-Alabama State matchup.

Jackson State then bought out Fort Valley for $9,000, opening that date for JSU to play Alabama State and thus open October 31 as the date USM and JSU could play in 1987. Reed said that at the time, "playing USM meant more to their program that playing Alabama State did."

Gorden was excited about the possibility of playing USM, despite the problems of an I-AA school playing a I-A program. Jackson State was allotted 70 football scholarships, while USM could offer 95.

Gorden said, "We are making history… There's a lot of interest, especially among our alumni, students, and supporters. I didn't think it would happen this soon. I would've thought I'd have been retired before it happened."

But Gorden was concerned about Jackson State's ability to compete, saying, "We don't have a computer scouting program here… We have to use the old-fashioned method of counting plays and figuring out tendencies."

Additionally, twenty years before, outstanding black athletes in Mississippi either went to HBCUs in the area or colleges out of state. Since historically white institutions began recruiting black athletes in the early 1970s, the pool of talented black football players in Mississippi that were available to HBCUs had been reduced.

Gorden said, "We don't get the athletes we got 20 years ago. In reality we can't match up with them, particularly on the offensive and defensive lines. I'm sure they're three deep in those positions. We're one and a half deep with quality athletes." Other factors that affected the ability of HBCUs to compete were the advent of big television contracts primarily for Division I schools and the ability of larger schools to improve their stadiums.

Carmody insisted that there is a fine line between I-A and I-AA athletes. "Years ago there was a good margin, but with the scholarship limitations there's less of a difference now. A lot of mistakes are made in recruiting. There are guys in I-AA who can play at our level just as there are players in I-A who were overrated in high school," he said.

The issue of scholarship limitations merits some discussion here. In 1973 the NCAA first placed a limit on football scholarships to offset the cost of increased scholarships for women as a result of Title IX that was approved by Congress as a major component of the Equal Opportunity in Education Act. The NCAA initially limited schools to 105 football scholarships. That number was reduced in 1978 to 95. In 1992 the number was again reduced to 85 for Division I football and 63 for Division I-AA.

Carmody and Gorden had surprisingly never met, despite recruiting many of the same players for years. Gorden told a reporter, "We were in the same place one time when we were recruiting Marcus Dupree, but we didn't meet. It's nobody's fault, actually, but no, we've never met. That is odd, isn't it?" But both had great respect for each other and for the success of each program.

Carmody knew this about Jackson State: "They have a tremendous tradition and following. It's a landmark game, very similar to when Mississippi State played Alcorn in basketball. (This) might be the most publicized game in the history of Mississippi."

Scheduling the game also excited JSU alumni and students, and JSU was expected to bring a crowd of 15,000 to 20,000 or more to Hattiesburg. Gorden might have been concerned about the lack of athletic equity, but Carmody was well aware of the motivation, talent, and coaching experience JSU would bring to the game. He warned USM fans to not take the game lightly. The players knew the stakes of such a matchup were high. Carmody said, "Surely, though, each realizes Saturday's game isn't just another game." He added, "It's a game that's got a lot of emotion. It should be a heckuva game. It's a game that is good for football. I think it's good for football in the state of Mississippi." But Carmody's boss, athletic director Bill McLellan, saw it the way most athletic administrators did, suggesting the game was simply a moneymaking venture.

While some fans and university administrators were concerned about any racial problems that might develop, the players and coaches were not. Jackson State wide receiver Ron Lewis remarked, "The game is a simple intrastate rivalry. It's not a racial point at all. It's just 18-, 19-, 20- and 21-year-old guys playing football. There's not anything to that. It's just two good football teams in the state of Mississippi playing a football game."

USM entered the game with a 4-3 record while JSU came in undefeated at 6-0-1. USM was listed as a heavy favorite going into the game, but Carmody said this would not affect his players because "they are familiar with the successful program they (JSU) have up there, and they realize the type of game it'll take to beat them."

Gorden said, "We respect them, but we are not in awe." He added, "We have no false perceptions about the people we play. Our people are going down there to win. Those who are making a living with this game know the enormity of it. Enthusiasm for the game might help us prevail."

Both coaches and players had genuine respect for their opponents. Carmody said that what concerned him about JSU was, "The ability of JSU running back (Lewis) Tillman to make the big play. He's very similar to Shelton Gandy (USM running back). You"ll need five yards on third down, and he'll get you six,"said Carmody. Another concern Carmody had was the speed of

JSU's receivers. "They can fly," he said.

Gorden knew that USM historically had a strong kicking game, especially using the punting game as both offensive and defensive weapons, and believed the kicking game would play a major role in the outcome.

As mentioned earlier, the game was played before a Roberts Stadium record sellout crowd of 33,687 fans — the first Roberts Stadium sellout in its history. Temporary bleachers had been constructed for the bands, freeing up space in the stadium to accommodate more fans. The game ended with a hard-fought USM 17-7 victory.

Carmody related, "Coach Gorden told me before the game that it was a great opportunity for Jackson State. I told him I thought it was a great opportunity for us to play a fine football team with great tradition like the Paytons, Robert Brazille, and Harold Jackson. I have a great admiration for those players and that football team."

The emotion of the JSU fans was especially evident. Just before the 1:00 p.m. kickoff as the team mascots were getting after each other, Tiger, the JSU mascot, body slammed the Golden Eagle mascot to the ground, further firing up JSU fans.

Jackson State and USM played a scoreless first half. Carmody admitted his offense had a difficult time moving the ball because his offensive line could not block 347-pound JSU nose guard Albert Coss, cutting off USM's highly touted ground game. Carmody told his offensive coordinator, Jack White, to quit trying to run the ball up the middle.

But with four minutes remaining in the third quarter USM's James Henry returned a punt 72 yards to give USM a 7-0 lead. It was Henry's first touchdown for USM. Gorden's pregame fears were realized. After the game Gorden said, "Whenever your opponent returns a punt for a touchdown, it really demoralizes your football team. There is nothing in the drugstore that will depress you any quicker than a punt return for a touchdown."

As demoralizing as the punt return is for the kicking team, it can be a major lift for the team returning the punt. Senior USM wideout Chris McGee said after the game, "James' punt return really fired us up. We were sort of standing around waiting for something to happen, which is unusual for us.

But that play turned us around. Everyone was fired up."

The Eagles inched further ahead when tailback Sheldon Gandy scored on a 7-yard run to make it 14-0. Near the start of the fourth quarter Chris Seroka kicked a 44-yard field goal to end USM scoring at 17-0. Later in the fourth quarter JSU's Lewis Tillman scored on a one-yard run to make the final score 17-7. JSU defensive lineman Deatrich Wise said, "Damn, we just ran out of time. All we did was run out of time. I knew we could play with these boys." Despite the game's being played in late October, heat was a factor. Several

Game Statistics		
	JSU	USM
First Downs	19	5
Yards Rushing	168	59
Yards Passing	131	64
Passes	11-27-2	3-14-2
Return Yards	40	113
Time of Possession	36:52	23:08

Collage of USM vs JSU game depicting Brett Favre (#4), The USM Dixie Darlings, USM and JSU players, Coaches Carmody and Gorden, the USM and JSU mascots, and the JSU "Sonic Boom of the South" Marching Band (Collage made by Noonie Carmody.)

JSU players suffered leg cramps.

Gorden's fears of the USM kicking game were realized. USM punter Billy Knighten was named Player of the Game, averaging 43.3 yards on 10 punts. Gorden pointed to USM's trademark of special teams, kicking and returning, as the main reason JSU lost. He would later say, "When I think back on it, it was their tradition in the kicking game that got to us. You think back to punters Gerald Wilson and Ray Guy, and that was a major factor in defeating us in this historic game. You'd have to put Billy Knighten down in history. He provided their offense great field position."

Game statistics back up Gorden's assessment. Statistics tell the story of the game, which was dominated by JSU. There were two outstanding defenses on the field that day, and the score could easily have been 0-0 had it not been for James Henry's game-breaking 72-yard punt return. JSU outgained USM in total yards, first downs, yards passing, (54 of the USM passing yards resulted from a 54-yard Brett-Favre-to-Darryl-Tillman pass just before the end of the first half.), and time of possession. JSU's running back, Lewis Tillman gained 164 yards rushing. On the other hand, USM's star running back Shelton Gandy, who entered the game ranked eighth in the nation in rushing, was held to 25 yards on 21 carries. USM quarterback Ailrick Young, who replaced Favre in the third quarter, commented, "We knew they had a good defense from looking at the film. But it seemed like they were faster in real life than on film."

As Carmody predicted, the game was played without major incident. USM's director of the department of public safety said, "We had an orderly crowd. They just wanted to see the ball game."

Both coaches were gracious after the game. When they met at midfield at the end of the game, the two coaches did more than simply shake hands. They understood that what they had witnessed on the field of Roberts Stadium that afternoon was more than just a football game and understood the long-term significance that the game would have on race relations in Mississippi. They talked at some length and then walked off the field with an arm on the other's shoulder.

It was truly a historic event. Gorden later called Carmody "a class person."

Carmody praised the Gorden-coached Tigers as one of the better teams they played. "One thing ought to be clear. Jackson State is as good, or perhaps better, than a lot of Division I teams that we play. They make few mistakes. They are sound fundamentally. They are well motivated and well coached. And when they tackle you, you stay tackled."

Gorden was equally gracious, "Give credit to Southern Mississippi. They have a fine defensive team. And a good football team finds a way to win."

After the game Carmody told Rick Cleveland, "I thought it was a tremendous spectacle and a hard-fought football game by two outstanding defensive football teams. We've beaten Mississippi State and Memphis State the last two weeks in the same type of ballgame." He went on: "I think the spectators, the news media, and certainly the players and coaches should realize first off that Jackson State is as good or better than the teams I just mentioned."

Gorden told Cleveland, "This solidifies my belief that we have an outstanding football program at Jackson State that can compete on a level with Division I-A teams. I know we have a Division I-A defense, and Lewis Tillman is a Division I-A back."

Carmody and Coach W.C. Gorden meet midfield following the USM-JSU game in 1987. (Photo from Clarion-Ledger Nov. 1, 1987 - photographer J.D. Schwalm)

Jackson State also gained the respect of USM players such as defensive tackle Ulysses Slaughter, who complimented and congratulated every Tiger player he saw. At one point he told several Tigers, "I'll tell you what. Ya'll are some bad dudes, the baddest dudes we've played."

USM center Jim Ferrell said, "They are good, very good. They have a lot of class. This should be a great in-state rivalry since Ole Miss bowed out on us, and it looks like State is going to. We ought to play them. I'll tell you this for sure — they're every bit as good, if not, better, than State or Ole Miss."

USM senior linebacker Sidney Coleman said, "We kind of underestimated them a little bit. We didn't start off that serious... I have all the respect in the world for them."

As Carmody was leaving the stadium he decided to visit the field one more time to absorb the significance of that afternoon. Most of the floodlights were still on as the cleanup crew did its job. Spread out in the bleachers that had been recently constructed to handle the record crowd attending the game was the Jackson State team. They were enjoying a post-game meal before the long, ninety-mile bus ride back to Jackson. Intermingled with the Jackson State players were several of Carmody's Southern players, black and white, eating, laughing, and socializing with the Jackson State players. A lot of the players had played with or against each other in high school. The social significance of this moment would have a long-term impact on race relations in Mississippi.

Surprisingly, as beneficial and meaningful as this matchup was for USM, Jackson State and, indeed, the whole state of Mississippi, the two schools would not meet again for fifteen years. Carmody had earlier expressed the opinion that, "I don't see any reason why we should not play them every year."

USM did not take advantage of the favorable publicity generated by this game and did not schedule a second meeting with JSU until they opened the season against the Tigers in Hattiesburg in 2002. The two schools have not played each other since then, although USM did play Mississippi HBCU Alcorn State in 2009 and 2014.

Nearly thirty years after this historic game Carmody and Gorden said that the game still generates interest. Carmody recalls that JSU fans still come up to thank him and USM for playing JSU, and Gorden says he gets more questions about that game than any other in his long career. He is convinced that the effects of that game have played a major impact on athletic and social relations in the state.

Gorden was born in Nashville, Tennessee, but moved to Magnolia, Mississippi, in 1956 as head coach of football, baseball, basketball, and track as well as athletic director at Eva Gordon High School and has remained in Mississippi ever since. He says he was fortunate that his coaching career enabled him to learn so much about Mississippi over the years.

That 1987 football game was a huge success for both USM and Jackson State, but primarily for the state of Mississippi. Gorden was one of the most successful coaches in Mississippi football history. During his career as head coach from 1977-1991, his JSU Tigers compiled a 118-47-5 record in fifteen seasons that included eight Southwestern Athletic Conference (SWAC) championships. In the period of 1985-1988, JSU won 28 straight games.

Gorden also served as the athletic director at JSU from 1991-94. He has been inducted into four halls of fame: the SWAC Hall of Fame in 1994, the Mississippi Sports Hall of Fame in 1997, the College Football Hall of Fame in 2008, and the newly established Black College Football Hall of Fame in 2015.

Michael Rubenstein, founder and director of the Mississippi Sports Hall of Fame, said Gorden was "representative of everything that's good about college football."

During the period of 1983-94 Jackson State led the nation in Division 1-AA football attendance (averaging 38,873 fans per game in 1977). Throughout his coaching career Gorden felt academics was more important than football, and in 1980 and 1981 JSU led the state of Mississippi college football programs with a graduation rate of 61.9%. His players consistently graduated at a higher rate than the rest of the JSU student body. Carmody, like most Division 1-A coaches, has a great deal of respect for W.C. Gorden, and the reverse was apparently true.

Noted Mississippi historian laureate, Dr. David Sansing, himself a University of Southern Mississippi graduate, commented on the significance of this game: "The University of Southern Mississippi and Jackson State University football game in 1987 was more than just a game. It was a confirmation of social progress and racial change in Mississippi. For more than a hundred years after the emancipation of African Americans, Mississippi's public schools were segregated. And when the dual system was abolished and a unified system was established in the spring semester of 1970, there was wide concern that the schools would be subject to chaos and disorder. Historians are in general agreement that high school athletics played an important role in the orderly transition from the dual educational system to a unified system, and that athletic officials were a major factor in that transition. The leadership displayed by Coach W.C. Gorden and Coach Jim Carmody in organizing, and conducting, that game in 1987 is a sterling example of the role sports played in the process of reconciling and unifying Mississippi's racial culture. And Professor Ron Borne's historical account of that game is an important contribution to an understanding of our complex history."

THIRD QUARTER

OVERLEAF PHOTOGRAPH
"Third Quarter"

1992 UM Goal Line Stand vs MSU
Artis Ford (#70), Dewayne Dotson (#33),
Chad Brown (top of pile)
(Carmody Family Collection)

13

Parting Ways with USM

The 1987 football season would turn out to be Carmody's last at USM. The crushing loss to Southwestern Louisiana at Lafayette, 37-30, in the last game of the season was totally frustrating. The Eagles entered that game headed for a nice bowl game but fell inexplicably flat. In the days following that season-ending loss, Carmody felt increasingly frustrated. It should have been one of Carmody's career highlight years as a head coach, yet it turned into being his worst.

But as the days went by frustration turned into optimism for the upcoming 1988 season. After all, 1987 was a year marked by the discovery of Southern's quarterback of the future, a player who would go on to become one of the great professional quarterbacks. Also, the Eagles had crushed the rival Louisville Cardinals 65-8 and defeated in-state rival Mississippi State 18-14. Carmody had put together and won the most historic football game in the history of the state of Mississippi — a game between one of Mississippi's "Big Three" historically white institutions against a historically black Mississippi institution. Roberts Stadium had been sold out for the first time in its history. Carmody began to feel re-energized and hit the recruitment trail.

But a sequence of events occurred the previous season that would have a major impact on Carmody's future at USM. On January 20, 1986, after serving as athletic director at USM since 1974, athletic director Roland Dale took a leave of absence for personal reasons and later retired, effective July 1, 1986. President Lucas established a search committee to find Dale's replacement. The search committee recommended Terry Don Phillips, athletic director at Southwestern Louisiana University, and Phillips initially accepted the job but then rejected the offer a few days later. The committee then select-ed John Schafer, assistant athletic director at the University of Georgia for six-teen years, but he subsequently rejected the offer. (Schafer later accepted the athletic director's position at Ole Miss in 1998). Subsequently, H.C. "Bill" McLellan replaced Roland Dale on July 19 — a change that would eventu-ally be ominous for some of the USM coaching staff. McLellan had been athletic director at Clemson for 14 years and set as his initial goals improving fund-raising and enhancing the athletic physical facilities.

McLellan quickly earned the nickname "Dollar Bill" for the way he ran the athletic budget with a tight fist. McLellan was highly successful at Clemson. While he was athletic director there Clemson's football program won three ACC championships and was in the nation's Top 25 programs five times, winning the National Championship in 1981 under coach Dan-ny Ford. However, McLellan's reputation was tarnished in November 1982 when Clemson's football program was placed on probation for two years for recruiting violations.

In the 1970s, Clemson's basketball program was placed on probation for similar violations. In addition, McClellan was athletic director when Clemson was accused, in a *Sports Illustrated* article in January 1985, of the widespread use of illegally obtained prescription drugs, including steroids, in several programs at Clemson. McLellan was replaced as athletic director the following March.

Despite these problems, McLellan remained popular among Clemson fans and alumni, and in 2013 the newly constructed North upper deck at Clemson's Memorial Stadium — which McLellan oversaw — was named in his honor. He was considered "a visionary" up to the time of his death in 2013.

When Dale retired, President Lucas named USM's faculty chairman of athletics as interim athletic director. It soon became apparent that the interim athletic director had a strong interest in being appointed full time athletic director. The appointment of the interim director did not win the approval of several USM head coaches, including Jim Carmody and basketball coach M.K. Turk. Carmody was aware of several USM alumni in the Hattiesburg area promoting the appointment of Bill McLellan as athletic director. Although they had never met, McLellan telephoned Carmody expressing his interest in the position. Carmody and Turk met with Lucas to discuss the opening and to express concerns about the interim athletic director appointed by Lucas. Lucas asked them if they had a recommendation, and both recommended Bill McLellan. Lucas was concerned that McLellan had had trouble with the NCAA while at Clemson.

Referring to the 1981 NCAA investigation, Carmody brazenly responded, "Well, sir, so have you." Lucas told both coaches that he would give the matter some thought, and eventually he hired McLellan. Ironically, McLellan would later fire both Carmody and Turk, as well as baseball coach Hill Denson.

Carmody's 31-24 record over his first five seasons gave him the best start of any Southern coach since Pie Vann, but some fans, now measuring success by the remarkable achievements earlier in the decade, began to complain, especially about lopsided losses to Kentucky (32-0) and Florida State (49-13) in 1986. Barely 11,000 showed up for the final home game, a 31-16 victory over Louisville that same year. In a less-than-subtle message to the disgruntled fans, McLellan extended Carmody's contract through 1990. USM won ten straight home football games in the 1985-86 seasons — why the crowds did not show is puzzling.

Less than a week after the 1987 season ended, President Lucas called a meeting of himself, Bill McLellan, and Carmody to "talk about some issues of the program and changes that were perhaps needed."

The attendance problem had raised its ugly head. Lucas obviously did not take into consideration Carmody's suggestion to play Jackson State in Hattiesburg, a game that drew a sellout crowd to Roberts Stadium. Carmody was surprised when he was asked to resign, despite the fact that in January 1987 his contract had been extended through December 31, 1990.

Carmody said, "I had no idea about the resignation. It was a surprise to me. I had not made any plans to do anything else (other than coach at USM). It was a mutual understanding after I met with Dr. Lucas." The attendance problem was the only reason Carmody cited for his resignation.

Jason Munz of the *Hattiesburg American* wrote that "attendance figures for Southern Miss home football games have never been eye popping." Carmody ssid, "My previous five years here we averaged 18,700 for home games in actual paid attendance, not announced attendance. The previous five years before I came here we averaged 18,400. And I think this year (1987) with the Florida State and Jackson State games, the average was probably larger." The problem has continued.

Although the attendance figures Carmody cites are not those USM reports as official attendance (which could be a reflection of paid attendance versus announced attendance), the trend he cites is accurate. In the period 1977-1980, the average attendance was 21,788 per game. Attendance during the period Carmody was head coach, (1982-87), average attendance actually rose to 22,936. He was also correct that playing Florida State at home and the scheduling of Jackson State would increase 1987 attendance over that of 1986. The average attendance in 1986 was 18,115, and for 1987 the figure increased to an average of 19,342. The year following Carmody's departure, attendance was an of average 18,836, despite USM's posting a 10-2 record.

In 2015, in the third year of Todd Monken's tenure as head football coach, he expressed his anger to let USM fans know that he was upset that only 23,000 fans attended the 52-6 victory over Austin Peay — one week after setting a Roberts Stadium record attendance of 36,641 for the opening season loss to Mississippi State, 34-16 — a crowd nearly half of which was presumably State fans. Roberts Stadium was expanded to a seating capacity of 36,000 in 2008.

Lucas said the university and Carmody agreed on a $100,000 buyout of Carmody's contract. He had just completed the first year of a four-year contract that had been extended to 1990. Few coaches had their own agent back then, so it can be assumed that a larger buyout could have been arranged if Jim had had legal representation. A Jackson *Clarion-Ledger* sports writer wrote that when asked if there was something Carmody could have done differently, Carmody replied, "Not a thing. I did the best I could, and every week I worked as hard or harder than anyone in coaching. I devoted all my time to getting a football team on the field. Building a winning football team was my job, and I did that." The obvious implication was that his job was to build a winning football team, and the job of filling the stadium fell on someone else's shoulders.

Lucas said, "This is painful for all of us. It really is." He admitted that the attendance problem may not be Carmody's sole responsibility and then employed the universally accepted academic method of solving a problem — he appointed a committee to look into the attendance situation.

Carmody was gracious in his comments following the resignation. "We're going to leave here with our heads held high...We're very much proud of what we've accomplished here at Southern Mississippi. I want to thank Coach Roland Dale and Dr. Lucas for the opportunity to be a head football coach at Southern Mississippi. We would have liked to win 11 games a year, but all of you know the situation here is extremely difficult to be a consistent winner."

Carmody called a team meeting that afternoon to announce his resignation to his players. Billy Watkins, Jackson *Clarion-Ledger* sports writer, talked to several players about the resignation after the team meeting.

Defensive tackle Ulysses Slaughter said, "Coach Carmody was down, really hurt. I've never seen him like that. He's a man who always holds his head up." Slaughter went on to say that firing Jim Carmody because of poor attendance is "hogwash. We have poor fans here; that's all."

Defensive back James Henry said, "I liked Coach Carmody. He is a very hard coach, a rough coach. He gets his point across, but that's the kind of coach you need. It wasn't his fault we didn't draw good crowds. Southern has never had good fans. Even when we were winning, the fans wouldn't come out."

Junior defensive back Vincent Rollins added, "Coach Carmody was doing what he was supposed to do — win games. The rest — ticket sales and all that stuff — is supposed to take care of itself."

Perhaps another factor in replacing Carmody was the appointment of his successor, Curley Hallman, an assistant coach at Texas A&M who also coached at Clemson during McLellan's tenure there. McLellan forgot that it was probably through the efforts of Jim Carmody and M.K. Turk that he was appointed Roland Dale's successor.

Carmody's career record at USM was 37-29, ranking him fourth at the time on the USM all-time head coaches' victory totals, behind only legendary Pie Vann (139-59), Reed Green (59-20), and Bobby Collins (48-30).

Carmody's record at USM was a proud one. He sent many players to the pros — including quarterback Brett Favre, running back Sammy Winder, quarterback Reggie Collier, tackle Glen Howe, defensive back Robert Ducksworth, wide receiver Louis Lipps, defensive end Richard Byrd, and defensive back Bud Brown. He should also be credited with the development of the career of Brett Favre. With his new quarterback, Favre, in place, 1988 would have been a great year. As it was, Big Nasty left the Eagles stockpiled in talent. The year after Carmody left, Hallman and USM went 10-2, but that was followed with a 5-6 record in 1989. Carmody was a relentless recruiter and brought many SEC-caliber players to USM and wherever he coached. He was never directly implicated or named by the NCAA in any recruiting irregularities.

Perhaps the end of Carmody's tenure as head coach at USM was inevitable — his relationship with President Aubrey Lucas was tenuous at best. Jim was the choice of athletic director Roland Dale, and probably not Lucas, although Lucas obviously had to support the selection since he recommended Jim to the IHL Board. Carmody never felt he had the complete support of Lucas, dating back to the 1981 NCAA investigation, which did not involve Carmody, and to the Jerry Bruner lawsuit.

14

BACK TO MISSISSIPPI STATE UNIVERSITY

The phone rang at the Carmody household, and son Chris answered the call. The caller asked for Jim, and Chris said, "He's not home right now. Who is this?

The caller said "Rockey Felker."

Chris said "Oh, yeah, right!"

Felker said, "No really, this is Rockey Felker."

Chris realized it really was Felker and said, "Oh, yes, sir, coach, yes, sir. I'll get him to call you when he gets in." And that was the start of Carmody's return to coaching at Mississippi State.

Former coach Emory Bellard had suffered through a 5-6 1985 season, was winless in the SEC, had four consecutive losing seasons (1982-85), and was fired by MSU athletic director Charlie Carr. Bellard's teams won only four SEC games in the previous four seasons. In replacing Bellard, Carr said, "Rockey Felker is our person. He belongs here."

Rockey Felker was an outstanding quarterback for the Mississippi State Bulldogs in the early 1970s, leading them to a Sun Bowl victory over North Carolina in 1974 and being named the SEC Player of the Year that season. He began his coaching career at MSU coaching the junior varsity as well as wide receivers and running backs. He then coached at Texas Tech, Memphis State, and the University of Alabama. Mississippi State had four consecutive losing seasons under Emory Bellard (1982-1985), and Felker's dossier as an experienced assistant coach and favorite son led to his being named head coach at Mississippi State in 1986.

Felker was only 32 years old and became the youngest head coach among the 105 Division 1-A teams. His first season at MSU was a winning one at 6-5, but then Felker suffered through two consecutive losing seasons in 1987-1988, including a miserable 1-10 season in 1988. Needing immediate defensive help, he hired Carmody as his defensive coordinator, hoping to turn things around in 1989.

After a year of non-coaching, Carmody, still being paid by USM, accepted Felker's offer to join his staff at Mississippi State University as defensive coordinator. Carmody was willing to return for a second stint at MSU, and he readily accepted the offer. He set his sights on the second game of the season. On September 9, 1989, Mississippi State was scheduled to play Southern Mississippi in Hattiesburg. Ironically, USM was still paying Carmody the remaining year of his contract with the Golden Eagles. Carmody could not help but feel nostalgia and bitterness when he returned to Roberts Stadium. Mississippi State and Southern had signed a 10-year agreement, and the 1989 contest would be the ninth in that deal. Mississippi State and USM played every year from 1964-1990 with the exception of 1971 and 1974. The series was tied at 12-12 prior to the 1989 matchup (not counting the two MSU games in 1975 and 1976 that MSU had to forfeit because of NCAA probation).

1989 Season

The highlight of the 1989 season for Carmody would be the September 9 game that would be the last time State would play in Hattiesburg for a while. Carmody would coach against players he brought to USM, players who led the Golden Eagles to a 10-2 record in 1988. When Mississippi State beat USM 26-23, USM was effectively paying Carmody to beat them! Carmody had set his defense to beat his former quarterback, Brett Favre. MSU employed a defense of five defensive backs and four down linemen to stop, or at least slow down Favre. USM was in its second year of Curley Hallman's tenure as head coach and, coming off the 10-2 season in 1988, was 7-point favorite to win the 1989 game.

MSU opened their 1989 season with a 42-7 thrashing of Vanderbilt to set up the MSU-USM match-up in Hattiesburg. A record crowd of 34,189 filled up Roberts Stadium, and the game turned out to be one of the more exciting games in the series. The crowd was intense and enthusiastic. The Eagles had won three straight over State and had defeated the Bulldogs in 10 of their last 12 meetings. USM, ranked No. 18 in the country after their opening season 30-26 victory over sixth-ranked Florida State, took a 3-0 first-quarter lead and MSU countered, scoring on a 7-yard pass play to take a 7-3 lead. But the Golden Eagles bounced back and scored on a one-yard run to take a 10-7 lead. MSU then returned the ensuing kickoff 96 yards to regain the lead. USM countered with a 33-yard field goal, and the Bulldogs went to the locker room at halftime with a 14-13 lead. A third-quarter field goal gave MSU a 17-13 lead, but the Eagles bounced back with a 12-yard touchdown run to take a 20-17 lead. Once again, MSU bounced back and scored in the fourth quarter to give State a 23-20 lead, but the Bulldogs missed the extra point. After another USM field goal, they tied the game at 23-23 with less than three minutes left in the seesaw contest.

State then began its game-winning drive from its own 37-yard line with 1:18 left in the game. MSU quarterback Eric Underwood completed a 38-yard pass to Kenny Roberts at the USM 25 yard-line. Two plays later Joel Logan kicked a field goal with less than ten seconds (some reports say four seconds remained, while other reports said there were eight seconds left on the clock) remaining to give MSU a hard-fought 26-23 victory. It was Felker's first victory in four tries against the Eagles.

USM lost their No. 18 national ranking and were knocked out of the polls. Favre completed fewer than half (18-39) of his passes against Carmody's defense.

Favre said, "We're the biggest game on their schedule. They wanted it bad and out-played us." Favre had wanted to shake Carmody's hand after the game but did not get a chance because several Bulldog defensive players carried Carmody off the field on their shoulders.

MSU defensive tackle Bobby Barlow said, "Football is the most important thing in Coach Carmody's life. Winning games is important to him, and that trickles down to all of us. We wanted this game more than Southern Mississippi did. Coach Carmody is such an organized coach. On the field we knew exactly what they were going to run. We couldn't always stop them, but we could slow them down. We knew their tendencies in certain situations. Heck, it was like a Tuesday practice on Saturday."

The USM victory was the season high point. The Bulldogs lost to the remaining six SEC schools on their schedule to finish the season 5-6. Following the thrilling victory over USM, the Bulldogs lost road games to Georgia (23-6) and Florida (21-0) before returning home and defeating Louisiana-Monroe (28-14) and Memphis State (35-10).

MSU had another miserable two-game road trip, losing to Auburn (14-0) and Alabama 23-10). A 27-7 victory over Tulane at home and another SEC road loss, this time to LSU 44-20, evened the Bulldog record at 5-5.

The LSU offense scored almost at will. However, with a chance to have a winning season still on the line, Ole Miss beat State 21-11 in the Egg Bowl in Jackson. Early in the second half MSU had a chance to take the lead but fumbled at the Ole Miss 7-yard line and could not recover from that lost opportunity. The impact of Carmody's defense was felt immediately. In the 1988 season MSU yielded an average of 30.2 points per game. The 1989 team defense improved almost two touchdowns per game, yielding only 18.8 points per game. The 1989 Bulldogs' pass defense ranked fourth in the nation and first in the SEC. The Carmody-led defense was ranked fifteenth in the nation for the season after ranking eighty-fourth in the nation in 1988, in spite of State's losing season.

1990 Season

The 1990 season opened on a sour note as the Tennessee Vols clobbered MSU 40-7 in Starkville. The Bulldogs bounced back with a 27-13 victory over Cal State-Fullerton at home to set up the final matchup against USM in the current 10-game agreement. USM opened their season with a victory over Delta State without their star quarterback Brett Favre, who was still recovering from a summer automobile accident. Favre amazingly returned the following week to lead USM to a 27-24 upset over Alabama in Birmingham. But the Eagles lost a close contest to Georgia the following week.

Favre has earned the reputation of being one of the toughest quarterbacks in the game, college or professional. Nowhere was his toughness more evident than the 1990 USM season. Favre entered the State game still not fully recovered from a summer automobile accident that caused severe injuries.

On July 14, 1990, Favre was involved in a one-car accident near his parents home in Pass Christian, Mississippi when, according to the sheriff of Hancock County, his car left the road, hit a culvert, flipped over three times and landed on the passenger side against a pine tree. Favre was admitted under an assumed name to the Forrest General Hospital in Hattiesburg. He suffered a hematoma on his liver and had a brief concussion. Favre was briefly knocked out and could not remember the accident. Doctors later removed nearly 30 inches of Favre's small intestine. Favre lost 35 pounds during his recovery, and there was some doubt that he would ever play football again.

Favre missed the opening game of the season against Delta State, but, amazingly, on September 8, less than two months after the near-fatal accident, Favre led USM to a 27-24 last-minute comeback victory over Alabama in Birmingham.

Favre's uniform draped his body and barely fit him. His return to the field was so emotional that supposedly some of his teammates cried.

Alabama coach Gene Stallings said, "You can call it a miracle or a legend or whatever you want to. I just know that on that day, Brett Favre was larger than life."

Carmody later said, "As far as toughness and leadership and grit and passion for the game, Brett was as good as they come. The guy loved to play."

Two weeks following the Alabama game, before the fourth-largest crowd in the history of Scott Field in Starkville, the 1990 matchup of USM and Mississippi State turned out to be a defensive struggle. This would be the final Carmody-Favre engagement.

USM entered the game as a five-point favorite. After the teams traded field goals in the opening quarter, MSU quarterback Tony Shell threw an interception at midfield in the second quarter that was returned 47 yards for a touchdown. Just before halftime MSU was at the USM one-yard line when MSU quarterback Sleepy Robinson completed a one-yard pass to Treddis Anderson for the game's only offensive touchdown. The teams played to a

10-10 tie at halftime.

The second half was a standoff until, with 3:01 left in the game, MSU's Joel Logan kicked a 41-yard field goal, and then MSU held off a USM drive. When a 47-yard field goal attempt by USM's Jim Taylor failed with 1:20 left in the game, Mississippi State had a 13-10 victory, and Carmody enjoyed his second consecutive win over his former team. In fact, other than Carmody, six of Felker's assistant coaches had come to MSU from USM before the 1989 season (Jim Tomkins, Gene Smith, Keith Daniels, Bill Clay, Ron Taylor, and Rick Trickett).

After the game Felker said, "It was the most important game of the year to our coaches, and they were gonna make sure that our football team was ready to play." Felker went on to say, "Over those 10 years from '80 to 90," — primarily the Carmody-USM era — "Southern embarrassed us. It was a game that we circled on our schedule. A game we knew we had to win." Felker went on, "The defense just played a tremendous game, keeping Southern out of the end zone. Time and time again they came up with big plays.

Favre said, "It's tough to lose to them like that. It's tough to lose any, but it's even tougher to lose to your big-time rival. We had the opportunity to win the game, but we didn't."

Newspaper reporter Mike Christensen wrote, "Playing no small part in this feat was State defensive coordinator, Jim Carmody, the former USM head coach."

Carmody was not available for comment after the game, but the State team knew he was very intense about the game and how important it was to him.

State lost its next two road games to Florida (34-21) and Kentucky (17-15), beat Tulane in New Orleans (38-17), and then lost consecutive home games to Auburn (17-16) and Alabama (22-0). The Bulldogs then beat Memphis State in Memphis (27-23) and LSU in Jackson (34-22) before ending another losing season with a 21-9 loss to Ole Miss.

After winning his first season at Mississippi State, finishing with a 6-5 record in 1986, Felker had four consecutive losing seasons in 1987, 1988, 1989, and 1990. In 1988 MSU posted the program's second-worst on-field record of 1-10. His five-year record at MSU was 21-34 and, following the 1990 loss to Ole Miss, Felker, one of MSU's greatest players and certainly one of its most popular players, resigned under intense pressure and assumed the offensive coordinator position at Tulsa.

Felker said, "I leave with my head held high. It is tough to win in the Southeastern Conference," an assessment many former SEC head coaches would make.

One report has it that thirty minutes after Felker resigned, athletic director Larry Templeton placed a telephone call to Jackie Sherrill, and shortly thereafter Sherrill was hired. This report is obviously not accurate. Carmody was interviewed for the position and thought he had reasonable support from Templeton. He certainly had the support of the popular and successful baseball coach at State, Ron Polk. According to Mike Knobler, reporter for the Jackson *Clarion-Ledger* newspaper, Polk wrote to Mississippi State President Donald Zacharias to support Carmody's efforts to secure the head-coaching job. Polk said he did so for several reasons, among which was his view that if there were a quality candidate from within, whatever the sport, they should be given consideration.

Polk said further, "Jim has talked to me about his interests. I told Jim Carmody that I would write a brief note to Dr. Zacharias. I would support him." However, Polk made it clear he would not get involved in favoring Carmody over another internal candidate, such as Bill Clay, State's defensive back coach, if he should also apply for the job. Clay did later express interest but was confident State would not be interested in him.

In Knobler's November 2, 1990, report he indicated that Templeton said interviews would begin soon. Felker resigned on Monday, October 29. Knobler cited a number of other coaches who would be candidates for the job. His list included Tennessee defensive coordinator Larry Lacewell, Alabama secondary coach Bill Oliver, former Southern Mississippi and SMU head coach Bobby Collins, former Clemson coach Dan Ford, and former Pittsburgh and Texas A&M head coach Jackie Sherrill.

Two days later Knobler reported that Carmody had interviewed for the position twice and felt positive about those discussions. Carmody felt he had

Larry Templeton's support. But the faculty council at State had apparently passed a non-binding resolution earlier in November urging Zacharias not to hire any coach who had a history of NCAA rules violations that directly involved the coach or anyone who led any program with a history of violations. The resolution was ignored with the hiring of Jackie Sherrill.

Several members of the media supported Carmody's appointment. One reporter, Marc Kuykendall, wrote, "Some people say that Carmody doesn't have the personality to be a head coach, that he's not outgoing or ingratiating enough to alumni. If you want laughs or an entertaining speaker, hire a comic. If you want to win a football game, hire Jim Carmody." Kuykendall added, "The point is this… hire Carmody. Do it now. Give him a five-year contract, and watch the wins begin."

However, Zacharias, under heavy pressure from Mississippi State alumni in Houston, hired Jackie Sherrill, despite his having led a program with a history of NCAA rules violations. Sherrill had been away from coaching for three years following the NCAA's placing Texas A&M on probation for two years for various infractions including unethical conduct and lack of institutional control. Sherrill was not directly found guilty of any violations. The assistant coaches at State had remained in limbo since their contracts ran through June 30, 1991.

When Sherrill arrived at State he called a meeting of the assistants and told them he had not made a decision on who he would keep. He directed the staff to continue recruiting for another week while he made up his mind. Carmody continued his recruiting.

A week later Sherrill called another meeting and said the same thing when the staff thought he would have made a decision about his coaching staff. Instead he repeated that he wanted the staff to go back out recruiting, and he would get together with them the following week.

When the meeting was over Carmody went to Templeton's office and told him, "Larry, I don't think I want to work for this guy. I want to know, my contract runs through June, do I have to be here working in some capacity? Or will you honor that contract for the year? I do not want to be here any more."

Templeton said he understood and would take care of it and would get back to him. When Templeton told Carmody later that State would honor his contract through June 30, Carmody left. Other assistants stayed. Carmody always felt Templeton treated him fairly throughout the process.

Sherrill formed his own coaching staff, including hiring Bill Clay as defensive coordinator, the position Carmody previously held.

Felker returned to MSU in 2002 as coordinator of football operations and served as running backs' coach in 2007-2008. He currently serves MSU as director of player personnel and high school relations.

15

Mississippi College

When Carmody left Mississippi State in 1991, coaching jobs were hard to find. Most colleges had filled their staffs by June 1991. He went to various coaching clinics and coaches meetings trying to re-establish contacts. The Carmodys had moved to Jackson, so he scoured the area for open jobs, including vacancies at the high school level. Carmody's last check from Mississippi State would arrive on June 30. He contacted former Ole Miss player Randy Rucker, who was head coach at Northwest Rankin High School, when he heard there might be a job possibility there. Rucker was a strong safety at Ole Miss when Carmody was on Ken Cooper's staff. Rucker was amazed that a coach with his experience was interested in returning to coaching at the high school level. Rucker saw this as a golden opportunity for himself, contemplating the benefits he would personally and professionally gain from working with Carmody and became excited about the possibilities of working with a coach of his caliber.

Carmody was getting his credentials (teaching certificate, etc.) together for the Northwest Rankin position when he was called by Mississippi College head coach Terry McMillan. McMillan learned that Carmody was available. Carmody knew McMillan because McMillan had visited Southern when he was coaching at Mississippi College. McMillan was MC's acting head coach at the time of their initial contact, but he was the leading candidate for the full-time job.

Following his graduation from Magee High School, where he quarterbacked the Trojans to two consecutive undefeated seasons, McMillan played quarterback for Southern Mississippi from 1966 to 1968. Following graduation from USM he joined the coaching staff at Biloxi High School in 1969 as assistant football coach and offensive coordinator. McMillan also served as Biloxi's head tennis coach and assistant baseball coach in addition to teaching physical education. Biloxi High football compiled a 24-7 record while he was coach. He then joined the staff at Mississippi College in 1972, serving as assistant head coach and offensive coordinator for John Williams for 19 years. He also earned a master of education degree in school administration from Mississippi College in 1974. He was named head football coach at MC in 1991 when Williams resigned and served until 2001.

Previous head coach John Williams ended his 19-year coaching career with MC by winning the national Division II 1989 championship and winning the championship of the Gulf Coast Conference, of which MC was a member, in 1990. The Choctaws enjoyed unprecedented success during 1981-91, enjoying an eleven-year stretch of winning seasons. During this period MC finished either first or second in the Gulf States Conference five years in a row. The Choctaws advanced to the semi-finals of the NCAA Division II championship in 1990. When the Choctaws won the 1989 Division II national football championship, Williams was named the Division II National Coach of the Year.

But reports of a NCAA investigation surfaced that placed the program, under Williams' leadership, under suspicion. Mississippi College reported itself to the NCAA. Although the NCAA investigation was not initiated until early 1992, Williams was forced to resign by MC President Lewis Nobles following the 1990 season.

Williams strongly maintained that he ran a clean program and refused to be interviewed by the NCAA. On Saturday, May 4, 1991 Nobles sent a letter to Williams, directing him to resign on May 8.

Williams declared, "I was backed into a corner" but resigned nevertheless.

After a lengthy investigation the NCAA found MC guilty of five rules violations including a lack of institutional control and misconduct on the part of head coach Williams. The NCAA charged that during the 1989 season Mississippi College had actually awarded twice the number of 40 scholarships that Division II schools were allowed to award. During the 1989-90 academic year MC was found to have awarded grants-in-aid to 98 players, amounting to 80.21 scholarships, and the next year, when MC was a Division II semifinalist, awarded grants-in-aid to 99 players, which totaled 77.26 scholarships.

The NCAA claimed that MC enjoyed a tremendous competitive advantage by awarding twice the number of scholarships allowed under their regulations. MC was also charged with providing extra benefits to student-athletes by allowing partial qualifiers to routinely participate in football-related activities. The 1989 Division II national football championship and the 1990 records were vacated as a result of the NCAA findings, and MC was banned from participating in postseason play through 1995. The NCAA also placed MC on four years' probation. The NCAA report claimed that Williams knew of these problems and acted contrary to the principles of ethical conduct. Williams consistently denied any guilt.

Before the end of June, Carmody had committed to joining the MC staff and to coach the Choctaws' defensive backs. Despite all of Carmody's experiences as a defensive coach and defensive coordinator, he had never coached defensive backs. On July 11, 1991, Mississippi College announced that former Southern Miss coach Jim Carmody was hired as assistant head coach, recruiting coordinator, and defensive assistant coach. Charlie Coles was named defensive coordinator. On July 26, Mississippi College named longtime assistant Terry McMillan as head coach and athletic director. McMillan had been a member of the Choctaw staff since 1972.

Mississippi College was established in 1826 as Hampstead Academy and is the oldest institution of higher learning in Mississippi and the second oldest Baptist college in the U.S. In 1831, MC became the first coeducational college in the U.S. to grant degrees to women. In 1850, the Mississippi Baptist Convention gained control of MC and abolished classes for women. The following year the name of the institution was changed to Mississippi Academy and then to Mississippi College in 1830. The Central Baptist Association established the Central Female Institute in 1853 as a sister college to MC. CFI became Hillman College in 1891, and Mississippi College bought out Hillman College in 1942. Once again, MC became a coeducational institution.

Enrollment gradually increased, and the college survived financial challenges presented by the Great Depression. Mississippi College has played intercollegiate football since 1907. They had avoided playing intercollegiate athletics on campus and, in fact, there was opposition to the formation of a baseball team in 1905 that would play intercollegiate competition. The trustees and the Baptist Convention soon saw the value of intercollegiate play and gave approval to the baseball team. Two years later football was introduced. MC won the first football game they played when they defeated Chamberlain-Hunt Academy 6-0 in 1907. The following year MC played the University of Mississippi football team and, despite losing, played competitively. That year witnessed the turning point in athletics in Mississippi College, "and from an incidental feature of the college work, it rises to be a permanent, potent influence, dominating the spirit of the college to a degree heretofore unknown."

In announcing the hiring of Carmody, McMillan said, "I hired Carmody because of his vast amount of experience, as well as the fact that he is well known throughout the state, which helps in recruiting. I thought he was the best man for the job, and he was. We feel like he is going to help us in recruiting with the contacts he has around the state. The experience he has picked up from all the places he has been is going to help us in a lot of areas of the program. We're using a lot of his suggestions. For one example, we're a little short in numbers for our scout teams. Coach Carmody suggested a practice plan they used when he was with the Buffalo Bills. We devote some days to offense, some to defense. It's been a big help in organizing our practices."

Carmody responded by saying, "I came to MC because of its prestigious academic and athletic tradition. I had the opportunity to work with a winning team and winning coaches, and I took it."

Carmody seemed to thrive in this newest addition to his coaching experiences. He enjoyed the challenges of hard work made necessary because of the small staff and the personal challenge of coaching the secondary, an area he had not coached before. McMillan said, "He's always in his office studying film. He's always looking for a new angle or a tendency or a weakness. As a head coach, I like that. The kids have responded well to him. He's fit right in.

He's been just one of us. It's been great."

Not surprisingly, Carmody was content with his new role and coaching at the Division II level. For the first time in many years he could concentrate solely on coaching football and not dealing with all the hoopla that surrounds coaching at the Division I level.

In an interview with Jackson *Clarion-Ledger* sportswriter Mike Christensen six weeks into his new coaching responsibilities, Carmody was forthcoming. "Preparing a game plan to me is one of the most exciting things about football. You look at a team on film and try to take apart their offense segment by segment. Figure out their strengths and weaknesses and tendencies. Make sure you've done everything possible to prepare your players from a technical standpoint to know everything about that offense. You want to feel comfortable about yourself on Saturday that you've given the players everything they need to win. I get just as excited about coaching a game at MC as I did when I was with the Buffalo Bills."

Carmody, always known for his intensity, appeared to some to be mellowing in his new role. One of the MC cornerbacks was a redshirt at USM during Carmody's last year there. He said, "I think he is more personable now. At USM he was kind of distant from his players. I was wondering if he would even remember me. Now, he's on the field with us every day, and he has a lot more personal contact with us. But he believes in a lot of hard work. That hasn't changed."

Carmody's oldest son, Steve, who played for his father at USM, agreed. "He's as happy as I've seen him. Maybe he's mellowed with age, and maybe it's because he is out of the pressure cooker of big-time football. It's probably a combination of both. I just know that he's doing what he likes best: coaching football. The kids he has here at MC are playing because they love the game, and so does he."

The 1991 season opened on an optimistic note for the Choctaws, who won at home against Central Arkansas (34-9) and North Alabama (31-3) and on the road at Henderson State (42-17). But then they lost the next two games on the road by nearly identical scores, 17-7 at Northeast Louisiana and 17-6 at Jacksonville State. They straightened the boat and beat Livingston at home 25-14 and West Georgia on the road 49-21. Following a 10-10 tie at home against Valdosta State, the Choctaws lost at Appalachian State, 31-23. However, they ended the regular season with a win at Delta State, 27-10, to finish at 6-3-1 and qualify for the Division II playoffs. MC defeated the Wofford Terriers, 28-15, in Spartanburg, South Carolina. MC decided to fly the team from Jackson to Spartanburg. Coaches were invited to bring their wives along. Turned out to be a nice trip, especially by defeating the Terriers — the highlight of the year. The one-and-a-half-hour flight over 555 miles was in sharp contrast to the game against Appalachian State in Boone, North Carolina, when the team bussed from Clinton to Boone, a driving distance of 661 miles that took more than 10 and a half hours!

But the Choctaws lost again to Jacksonville State in the next round, displaying their poorest showing of the year, this time by a wider margin, 35-7. Nevertheless, they had a good season, finishing at 7-4-1 and 4-1-1 in the Gulf States Conference.

Carmody's debut as a defensive backs' and punt return coach was successful. The Mississippi College defense was ranked 11th in the nation, allowing 13 points per game, and they ranked second in the nation in punt returns, returning 37 punts for an average of 16.0 yards per punt return. The Choctaws gave up only five passing touchdowns.

The 1991 Choctaws were led by University of Florida transfer Kyle Morris. Morris and Florida back-up quarterback Shane Matthews were found to have placed bets on professional and college football games, a NCAA violation, and were declared ineligible for the remainder of the 1989 season. Both players admitted the violation but also stated that they did not place bets on Florida games and only small amounts of money ($25-$100) were wagered. They further made clear that the bets were placed using personal funds. Morris then transferred to Mississippi College.

Carmody said he liked Mississippi College, the school and the players. They had nice facilities for a Division II school. But he was ready to return to Division I football.

16

BACK TO OLE MISS

Ole Miss football had undergone several twists and turns in the fifteen years since Carmody left the first time in 1977. The promising Sloan-era (1978-82) failed to materialize, and when that era ended at Ole Miss, the Rebels turned to former Ole Miss standout Billy Brewer, who was the head coach at Louisiana Tech, to salvage the program. The excitement that was generated when Sloan was hired in 1978 faded with five consecutive losing seasons. Most attributed his lack of success to poor defensive efforts. Sloan selected his former Alabama roommate, Paul Crane, as his defensive coordinator — rather than retaining Carmody as defensive coordinator — and the result was a 20-34-1 career record at Ole Miss.

Crane resigned from Ole Miss following the 1980 season after the Rebels finished with a disappointing 3-8 record. One can only guess what record Sloan's Ole Miss career would have produced had he retained one of the best defensive coaches in the country, Jim Carmody, on his staff.

Brewer produced a winning season his first year at Ole Miss — with the help of some wind, known as "The Immaculate Deflection." Brewer's career at Ole Miss got off to a slow start, with the Rebels going 1-5 to begin the season. However, Ole Miss put together four straight victories to enter the Egg Bowl of 1983 with a 5-5 record. With Ole Miss leading 24-23 with 24 seconds remaining on the clock, Mississippi State lined up to kick a game-winning 27-yard field goal. Ole Miss fans groaned, and cowbells rang loudly, as freshman State kicker Artie Crosby kicked the ball dead center and seemingly through the uprights when a 40 mph gusting wind stopped the ball in mid-flight and blew it back to the playing field. The ball amazingly landed in the end zone, barely short of the goalpost, and the Rebels won. Brewer's 6-5 team went to the Independence Bowl, the first bowl appearance for the Rebels since their Peach Bowl game under Billy Kinard in 1971.

Ole Miss quarterback Kelly Powell recalled Brewer's reactions after the unbelievable ending. "He was just as elated as we were, excited. He had taught us from Day 1 that every time you go out on that field, it's a war. The last man standing is going to win. Don't ever give up. I guess we held to that motto. We did not give up. It was a war today; we're the victors." *The Clarksdale Press Register* would later proclaim, "God was an Ole Miss Rebel in 1983."

Entering Brewer's eleventh season the Rebels had appeared in five bowl games during the Brewer regime and started the 1991 season with a 5-1 record. However, Ole Miss lost its final five games to end with a losing season for the first time in three years. The Rebels collapsed on both sides of the ball. During the losing streak the Rebels averaged less than 220 yards a game and scored 20 points per game. The defense yielded over 430 yards and 30.4 points a game.

Brewer fired offensive coordinator Red Parker and defensive coordinator Robert Henry but not without controversy. Both Parker and Henry claimed they were caught by surprise. Ironically, Henry was a graduate assistant for Carmody at USM. Brewer admitted that injuries on both offense and defense played a major role in the losing streak, but he felt it was time for a change. He began his search for replacements.

Ole Miss fans immediately began a campaign to get the unconventional defensive coordinator at Memphis State, Joe Lee Dunn, hired as defensive coordinator at Ole Miss. Earlier in the 1991 season Ole Miss defeated Memphis State 10-0, but fans were impressed with the Memphis blitzing defense and were intrigued with Dunn's lifestyle — no socks, no playbook, no cell phones, no email, etc.

Dunn made it clear he was interested in the position and announced, "I would say I'm a candidate."

Reporters referred, in a complimentary way, that Dunn' s defensive schemes were "a version of controlled insanity" designed to confuse the opposition. His defense was characterized by players constantly moving, or they would kneel, then stand up and shift from position to position, then finally they blitzed. Other coaches were being mentioned for that position including Charlie Bailey, former Memphis State head coach, and Mississippi College assistant coach Jim Carmody.

The accounting below may suffer from a lapse of some memory over time, but the bottom line is that Big Nasty joined the coaching staff of his one-time rival, Billy Brewer, at Ole Miss, but not as defensive coordinator. Following the dismissals of Parker and Henry, a mutual friend of Billy Brewer and Jim Carmody asked Brewer if he would be open to considering Carmody for the defensive coordinator position. Brewer replied that he was about to offer the defensive coordinator position to Joe Lee Dunn, but noted that the position of defensive line coach would be open. Brewer indicated that he would be open to exploring the possibility of Carmody's joining his coaching staff if his one-time rival was, in turn, interested in joining his staff. The friend then telephoned Carmody's oldest son, Steve, to ask his father if he would be interested in the position. Steve called back shortly to indicate that indeed his father, who had just completed the season at Mississippi College, would be interested. The friend then called Brewer and related Carmody's interest in joining his staff. Brewer and Carmody then met at the Ramada Inn in Oxford, and Carmody was offered the positions of assistant head coach and defensive line coach. He readily accepted Brewer's offer. Thus, Carmody returned to Ole Miss for the second time.

Five years earlier no one would have predicted that Billy "Dog" Brewer and Jim "Big Nasty" Carmody would join forces. The Jackson *Clarion-Ledger* had reported that in December 1987, at his Monday press conference following the disappointing USM 37-30 season-ending loss to the University of Southwestern Louisiana (Louisiana-Lafayette), Carmody, uncharacteristically, and most likely in response to the frustrating but winning 1987 season, vented his frustration and listed several other major football programs as being "big-time losers."

The Golden Eagles were being criticized for its 1987 performance, and Carmody was attempting to rebut negative criticism by the press and fans. Carmody would be forced to resign a few days later, so this was, indeed, a stressful period. While admitting the obvious, that the USM program was not like that of Oklahoma and Miami, Carmody said, "but we're not like some other people who should be a heck of a lot better than we are." He then cited the programs at Illinois (3-7-1), Purdue 3-7-1), Wisconsin (3-8), California (3-6-2), Kansas (1-9-1), Georgia Tech (2-9), Virginia Tech (2-9), and Duke (5-6), all of whom had losing seasons in 1987. But a furor was initiated when he also included the programs at Ole Miss (3-8) and Mississippi State (4-7) — both of whom had losing seasons — in his big-time losers' category. Carmody then went on to say, "If you have ever been to any of those places, and I have been, you'd say they had a heck of a lot more going for them from the standpoint of finances, resources, tradition, crowd support, facilities, a heck of a lot going, and all of them are big-time losers. But we are winners and still getting more for our dollar than anybody in the country."

When asked to comment on Carmody's remarks, USM Athletic Director Bill McLellan said he never gave these comments a second thought and took them with a grain of salt.

Billy Brewer was also asked to comment and said, "I don't think I'll respond to it other than the person who said that. You have to consider the source."

Carmody later tried to clarify his comments by saying they were taken out of context.

Sports writer Don Hudson of the Jackson *Clarion-Ledger* quoted Carmody, "I am not apologizing, I just want to explain because it is embarrassing to me." He went on to say that his remarks were directed to those programs that have had winning programs in recent seasons but did not have success in 1987. He further claimed that Brewer showed bad judgment in his response because of the stress he was under. In truth, both Carmody and Brewer were under a lot of stress — Ole Miss finished the 1987 season with a losing record, and the season-ending loss to Southwestern Louisiana most probably cost USM a bowl bid, despite finishing with a winning 6-5 record. Brewer had been known to vent his frustrations to the press as well. The verbal exchange between Carmody and Brewer apparently did not leave permanent scars in the egos of either coach. Brewer subsequently hired Carmody for his staff in 1992.

"Jim Carmody is an outstanding football coach," Brewer said following Carmody's hiring. "He's been an opponent for years, and I've always wanted him on my team. I welcome him back to Ole Miss, because he'll be a tremendous asset. He's just a proven winner." If any bitterness remained from the Carmody-Brewer war of words in 1987, there was no evidence of a rift in 1992.

Despite their different backgrounds, Brewer and Carmody had much in common. Both were tenacious, highly disciplined, excellent recruiters, excellent game tacticians, motivators, fierce competitors — coaches who knew how to relate to their players, white and black alike. Both worked for chancellors or presidents with large egos. When the opportunity to make a change in the head coaching position at USM presented itself, President Lucas did so, and he let Carmody go rather unceremoniously. Interestingly, a parallel situation would occur at Ole Miss shortly thereafter.

Billy Brewer was the choice of athletic director Warner Alford and Chancellor Porter L. Fortune when Brewer was hired in 1983. When Chancellor Fortune retired shortly thereafter and R. Gerald Turner succeeded him, Brewer and Turner often clashed. In the past, at alumni meetings, the football head coach, when he was on the program, spoke last to wrap up and garner alumni support. That role was taken over by the new chancellor. Besides, Brewer was Fortune's choice, not Turner's, and when the opportunity to make a change in the head coaching position presented itself, Turner did so. Despite the bitter on-field-struggles Carmody and Brewer staged in the USM-Ole Miss rivalry, it was inevitable that these two highly principled men of character and strong egos would eventually be drawn together. Carmody accepted the position of assistant head coach and defensive line coach for Ole Miss in 1992.

Another nice benefit to the Carmody-Brewer relationship was the close friendship that formed between Jim's wife, Noonie, and Billy's wife, Kay. Both were keen bridge players and would often team up at local bridge games and various bridge tournaments. They were a highly successful team.

Brewer hired Joe Lee Dunn as his new defensive coordinator; Dunn had served as the Memphis State defensive coordinator for the past three years.

In announcing the hiring Brewer said, "Joe Lee Dunn is a unique football coach." Unique indeed. When he coached on the sideline as a defensive co-ordinator he did not wear a headset to communicate with press box coaches. He did not believe in wearing socks. Dunn is widely credited with coming up with, or at least tweaking, a 3-3-5 defensive scheme in 1991 (although some credit Coach Charlie Strong with developing that defense while he was at South Carolina).

As recounted by Chris B. Brown, "Under Dunn, the 3-3-5 opened with a splash. Just two years removed from being a graduate assistant, Dunn was Memphis State's defensive coordinator in the fall of 1991 when the team was set to play Southern Cal. Dunn knew he did not have enough players with the brute strength to line up in a traditional front and compete against the Trojans. The solution involved Dunn swapping out one of his linemen from the team's 4-3-4 set and replacing him with a defensive back. With that, the 3-3-5 defense was born. Dunn shifted the alignments around — moving the defensive linemen to the spots now custom for the 3-3-5, with a nose tackle over the center. The move worked: on September 2, 1991, Memphis State upset Southern Cal 21-10. However, it should also be noted that Carmody and Dunn worked together on what became known as the "organized chaos" defense.

Dunn considered himself an old-school guy teaching "smash-mouth" football. However, his defenses proved to be inconsistent, giving up 50 or more points six times and 60 or more points three times. Yet, his defenses also held the opponents to scoring 20 or fewer points fifteen times.

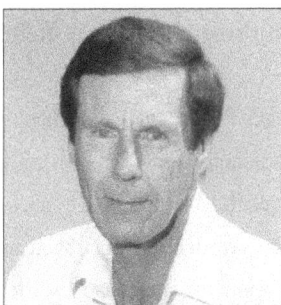

1992 Season

Ole Miss opened the 1992 season with a stunning 45-21 victory over Pat Dye's Auburn Tigers. Joe Lee Dunn's 3-3-5 defensive scheme received most of the credit for confusing Auburn's quarterback, Stan White.

Dye said, "Ole Miss took us to the woodshed." The Ole Miss defense forced six turnovers and scored two touchdowns. Auburn was held to -16 yards rushing. The play of Carmody's defensive line was of particular note. Cassius Ware, a transfer from Northwest Mississippi Community College, had an outstanding day. Ole Miss was leading 21-14, and Auburn had first-and-goal at the Rebel 5-yard line. Ole Miss blitzed, knocking the ball out of White's hands and into the air when Ware grabbed it and returned the fumble 91 yards. Ware ended up making 14 tackles in the game. The Rebels intercepted four Auburn passes, one for a touchdown. Brewer had a season-opening victory. Ole Miss sent notice that this defense was for real.

The Rebels crushed Tulane the following week, 35-9, holding the Green Wave to less than 100 yards rushing. Inexplicably, the following week Vanderbilt manhandled the Rebels 31-9 at Vandy. The Rebels failed to score a touchdown for the first time in a regular season game since 1988. Ole Miss' woes continued on the road the following week, losing to Georgia 37-11, but the Rebels bounced back, beating Kentucky 24-14 and Arkansas 17-3. Ole Miss held the Razorbacks to only 13 yards rushing and sacked the Razorback QB eight tines.

The Rebels could not handle Alabama in Tuscaloosa, suffering a 31-10 loss, but bounced back to shut out the LSU Tigers in Jackson 32-0, then following that up with a 17-12 win over Memphis State in Oxford.

Cassius Ware recorded three sacks as the Rebels had eight sacks for the game.

The Rebels then squeaked out a 13-6 win over defensive-minded Louisiana Tech in Oxford. Louisiana Tech was ranked second in defense in the nation while Ole Miss was ranked ninth. Ware recorded eight tackles and two sacks. Following the victory, the Rebels accepted an invitation to play in the Liberty Bowl. Ole Miss capped off the season with a 17-10 victory over Mississippi State in Oxford in a game featured by the famous amazing goal-line stand highlighted in a separate chapter (See Chapter 17).

Ole Miss then capped off a 9-3 season with a Liberty Bowl 13-0 victory over Air Force. The Rebel defense kept opponents out of the end zone for the fourth game of the season, and the Ole Miss defense moved up to sixth best in the nation. Ware again led the defense, recording 10 tackles and two sacks.

The Rebels finished 5-3 in SEC games, ranked second in the SEC West, and Ole Miss ended its season at No. 16 nationally overall. The Carmody-Dunn defense had brought the Rebels back from the disastrous 1991 season. The defense ended the season ranked No. 6 in the nation.

1993 Season

Unfortunately, the success enjoyed with the 1992 season could not be repeated in the 1993 season as the Rebels finished at 5-6. And the situation worsened at the end of the season. The Rebels suffered a season-opening 16-12 loss to Auburn, playing without linebacker Cassius Ware, who had been declared ineligible by the university three days before the game after the NCAA accused Ware of accepting a questionable car loan. Ware did not travel to Auburn. The Rebel offense was ineffective.

The Rebels did bounce back to crush UT-Chattanooga 40-7 and Vanderbilt 49-7 the following two weeks. It appeared as if Ole Miss had righted its offensive ship. Cassius Ware, who missed the first game because of a university suspension after the NCAA questioned his eligibility, made his 1993 debut in the UT-Chattanooga game, making seven tackles, including two sacks.

The Rebels made it three wins in a row by beating Georgia 31-14 in Oxford. Ware again stood out defensively, making 10 tackles and causing two fumbles. Ole Miss held the Bulldogs to one yard rushing.

Ole Miss was shutout in Kentucky, 21-0, but bounced back to shutout Arkansas in Jackson, 19-0. The Rebels then went into a three-game tailspin, losing 19-14 to Alabama (who played for the first time in Oxford, drawing a record crowd of 43,500 fans), 19-17 to LSU in Tiger Stadium, and 19-3 to Memphis State, who exacted a measure of revenge against Joe Lee Dunn by holding Ole Miss to -4 rushing yards.

The Rebels then took its revenge against Northern Illinois by shutting them out 44-0 to even its season record at 5-5. But Ole Miss lost its chance for a winning season by losing the Egg Bowl to Mississippi State, 20-13, in Starkville. Despite finishing with a 5-6 record, Ole Miss did win the national rushing defense title for fewest yards allowed per game and ranked first in the nation in total defense.

But the Ole Miss program took a downward spiral the summer of 1994 when Ole Miss announced that the NCAA had accused the Rebels of 15 violations. On July 10 (three and one-half weeks after Ole Miss announced the NCAA inquiry) Ole Miss athletic director Warner Alford resigned, effective August 31, stating that he was embarrassed that Ole Miss had been charged twice under his watch of rules violations. The day after Alford resigned Ole Miss fired Billy Brewer, without pay. Chancellor R. Gerald Turner placed the decision for the firing in the hands of the University's Committee on Intercollegiate Athletics, stating that when that committee had been informed of the NCAA allegations it unanimously voted for a change in leadership of the football program. Coach Brewer had hired the current staff, and now he was gone.

Brewer coached 11 years (1983-93) and compiled a 67-56-3 record, making him the second winningest Ole Miss football coach behind legendary coach Johnny Vaught. He also led the Rebels to five bowl games in those eleven years, with Ole Miss winning three of those bowls. Brewer also led Ole Miss to eight Egg Bowl victories over rival Mississippi State, losing only three times.

1994 Season

The 1994 season opened on a note of uncertainty. With Coach Brewer's having been dismissed after the 1993 season, job security was non-existent for the interim coaching staff. The first game of the 1994 season against Auburn was less than two months away. The interim appointment of Coach Joe Lee Dunn was not without some controversy. Many Rebel fans and players preferred to see Jim Carmody named as interim head coach, but also many players and fans supported Dunn's appointment mainly because of his personality and personal traits.

Carmody realized that he had been passed over for the head coaching position when, shortly after the season was over, he and the author went to play golf at the Shiloh Falls Golf Course. As they waited in the clubhouse for their tee-time, Dunn and Steve Davenport, CEO of TeleSouth Communications (which handled Mississippi sports programming), came into the clubhouse. Carmody immediately, and correctly, surmised that Dunn was to be named interim head coach, and Davenport had taken him out of Oxford until the announcement could be made. Apparently, Dunn was offered the interim head coach position the day after Brewer was fired.

The general feeling was that the university administration would not be naming any of the current coaches as the new 1995 head coach. Yet, as professional as they were, the interim staff approached the 1994 season with a degree of optimism.

On November 17, 1994 — the week before the Mississippi State game, the NCAA announced the sanctions against Ole Miss. Ole Miss was found guilty of 15 violations that included members of the Ole Miss staff, as well as boosters, making illegal offers of cash, plane tickets, and cars to prospects. The university was also found guilty of lack of institutional control. Ole Miss pleaded guilty to nine of the charges. The program was placed on four years' probation, was given a two-year postseason participation ban along with a one-year television ban, a loss of 12 scholarships a year for the two years, and a reduction in the number of official recruiting visits from 56 to 40 — an almost crippling punishment. Brewer was found guilty of unethical conduct, a charge filed after the original letter of inquiry was sent to the university. Ole Miss did not pay Brewer for the three years remaining on his original contract, but Brewer would later sue the university for breach of contract. Five years after being fired, Brewer won his lawsuit against the university. A Lafayette County Circuit Court awarded Brewer $221,385 in damages while denying him $2 million in damages he had sought.

The 1994 season opened with a 22-17 loss to Auburn at home, followed by wins over Southern Illinois (59-30) and Vanderbilt (20-14). The Rebels then went into a four-game losing streak to Georgia on the road, Florida in Oxford, and Arkansas and Alabama on the road. They won a nice upset over LSU at home (34-21) but lost to Memphis State the following week (17-16). They notched a shutout against Tulane in New Orleans (38-0) but lost the season finale to Mississippi State in Oxford (21-17). The Rebels ranked 17th in the nation in defense.

During Carmody's three-year stint as coach of the defensive line, four of his defensive linemen went to the NFL: Tim Bowens (who made All-SEC as a defensive tackle, was a number-one NFL draft pick, and was named A.F.C. Rookie of the Year for the Miami Dolphins), Chad Brown (an eighth-round draft pick of the Arizona Cardinals), Norman Hand (a fifth-round pick of the Miami Dolphins) and Artis Ford (who signed with the Cincinnati Bengals). In addition, two linebackers were drafted: Marquise Thomas (an eighth-round pick of the Indianapolis Colts) and DeWayne Dotson (a fourth-round selection by the Dallas Cowboys). Bowens played eleven seasons; Hand played for nine seasons, and Dotson played for three seasons in the NFL.

After the season it became obvious that Dunn would not be named head coach, but Carmody still held out some hope since he had the support of some key alumni, university and athletic department administrators, and Rebel staff members. But Chancellor R. Gerald Turner was determined to clean house and remove any vestiges of the Billy Brewer era.

On December 2, 1994, Texas A&M defensive coordinator Tommy Tuberville was selected as the head football coach charged with getting the Rebels back to their winning ways. Tuberville enjoyed success at Ole Miss, going 6-5, 5-6, 8-4, and 6-5 in his four seasons there. His success attracted attention from other programs, but he said, "They'll have to carry me out of here in a pine box." Two days later he accepted the head coaching job at Auburn at double his Ole Miss salary. He reportedly never said good bye to his players.

As things would develop, this would be Carmody's final season as a college coach as he made a major career move when he began his new career as a professional scout with the Arizona Cardinals.

17

The Goal Line Stand - UM 17, MSU 10

There have been several memorable goal line stands in college football history —among the most memorable being Alabama's famous stand against Penn State in the 1979 Sugar Bowl with the national championship on the line. But even that goal line stand cannot match the game-ending stand Ole Miss put up against Mississippi State in their 1992 Egg Bowl battle. Who would believe stopping an opponent eleven times inside the ten-yard line with less than three minutes to play? The Rebels did it with some help from the boisterous "South End Zone Rowdies."

Writer and publisher Larry Wells recalled events that took place in the south end zone on November 28, 1992, in an article recently published by HottyToddy.com. In the 1980s the south end zone stands of Vaught-Hemingway Stadium had historically attracted relatively few fans until a group of fanatics led by writer Willie Morris, Larry and his wife, Dean — niece of William Faulkner — began to assemble to watch games from that vantage point. They were occasionally joined by their sons, David Rae Morris and Jon Mallard. Watching Ole Miss games from the south end zone with Willie quickly became the rage of a group of Oxonians. Soon Ole Miss history professor David Sansing — later named Emperor of the South End Zone — and the author joined the group with our spouses, and as Larry writes, "the south end zone began to take on a whole new kind of diversity."

Writer Barry Hannah and his wife, Susan, had become regulars along with longtime Rebel fans Ron Shapiro (owner of the Hoka Theater and Cafe), bon vivant Semmes Luckett, photographer Jane Rule Burdine, Square Books owners Richard and Lisa Howorth, author Jim Dees, and writer-producer

Elizabeth Dollarhide, who formed a group named by Susan Hannah as the "South End Zone Rowdies." Susan even created a banner with that name.

The South End Zone group began to grow and quickly became a football happening, serving as a haven for Oxford visitors such as writers Raad Cawthon and John Little, numerous movie producers, actors, magazine editors, literary agents, noted photographer Bill Eggleston, and even former Rebel football players.

The attraction, of course, was more than Ole Miss football; the real attraction was Willie Morris. Larry quoted Willie asking, "Where else could this have happened except in a stadium named Hemingway?" (It should be noted that in this case the stadium was originally named in 1915 not after Ernest Hemingway but rather after Ole Miss law professor and chairman of the university athletic committee, William Hemingway).

Pep rallies were held at the Hoka Theater on Friday nights before home games. Noonie Carmody; Billy Brewer's wife, Kay; and Dean Faulkner Wells were part of a group of women who played bridge on a regular basis, so it was only natural that coaches Jim Carmody and Billy Brewer became favorites of the Rowdies. The women would make voodoo sticks, Haitian mojo sticks, and shake them at the visiting team, hexing them as they warmed up just below the Rowdies. In 1992, that hex took on special meaning.

Ole Miss Coaching Staff, 1992 (Photo Carmody Family Collection)

On the night before the 1992 Ole Miss — Mississippi State game, Larry, Dean, Shapiro, Dees, and Luckett paid a midnight visit to Vaught-Hemingway, which was surprisingly not locked or secured, and standing at the 50-yard line, Dean read a passage from "The Bear," written by her uncle, Pappy (William Faulkner), to gain his blessing and to complete the hex the Rowdies would place on the visiting Bulldogs. Despite these preparations, little did the Rowdies anticipate what would happen in the South End Zone the next day.

The Ole Miss-Mississippi State rivalry began in 1901 and is one of the most intense in the country. The two teams have played every year since with the exception of a three-year break in the series in 1912-1914 and the cancellation of the 1943 contest because of World War II. This rivalry has been rated among the Top 25 rivalries in college football. Ole Miss leads the long series 62-43-8 (Mississippi State was forced to forfeit its 1976 and 1977 victories over Ole Miss because of NCAA penalties). In 1927 the schools created a trophy called the "Golden Egg" to be awarded to the winner.

In 1978, executive sports editor of the Jackson *Clarion-Ledger*, Tom Patterson, suggested changing the name of this game from the "Battle for the Golden Egg" to the "Egg Bowl," and that name has stuck ever since. The 1992 Egg Bowl was played in Oxford at Vaught-Hemingway stadium on November 28, and the South End Zone Rowdies were fired up.

Ole Miss entered the game a two-point favorite because of the home field advantage. Both teams entered the contest with 7-3 records. Mississippi State was nationally ranked number 16, while Ole Miss was ranked number 24. The game began in grey, cloudy, cold November weather, but events would soon heat things up. Ole Miss and State entered the game with bowl games secured — the first time since 1963 that both teams were bowl-bound. Ole Miss was coached by Billy Brewer and State by Jackie Sherrill. The Egg Bowl returned to the Oxford campus for the first time in 20 years. Carmody was Ole Miss assistant head coach and coached the defensive line in his second stint at Ole Miss. Needless to say, no love was lost between these two teams and their coaches or their fans. This would be the tenth Ole Miss-Mississippi State game in which Carmody coached, so he was well aware of the importance of this game.

With about four minutes to play and Ole Miss protecting a 17-10 lead, MSU put together a drive toward the south end zone that gave the Bulldogs a first and goal at the Rebel 8-yard line. What happened during those final minutes could only be attributed to the effects of the voodoo sticks and great defensive coaching. Carmody's defensive line, led by Chad Brown and Artis Ford, played magnificently. The Rowdies' roller coaster ride, fueled by Jack Daniels and Jim Beam, was about to begin.

A running play advanced the ball to the 6-yard-line, and then MSU quarterback Todd Jordan was sacked by Chad Brown at the 10. On third down and 2:27 left to play, the Rebels seemingly staved off the threat when Michael Lowry picked off a pass from Todd Jordan in the end zone and ran it out to the 4.

The Rowdies' voodoo sticks were shaking, and a celebration began. But then on second down, running back Corey Philpot fumbled, and MSU's Frankie Luster recovered the ball at the 8, giving MSU a fresh set of downs. The Rowdies became silent except for Susan Hannah, waving her Haitian mojo stick, pleading, "Stay out of our end zone! Stay our of our end zone!"

On first down Jordan threw the ball away and then was tackled at the 4. His third down pass under intense pressure was overthrown in the end zone. A fourth-down pass into the end zone fell incomplete, but Rowdie cheers became Rowdie groans because Ole Miss was flagged for pass interference, and now State had a fresh set of downs from the 2-yard line.

State replaced quarterbacks and brought the previously injured Gregg Plump into the game. On first down MSU running back Randy Brown was stopped on the 1-yard line. Then, on perhaps the key defensive play of the stand, defensive tackle Chad Brown broke through the offensive line and tackled running back Brown for a three-yard loss. Brown got such a jump on the play when he saw the Bulldog guard pulling to his right that he almost took the handoff from Plump himself.

After Brown's brilliant defensive read, Carmody called Brown's big play: "It was a big-time play by a big-time player."

Following a timeout Plump then attempted a naked bootleg reverse but was thrown for a 2-yard loss by strong safety Johnny Dixon and linebacker

Dewayne Dotson, who were not fooled. On fourth down Plump nearly connected with Willie Harris on a pass into the end zone that was thrown slightly behind the receiver.

Jackie Sherrill begged for a flag to be thrown to no avail. The Rowdie voodoo sticks had won. Ole Miss ran out the final 19 seconds, and the Rebels had pulled off one of the greatest goal-line stands in collegiate history. Carmody's defensive linemen were the heroes of the game. Ole Miss had played the entire season with only two defensive tackles, Artis Ford and Chad Brown. Carmody referred to the pair as "My Warriors" and said, "When you only have two, it gives you a lot more time to coach them. Thank God, one never got hurt."

Goal-Line Stand Detail: Artis Ford (#70) and Chad Brown (top of pile), "My Warriors"

The Ole Miss defense held MSU to 39 rushing yards on 41 attempts, marking the sixth straight game that the defense held their opponent to less that 88 rushing yards. In the celebration that took place on the field, Dean Wells ran onto the field and ripped up pieces of turf that she displayed in her kitchen window along with her Haitian cross.

When Chad Brown came off the field he went up to Carmody and apologized for following his instincts rather than playing the defense that was called. Brown told Carmody, "Coach, sorry, but I was supposed to slant left on that play, but when I saw the guard pulling to my right, I just charged straight ahead."

Carmody told him, "Chad, sometimes the players are smarter than the coaches."

Brown was named SEC Player of the Week for recording 13 tackles — two of them sacks. The game was a defensive struggle and featured eleven total turnovers. Ole Miss fumbled five times and lost all five fumbles. MSU fumbled three times and lost all three fumbles. Ole Miss had two passes intercepted while MSU had one pass intercepted — that being the one by Michael Lowry during the goal-line stand. Carmody and the Ole Miss coaching staff were stunned. Carmody would remember later, "That was unbelievable, really. I had never seen anything like that before, and I haven't seen anything like it since."

Carmody understood the Ole Miss-Mississippi State rivalry as well or better than most coaches. He coached in a total of twelve Egg Bowls — seven while at he was coaching Ole Miss and five while he was at Mississippi State.

The 8-3 Rebels went on to defeat the Air Force Academy 13-0 in the Liberty Bowl. Mississippi State went the Peach Bowl and lost to North Carolina 21-17. Willie, Dean, Barry, and Susan are gone now, and other Rowdies have scattered, but Larry Wells, David Sansing, and I and our families still sit in the south end zone at Vaught-Hemingway, doing our best to create some magic for the current Ole Miss Rebels.

FOURTH QUARTER

*"Jim Carmody talking to Bob Davie, Head Coach
for Notre Dame, while scouting a
Notre Dame football pratcice, 1999."*
(Carmody Family Collection)

18

PROFESSIONAL SCOUT

Just as recruiting is the lifeblood of college football, so is scouting the lifeblood of professional football. The success or failure of a franchise is often the result of great or poor scouting. A prospect's size and speed become the ultimate measuring points in scouting. NFL writer and reporter Conor Orr's *The History of Scouting* is a rich source of the development of the art and science of scouting. Teams had little or no time to scout players and in the beginning of the league; there were few scouts on the road.

Eddie Accorsi, former general manager of the New York Giants, recalls that in the early days teams would draft off the list of All-American teams that appeared in the newspapers. "They would have someone clip all the newspapers, compile all the numbers, and that was it." Teams would also rely on trade magazines such as "Street & Smith" or "College Football Illustrated." Small colleges and black colleges whose teams were often loaded with undiscovered talent, were mostly ignored. The first three rounds of the 1956 draft were held in November 1955 while games were still being played!

Since that time, professional football organizations have developed huge scouting departments. The NFL developed the Scouting Combine in 1982 where players were invited to appear before scouts of every team to have their height, weight, speed, power, and agility measured. Even arm length and hand size are measured. Medical records are thoroughly examined. Now each scout is assigned to an area of the country to seek the best professional prospects.

In his "History of Scouting" article, Orr states that "The life of a scout is often humorless and heartbreaking; there's endless blame to shoulder and a coach who takes credit when the roster takes shape. Just long hours, endless car rides (he could have added long airline flights), warm Pepsi in the trunk."

But success or failure of draftable players depends, in the end, on what's in a prospect's heart and a scout's eye and instinct. Size and speed are easily measurable. Accorsi surmised, "If you start making exceptions to size and speed, you're going to have a slow and small team." Thus, measuring the intangibles becomes of increasing and utmost importance.

New England Patriots head coach, Bill Belichick, one of pro football's most successful coaches, said, "When we evaluate players, it's a long, thorough process we go through; obviously, its very inexact. We do the best we can, and that's a long process that's involved. Visiting the school, interviewing the player, talking to the people who have had the most involvement with him — like his college coaches, even high school coaches, even beyond that. Other people that have had associations with him — former teammates, so forth, so on. It's a mosaic composed of a lot of different pieces, and you try to fit them all together and put some type of valuation on the player. And you do that for all the players. Each one's different. Each one's unique."

Writer Danny Kelly wrote, "There's evidently no hardline guide to scouting — it's as much an art as it is a science."

Pete Carroll, coach of the 2014 Super Bowl Champion Seattle Seahawks, feels "The most important characteristic is grit. That's the most crucial characteristic that helps somebody be successful. If they continue to hang, continue to fight — and that's the competitiveness we're looking for — there's always a chance they can pull it together. If you do a little homework, read up on what grit is all about, it's persistence and resiliency, and an inner strength and belief you can get it done. That's what's most important. If guys don't have that, you can only take them so far."

Once Carmody was formally released from his contractual obligations to Ole Miss he began making calls to former colleagues, seeking a job. He called Ralph Hawkins and George Boone, with whom Carmody coached at the University of Kentucky. He also knew Hawkins from coaching with him for the Buffalo Bills in 1981. Hawkins worked in the NFL for 35 years and was a scout for the Arizona Cardinals from 1991-93. Boone spent 28 seasons with the Arizona Cardinals, serving as a scout from 2001-05. Hawkins and Boone both knew the director of scouting for Arizona, Bo Bolinger. Carmody called Hawkins and Boone and asked if they knew of any scouting jobs becoming available. They said they would check things out. They called Jim back and told him there was a scouting job available at Arizona, and both recommended him to Bolinger. Carmody flew to Arizona for an interview and was offered the position of area scout. He accepted and became a full-time scout.

Carmody, an outstanding recruiter, immediately saw the major differences between recruiting and scouting, although both were highly competitive processes. Recruiting involved selling oneself and one's college or university to the recruit and his family. In scouting the player has essentially no choice of where he will go or when he will get drafted. There is not the same type of competition in recruiting and scouting. Professional scouting does not get as personal as college recruiting.

Scouting can be considered as the lifeblood of a professional football franchise, and the scouting department constitutes a large segment of a team's operations. The scouting staff of the Arizona Cardinals consisted primarily of a director of scouting, two regional scouts, one on either side of the Mississippi River, and four area scouts, two in each region. The team's general manager is also involved, and sometimes the director of scouting would ask coaches to review film of potential draftees at their coaching positions. The head coach is also involved in the selection process. Area and regional scouts are often asked to cross-check and provide their opinions regarding prospects in other areas or regions.

In addition to having their scouts' opinions on players they have most probably seen in game situations, the NFL holds a Scouting Combine before the draft. More than 300 prospects are invited to spend up to four days essentially being interviewed. Each of the 32 NFL teams will send their top executives, their player personnel departments, and medical personnel to observe various physical and mental tests. Physical measurements are taken and physical skills such as measuring speed in the 40-yard dash, strength in bench pressing, physical agility skills such as vertical leaping and broad jumping, agility drills such as the three-cone shuffle, and measurement of joint movement are all evaluated. The prospect then undergoes interviews by each team and is given the "Wonderlic Cognitive Ability Test," a group of intelligence tests designed in 1936 by E.F. Wonderlic, at the time a psychology graduate student at Northwestern University, to assess learning and problem-solving skills. The test is used as a measure of how well people make decisions under pressure. The Combine has become a popular television event on the NFL Network. Not a group averse to taking in money, the NFL sells tickets to thousands of fans, who become "Drafted Fans" and get to see the Combine activities in person.

While it is possible to measure obvious physical skills, a big part of scouting is personally knowing the background of the prospect and not relying on the opinions of others. The more important the player, the deeper a scout checks his background. A scout cannot afford to make a mistake here, so several scouts will scout good players. The player's character can play a big role in the draft rankings. It is particularly difficult to measure the impact of criminal activity, if any, major or minor, on the desirability of drafting a particular prospect. Criminal mistakes can take on paramount importance. How much players get downgraded depends on what offense the player committed, and the consequences vary from team to team. What a player did plays a key role. Illicit drug use and domestic violence are important, particularly in these days, and can drop a player several rounds and thus a significant amount of money. Being found guilty of a DUI may not hurt a potential draftee as much, but it will not help him.

Carmody remained at Ole Miss after the 1994 season and made Oxford his base of operations, flying, when necessary out of Memphis, some 85 miles north. During 1995-2003 he scouted all of Mississippi, Alabama, Florida, Georgia, South Carolina, North Carolina, Virginia, Kentucky, Tennessee, New Hampshire, Massachusetts, and the east coast, rating the exceptional players as "draftable" and others with potential as "free agents." Carmody would be on the road two weeks at a time during the football season. He would come home and spend about as much time as it took to wash his clothes and then head back to the airport. He was expected to watch Saturday college games and go to all All-Star and bowl games.

In 2003, after serving eight years as an area scout, Carmody was promoted to Western regional scout. His new area of scouting consisted of schools west of the Mississippi River, and he spent most of his time in Washington, Utah, Texas, Minnesota, California, and Colorado. He also picked up Louisiana, Texas, Oklahoma, Arkansas, Nebraska, Kansas, and Montana. As a West regional scout he was now working with a more select list of players — primarily players who were deemed "draftable" by area scouts. He did not have as many schools to scout as he did when he was an area scout, going instead to schools that had highly rated players. If a school also had players who were deemed possible free agents, he would scout those players as well. He would give his reports to a draft secretary, who would organize them according to area and region. After October a regional scout might be expected to cross over and cross-check players in another region.

On draft day, usually toward the end of April, the "War Room" would usually have all scouts including the director of scouting, the head coach, the general manager, the offensive and defensive coordinators, and team doctors prepared to give medical reports. A player may be rated as, for example, a second- or third-round pick, but medical problems could drop him down in value. Barring trades, teams drafted in the reverse order of their league standing the previous year. In the first round, teams have ten minutes to make their selection then seven minutes in the second round and five minutes in the following five rounds. This is also an opportunity for teams to trade draft picks to pick up proven talent.

The atmosphere in the War Room can get intense, and feelings can be easily hurt. Some discussions might get personal. Whatever the eventual list of players, the atmosphere in the room relaxes when the draft is over. One year as he was leaving the War Room after the draft, Carmody observed to fellow scout, Cole Proctor, "All that work for seven players?"

Proctor said, "Shhhh, don't say anything, we might be out of a job."

When the draft is over, all free agents would be told to make no moves until they talked to an interested club. Clubs would often fight over free agents. At this point, all the hard work the previous nine months would pay off. Following the conclusion of the draft, scouts would have May, June, and

July off, a benefit well earned after the amount of effort put into scouting the previous season and filing all those daily reports.

Jim and Noonie took advantage of having their summers free by making trips to Europe. Particularly memorable was a trip that involved flying into Barcelona, Spain, and then taking a cruise from Barcelona to Marseilles and then on to Monte Carlo, Rome, the Isle of Capri, Naples, and Florence. They took another memorable trip to Ireland and Scotland another summer. The trip to Ireland and Scotland was particularly memorable since it gave Jim an opportunity to explore his family's Irish heritage and for Jim to try to play golf at the fabled Old Course at St. Andrews, Scotland. On their Ireland trip he and Noonie flew into Shannon and then visited Ballybunion, home of one of the world's most beautiful and famous golf courses. Jim wished he had brought his clubs along. They then travelled to the Ring of Kerry and Dublin, before taking a train to Belfast and a ferry to Scotland.

Once in Scotland they made their way to the Home of Golf at St. Andrews and stayed at a hotel within walking distance of The Old Course. One afternoon Jim walked to the Old Course. Carmody could not resist an opportunity to try to play the fabled Old Course. He went to the starter's booth and asked the starter how far ahead of time players had to request a tee time. He was told that golfers booked the Old Course months in advance in order to play. Carmody then asked if it would be possible to play the course with no advance tee-time, no clubs, and no golf shoes. Obviously, the starter had been asked these questions before and resisted the temptation to laugh. The starter told him that golfers with no advance tee times would queue up at 5:30 in the morning, hoping a group with an advanced tee-time would not show up.

Jim decided to give it a try and rented a set of golf clubs and a pair of golf shoes from one of the nearby golf shops just in case a tee-time opened up. Then the next morning he queued up at 4:30 a.m. rather than 5:30. To his surprise there were already six guys ahead of him, and a long line began to form behind him. The first guy in line slept in a sleeping bag, having spent the entire night on the course. Finally a group of only three players showed up, and the starter asked them if one of those in the queue could join them to complete a foursome. When they shook their heads, those in line booed them. It was the first week in June, and it was cold.

In mid-morning Noonie came to the course expecting to greet her husband when he finished playing. Instead she saw him still standing in the queue waiting to tee off. He was hungry. Jim sent her after some coffee and a scone. He finally got to tee-off at 10:30 a.m. A whole foursome failed to show up, so Carmody played with three guys from Minneapolis who had been in queue: a father, a grandfather, and the son. When Jim finished playing in mid-afternoon, Noonie was waiting for him. He finished the round with a par at the 18th, having avoided the famous, or infamous, Valley of Sin. It was a long day but well worth it.

Then in August, as teams began their fall practices, Carmody would return to the camp at Flagstaff, Arizona, and watch practices, constantly evaluating. He would stay a week to ten days and then return to watch college practices, watch film, talk to coaches, and file those daily reports. Oftentimes a scout at the Cardinals' practice would go up to a player he had rated and who was subsequently drafted and say to the player, "I'm the one who scouted you; I recommended you."

Without being flippant the player would usually respond, "That's right, that's what all of you say. Sorry, but I do not remember you." There is no way to tell how many scouts scouted the good players in practices and games, All-Star games, and bowl games. Literally hundreds of scouts would go to a school. There was no way a player could possibly remember a particular scout.

Despite the hard work those eight or nine months of the season, Carmody enjoyed the challenge and the feeling of success he had when a player he strongly supported was drafted and played well in the NFL. Two Arizona first-round picks were selected from his territory, both in the 1999 draft: David Boston, a wide receiver from Ohio State, and L.J. Shelton, an offensive tackle from Eastern Michigan. Boston was the eighth selection and was selected for the Pro Bowl in 2001. He enjoyed a nine-year professional career with Arizona, the San Diego Chargers, the Miami Dolphins, the Tampa Bay Buccaneers, and the Toronto Argonauts in the Canadian Football League. Shelton was the twenty-first overall pick and had a ten-year career in the NFL with Arizona, the Cleveland Browns, the Miami Dolphins, and the San

Diego Chargers.

Ron McKinnon was a linebacker from North Alabama who was signed as an undrafted free agent in 1996. He was the leading tackler in the NFL for five consecutive seasons, from 1999 to 2003. He ended his ten-year NFL career with the New Orleans Saints.

Mark Smith, a defensive tackle from Auburn, was also in Carmody's scouting territory. Smith was a seventh-round draft choice and enjoyed a six-year NFL career with Arizona and the Cleveland Browns.

Also from Carmody's territory was Cory Chavous, a safety from Vanderbilt, who was drafted in the second round (33rd overall pick). Chavous had an eleven-year NFL career with Arizona, the Minnesota Vikings, and St. Louis Rams. He made the Pro Bowl in 2003.

Another player signed out of Carmody's territory was Arnold Jackson, an undrafted free agent wide receiver from the University of Louisville. He played for Arizona for two years. Smith, Chavous, and Jackson made the NFL All-Rookie team in 1997, 1998, and 2001, respectively.

Carmody also takes pride in the fact that the Arizona Cardinals went to the playoffs in 1998 for the first time in 26 years and defeated the Dallas Cowboys in the wild card game before falling to Minnesota in the NFL divisional playoffs.

After ten years of traveling and scouting, Carmody felt that the time to retire had arrived. He talked retirement over with Noonie and, as was the case most of the time, she supported Jim's decision. Travel had become very difficult following the Twin Towers attack on 9/11, and Carmody was getting tired of all the hassle involved with airline travel. Prior to the February 2005 Scouting Combine, he told the Cardinal's General Manager Rod Graves that he planned to retire after the draft but wanted to wait until after the draft to announce his retirement. Carmody told Graves that he would rather his retirement not be brought up until after the draft because Graves would be inundated with people seeking the job. Graves agreed with him and said he would indeed be swamped with applicants knocking on his door at midnight looking for a job.

Graves had been the Arizona general manager since 1997 and understood Jim's reasons for wishing to retire. Graves honored his wishes and kept his discussion with Carmody confidential. On the morning after the draft, the scouts met as usual before going home, and Graves announced that Jim had decided to retire.

After the meeting, Carmody met briefly with Head Coach Dennis Green and Bill Bidwell, owner of the Cardinals, to say goodbye. The Cardinals honored his contract and paid him through June. For the first time in 58 years, Big Nasty stepped away from football.

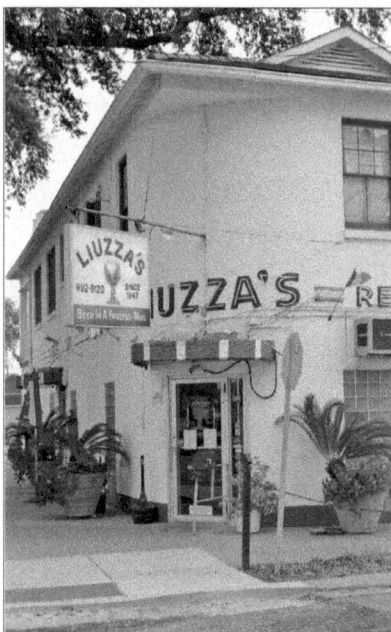

Liuzza's was nearly destroyed by the flood. The water rose half way up the building. It was under construcion and had not reopened.

Parkway Bakery and Tavern suffered serious damage in the storm. We were glad to see the restaurant had reopen and was serving lunch.

Parkway Bakery, on Hagan Street, is not far from Liuzza's. (photos provided by Deborah Freeland)

19

Katrina — NOLA Revisited

In the aftermath of Hurricane Katrina, New Orleans suffered three major breaks in its canal levees, causing devastating flooding throughout parts of the city. Two of the three canal breaches directly affected Carmody's upbringing in the city. The London Avenue Canal levee breach occurred in Gentilly, the area where Jim grew up. The Industrial Canal levee breach destroyed the Lower Ninth Ward, the area of Holy Cross High School, his high school alma mater. A third canal levee breach, the 17th Street Canal levee, devastated the Lakeview and Mid City areas of the city where the author's high school was located. The 17th Street Canal marked the dividing line of Orleans and Jefferson parishes. The breach occurred on the Orleans Parish side of the canal — if the breach had occurred on the Jefferson Parish side, there is no doubt that the area of my boyhood home would have been devastated.

Less than five months after Hurricane Katrina devastated most of New Orleans, Carmody, his long-time friend Bruce Howe, and the author, all New Orleans natives, returned to our hometown. Bruce and Jim grew up a block apart and went to Gentilly Terrace School together. Bruce went to high school at Warren Easton on Canal Street and college at Southeastern Louisiana before transferring to LSU. He and Jim have remained friends through the years. We wanted to check out the damage Katrina had done to our city, our neighborhoods, and our respective archrival high schools — Jim went to Holy Cross, of course; Bruce went to Warren Easton (the high school where Lee Harvey Oswald briefly attended tenth grade in 1955 when he lived in New Orleans), and I went to Jesuit. We also wanted to check on the damage, if any, to three legendary New Orleans restaurants and bars: The Rivershack Tavern (one of my old neighborhood favorites), Liuzza's, and Parkway Bakery and Tavern (the latter two being favorites of all three of us).

We all met in Jackson and drove to New Orleans, Bruce at the wheel. Driving into the city from the west on I-10, the city looked like a field of blue tarps covering nearly every roof of nearly every building. Traffic lights in most parts of the city were still not working — in fact, it looked as if Katrina had just struck. We left the interstate to drive to my old house on Shrewsbury Court in Jefferson Parish and The Rivershack Tavern on River Road, just around the corner. The house I grew up in seemed smaller than I recalled and still needed repairs. I joked that Katrina might have improved my old house!

We found little or no damage to The Rivershack — the canal breaches did not affect this part of Jefferson Parish. We then drove down River Road to Oak Street and on to Carrollton Avenue and the Mid-City area. The farther we drove into the city, the more evident were the results of flooding. High water lines from the floods that nearly wiped out the city marked nearly every home or business on Carrollton Avenue.

Jesuit High School, located on the corner of Banks St. and Carrollton Ave., despite being flooded, was among the first schools to re-open in New Orleans after the storm, and it apparently suffered no structural damage except water damage.

We then drove to Bruce's old high school on Canal Street, Warren Easton, and it looked untouched. We decided to see if one of our favorite restaurants, the Liuzza's on Bienville Street (there is another Liuzza's near the Fair Grounds Racetrack), was open before going to the devastated Lower Ninth Ward where Holy Cross was located.

The great food served at Liuzza's was a distant memory when we pulled up. Liuzza's and the houses surrounding it were marked with waterlines six feet high. The floodwaters nearly reached the top of the doors. There is a famous photograph of a man in a motorboat passing by Liuzza's when the water was halfway up the building. We got out of the car to get a look at the damage inside, thinking the place was abandoned. But when we entered the building, we saw one of the owners, Michael Bordelon, working alone trying to restore the restaurant. We introduced ourselves and asked if we could come in and take some photos.

"Come on in," Michael said, "but there's not much to see." The restaurant looked as if it was nearly destroyed by the flood. What a sad sight. I asked Bordelon when he thought he would be able to re-open, and he turned to me with tears in his eyes and said, "Man, I am trying to do the best I can." I thought I detected tears in all of our eyes. Liuzza's has since re-opened.

While we were in the area we went to another of our favorite lunch places, the Parkway Bakery and Tavern on Hagan Street near Bayou St. John, not far from Liuzza's. This area experienced serious flooding as well. Parkway was famous for its po-boy sandwiches, and we were hungry. We were happy to see that Parkway had just reopened and was serving, but roast beef po-boys only. Parkway had suffered tremendous water damage, but the po-boys were delicious. As we were ordering lunch, a middle-aged man — presumably the owner or manager — sat at a table by himself writing a menu and a grocery list on a piece of cardboard with a Sharpie, all the while talking and mumbling to himself, occasionally crying. Statistics from Hurricane Katrina do not include the storm's and flood's permanent scars on Michael Bordelon and this man.

We then went to the Lower Ninth Ward, which was essentially wiped out by the flooding from the breach in the Industrial Canal levee. We traced most of Jim's daily route to Holy Cross High School. We turned off St. Claude Avenue then on to Dauphine Street. When we crossed the bridge over the Industrial Canal, the scene was reminiscent of the photos of Hiroshima and Nagasaki after the atom bomb attacks. Complete devastation — almost every home wiped out, flattened by the flood.

Bruce said, "Gentlemen, we have landed — Ground Zero." Sitting practically in the middle of the Lower Ninth Ward neighborhood was a huge red barge that had torn loose of its moorings, ridden the floodwater after the canal breach, and come to rest on the top of several houses and a school bus. The barge was thought to cause the breaches in the canal levee, but a federal judge would rule otherwise.

As we were looking around, a black family drove up and got out of their car. They walked around, appearing lost. The older woman in the group, presumably the mother, said, "I can't even find our house. I don't even know where our street was. Everything's gone." No street signs remained. Each corner looked like the other — devastated, there was nothing standing.

Many brick and concrete buildings that comprised Holy Cross High School were still standing, but the insides were totally destroyed. The campus was a ghost town. Holy Cross was situated just adjacent to the Mississippi River levee, south of the city of New Orleans. Carmody walked around, stunned, spending more time in some areas than others. I presumed that those were the areas of his old classrooms. The three of us then climbed the levee to get a unique and pleasant view of New Orleans, located upriver.

Carmody noted, "When I went to school here, if you were caught by one of the Brothers on top of this levee, you were automatically dismissed from school. This is the first time, fifty years later, that I have been up here. What a great view I missed all these years."

As a joke I said loudly, "Look out, here comes a Brother!" Jim flinched and momentarily seemed alarmed. Fifty years later the levee ban was still in effect in Jim's mind. Bad joke on my part.

Holy Cross has rebuilt in another part of the city — in the Gentilly area

The aftermath of Katrina, 9th Ward, New Orleans (photo provided by Sarah Simonson)

in which Carmody grew up — and is once again offering an excellent academic program and fielding competitive athletic teams. As recounted earlier, less than two months after Katrina, on October 22, 2005, Jesuit and Holy Cross patched together football teams and played a game at Joe Yenni Stadium in Kenner (Jefferson Parish), which had been undamaged by the storm. With less than a week's practice Holy Cross beat Jesuit 20-10. The renewal of this rivalry had a far greater impact than just another game in a long-standing rivalry. The game uplifted the spirits of many New Orleans citizens and sent a signal that New Orleans was making a comeback.

On the way out of New Orleans, we drove to the Gentilly area in which Carmody grew up — the area of the London Canal breach. Unlike the Lower Ninth Ward, this neighborhood was alive with new construction. The area near Jim's boyhood home on Vermillion Boulevard was making a comeback. Carmody had come full circle and was back home.

The aftermath of Katrina, Ninth Ward, New Orleans (photo provided by Sarah Simonson)

Carmody and David Ballentine, Mississippi Sports Hall of Fame, July 31, 2009

Carmody, Mississippi Hall of Fame, July 31, 2009 (Photos provided by Mississippi Hall of Fame)

20

RETIREMENT — FAMILY CRISIS

Jim and Noonie Carmody remained in Oxford following his second stint at Ole Miss, when as he began his career as a professional scout for the Arizona Cardinals. Carmody found it convenient to use Oxford as a base for his travels as an area scout and as a Western regional scout. Oxford is only a little over an hour from the Memphis International Airport, which had excellent connecting flights across the country. The commute to the Memphis airport was not all that bad. With all the extensive travel over the ten-year period, he would accumulate many frequent flyer miles.

Since his Arizona schedule gave Carmody the months of May, June, and July essentially off, he played a lot of golf and traveled. He played golf mainly at the Ole Miss Golf Course but also at different courses in the north Mississippi area as well. He usually played with a group of local and Ole Miss friends such as oil and gas man Leroy Rooker, Ole Miss football and baseball legend Jake Gibbs, senior federal judge Neal Biggers, Ole Miss women's basketball coach Van Chancellor, City Grocery restaurant manager Jim Weems, former Ole Miss football player Reed Davis, generic drug manufacturer Bill "Cuz" Rucker, and a university pharmacy professor (the author).

He played a big role in the formation of two local golf tournaments. The Happy Hour Scramble Tournament was the result of many discussions held on Friday Happy Hour at the Holiday Inn. The tournament grew from a group of 16 locals to a tournament of 136 players from all over north Mississippi. The tournament outgrew its purpose and was discontinued. A second tournament was even more fun. Named the Shrimp & Grits Scramble — after City Grocery owner John Currence's signature dish of Shrimp and Grits

— the tournament featured City Grocery customers against employees of Currence's four restaurant enterprises. There were eight Shrimp & Grits tournaments, the patrons winning seven. Whatever the tournament, Carmody would tell his partner, "Play hard when you're ahead and never give up when you are behind," a nice summary of his approach to coaching football.

Once, when Carmody was playing a "friendly" match in Oxford with Jim Weems, one of the better iron players in the area, Weems found himself in the uncharacteristic position of having a tree between his second shot and the green on a long par-4 hole. There was a narrow opening between the limbs of the big willow, and Weems was studying his chances of hitting an iron approach through that opening. Carmody, on the opposing team, offered the following friendly advice: "Hell, Weems, a faint heart never won a fair maiden." Inspired, Weems decided to try going through the small opening, and the ball made it through, landing almost on the green.

When Carmody retired from scouting for the Arizona Cardinals he and Noonie moved from Oxford to Madison, Mississippi, to be closer to their sons and grandchildren. Noonie figured that was the sixteenth move she and Jim had made since they were married. Not surprisingly, they moved into a home that bordered a golf course — the Annandale Golf Club (that at one time had hosted a Mississippi PGA Tour tournament) — and was adjacent to the Whisper Lake Country Club. Golf ranked second as a sport for Carmody only to football. No doubt, playing decent golf requires many of the same attributes as football — discipline, patience, respect for the game, etc. Carmody played most of his local golf at Whisper Lake — a short golf cart ride from his home. And he played as often as he could.

Carmody did not completely dissociate himself from football. He enjoyed watching two of his grandsons, Chase and Connor, play high school football. He also had time to watch his granddaughters participate in various high school sports. He enjoys providing advice to Chase since Chase recently assumed the position of defensive coordinator at Pearl High School.

Carmody would occasionally make his way back to Oxford, particularly to watch Ole Miss play LSU in football. His nephew and friends from Baton Rouge, Louisiana, would make the trip with him, bringing Cajun specialties like hog head cheese and boudin with them.

Every Christmas holiday the Carmodys and friends from Louisiana and Mississippi would gather at the Fair Grounds Racetrack in New Orleans for a day at the races. Noonie usually came home a winner. Carmody met new Happy Hour friends in the Jackson area, first at the Cherokee Bar and Restaurant in Jackson and then at the Georgia Blue Restaurant in Madison, where he continues to lead Monday "seminars."

Then, in 2009 Jim received one of his highest honors — he had been selected for induction into the Mississippi Sports Hall of Fame — an honor reserved for Mississippi's best athletes, coaches, and contributors to Mississippi sports.

The Mississippi Sports Hall of Fame opened on July 4, 1996, its purpose being to preserve the sports history of Mississippi and to recognize the great athletes and contributors to Mississippi sports. The hall also features memorabilia, artifacts, and film footage of great Mississippi athletes. The major driving force behind the establishment of the hall was Michael Rubenstein, a sports director for local television station WLBT in Jackson. Rubenstein was director of the hall from 1993 — before the hall officially opened — until 2011, when he passed away. Rubenstein was himself inducted into the hall in 2013. Noted Mississippi sportswriter Rick Cleveland succeeded him.

The hall has inducted more than 290 members to date including (at the risk of leaving out other Mississippi greats) college and professional football players and coaches including Lance Alworth, Doc Blanchard, Bobby Collins, Charlie Conerly, Reggie Collier, Eddie Crawford, Brett Favre, Tom Goode, Ray Guy, Glynn Griffing, Bruiser Kinard, Archie Manning, the Pooles (Barney, Buster, and Ray), Jerry Rice, Johnny Vaught, Warner Alford, Walter Payton, Ben Williams, and Sammy Winder; basketball players and coaches including Coolidge Ball, Bailey Howell, Denver Brackeen, Van Chancellor, Jennifer Gillom, Country Graham, and Margaret Wade; baseball players including "Cool Papa" Bell, Dizzy Dean, Boo Ferriss, Jake Gibbs, Don Kessinger, Will Clark, and Ron Polk; golfer Cary Middlecoff, track and field star Ralph Boston; administrators and announcers such as Jack Cristil, Ace Cleveland, and Reed Green.

To be inducted into a group containing these sports stars is quite an accomplishment (a notable exception among the inductees, at least in the opinion of the author, is Billy Brewer, outstanding player and coach for Ole Miss and a former member of the NFL's Washington Redskins who, inexplicably, is yet to be inducted).

Jim Carmody was inducted into the Mississippi Sports Hall of fame on July 31, 2009. This marked the third hall of fame into which he has been inducted — along with former USM head football coach Jeff Bower; former NFL star Hugh Green; former PGA tournament director Robert Morgan; former Mississippi State University and member of the NFL Chicago Bears, Tyrone Keys; and Ole Miss basketball great John Stroud. Carmody, ever the perfectionist, had written his acceptance speech but committed it and deliv-

"I want to extend my deepest appreciation to the selection committee of the Mississippi Sports Hall of Fame for the honor they have bestowed on me. My thanks go out to my wife of nearly fifty years, Noonie, and to our four sons — Chris, Keith, Brian, and Steve, and their families. The wife of a football coach has a difficult job. The constant moving takes a great deal of patience and understanding. Thank you, Noonie, for a great job of managing our family. There should be a Hall of Fame for coaches' wives, and you should be the first inductee. I love you, and I salute you for your many years of hard work.

Thanks to my parents and my sister, Elizabeth. My parents taught me at an early age the values of honesty, loyalty, dependability, and pride. My coaches at Holy Cross High School, Copiah-Lincoln JUCO, and Tulane University were great role models for me, stressing hard work, setting goals, self-discipline, attitude, unselfishness, persistence, preparation, courage, and confidence.

A special thanks to the head coaches in Mississippi who gave me the opportunity to coach in this state. Paul Davis was the first, offering me the defensive line job at Mississippi State in 1964. Coach Davis was an outstanding coach, and I learned a lot under him. In 1989, a quarter of a century later, Rockey Felker hired me as defen-

sive coordinator at Mississippi State, and I appreciate his confidence in me. Two Ole Miss coaches were very influential in my career in this state. Ken Cooper brought us to Oxford in 1974, and it was a great pleasure to work with him. He is the most underrated head coach ever in this state, with some very big wins in a short period of time. We were back in Oxford 18 years later, thanks to Billy Brewer, a player's coach, a coach's coach, and a winner at every place he's been. I had the pleasure of coaching with Bobby Collins at USM beginning in 1978, and we had three enjoyable years together. Bobby is a classy guy, and we have been friends since our years as assistants together at North Carolina. Roland Dale was the AD at USM, and he gave me my opportunity to be a head coach after many years as an assistant. Thank you, Coach Dale, for your confidence in me. I do not want to forget Terry McMillan, who gave me the opportunity to coach at Mississippi College. I was only there one year, but we won a lot of games and got into the national playoffs. Terry did a magnificent job.

And so, tonight when you honor me, you also honor the coaches I just talked about. You honor my family. You honor the assistant coaches I had the privilege to work with at these schools. You also honor a multitude of outstanding players who I had the good fortune to coach through the years.

In conclusion, I would like to say it has been an incredible ride — I'm humbled and honored by this induction, and I will treasure these moments forever. Thank you and God bless you."

ered it from memory. Following is the text of his speech:

Among those attending Carmody's induction was his long time U.S. Army and University of Kentucky coaching friend, Bob Ford. Their friendship goes back to their coaching careers in Korea. Ford was inducted into the Arkansas Sports Hall of Fame in 2011. Their friendship spanned a period of over 50 years. Carmody also coached the following members of the Mississippi Sports Hall of Fame: Tommy Neville (MSU), D.D. Lewis (MSU), Sammy Winder (USM), Ben Williams (UM), Hanford Dixon (USM), Reggie Collier

Carmody Family gathered at Jim's induction in the Southern Miss Hall of Fame, 2009
(Photo Carmody Family Collection)

(USM), and Brett Favre (USM).

"Retirement is good," Carmody told reporter Larry Mixon, I play a little golf, do a little speaking here and there, and we've traveled some. The only games I really care about now are the ones the grandkids are playing."

But then, in 2010, disaster struck the Carmodys. Noonie suffered a severe stroke and was hospitalized for a considerable length of time. Noonie had been the backbone of the Carmody family for over fifty years. While Jim did the coaching, Noonie ran the Carmody household, writing all the checks, paying all the bills, for the most part raising their four sons, doing the grocery shopping, handling all the family moves, etc. Jim never had to write a check or balance a checkbook but with Noonie being hospitalized, he found himself in the position of asking his son Keith for help. Jim is proud of the fact that in the first month of balancing the checkbook he was off by only $200!

Jim essentially gave up most of his activities in order to care for Noonie. He said, "Noonie took care of me all these years; now it's my turn to take care of her." He has essentially given up golf and, with the help of his sons and an improving wife, is running the Carmody household.

Noonie suffered numerous setbacks during her recovery but, in true

Dwayne Massey, Glen Howe, Fred Richards, Jim Carmody, Steve Carmody, Jeff Bower,
(Photo provided by Mississippi Hall of Fame)

Carmody fashion, she is a battler and has never given up. She continued to improve, and gain mobility. She contributed to this biography in numerous ways. During this recovery period she did not use a wheelchair or a walker. Carmody liked to say, "Those St. Joseph Academy girls are really tough."

Unfortunately, Noonie suffered a second stroke on Easter Sunday morning in 2016. She underwent surgery to stop the brain hemorrhage and spent time in intensive care but is improving. Given the Carmody spirit, she will continue to improve.

In August 2016, Brett Favre, one of Carmody's all-time favorite players, was inducted into the Pro Football Hall of Fame in Canton, Ohio. In a class act, Favre, who highly respected Carmody, invited Jim and members of his family to attend all of the induction activities in Canton.

Jim, his sons Steve and Keith, and Steve's son Connor spent the weekend in Canton celebrating Favre's induction. At the induction ceremonies Favre gave a deeply emotional speech. In addition to thanking his family he thanked Jim Carmody and his coaches. No coach would be foolish enough to risk singling out one of his former players as his favorite, but I suspect that if Carmody were to be administered truth serum, one would not be surprised if he would single out, other than his sons Steve and Keith, Brett Favre as his favorite player because they had in common such a deep appreciation for the game of football. They were all fierce competitors; they loved the game and what it stood for; they all considered their football families to simply be extensions of their own families; they all played or coached hard every single down, and they all subscribed to the Carmody tenet of playing hard when they were ahead and never giving up when they were behind.

21

RELATIONS WITH FORMER PLAYERS/COACHES/COLLEAGUES

It is relatively easy to measure the success of a football coach. One can easily count the number of wins and championships during a career. Much tougher to assess, but still assessable, is the effect a coach has had on the character of his players. How did his players respond as human beings? Big Nasty earned the respect of his players and fellow coaches. The influence he exerted on not only the more famous players on his teams was felt, perhaps, most strongly by those players who were not stars but who had to grind their way at every play in practice and games — the so-called grunts. The ability of a coach to motivate players to excel beyond the level of their abilities was a key to Carmody's success. He was well aware that motivating players is one of the biggest keys to winning a game and to leading a successful life after football.

In 2011 Carmody gave an interview to Larry Mixon for a USM magazine "To the Top." He related to Mixon his coaching philosophy and the role motivation played in his success as a coach. Carmody discussed how motivating players is one of the biggest keys to winning any game. "It's a big part of the game, but it requires study just like managing the game and putting together a game plan. You have to manage emotion and motivation. You've got to do it in a sensible way. Motivationally, the best thing you can do is let guys see how important football is to you. It rubs off on the players. Coach with passion; coach with sincerity; they'll see that. If it's important to you, it'll be important to them."

Carmody then related to Mixon an incident in a game at Memphis State when he realized that his players, The Nasty Bunch, had gotten on the same page with him. "We were up at Memphis, and it was the first series of the game. We had kicked off to them, and they were just coming out of the huddle for the first play. The whistle blew for an offsides or something, and their little quarterback was running, and some of the guys stopped, but Rhett Whitley kept after him. He ran him over to our sidelines and kind of picked him up and slammed him on his head. The kid's helmet popped off, and he got up yelling, 'What are you trying to do? This is just a game!' Whitley spit out his mouthpiece and said back to the Memphis quarterback, 'Maybe it's a game to you, but it's a way of life to us.' I knew right then we were going to be all right."

Carmody's philosophy applies both on and off the football field. There are many examples of the long-term effect Big Nasty had on all of his players. Carmody's son Brian helped identify many former players and asked them to contribute their recollections of their coach for this biography. Other accounts of his influence had been reported in the printed media. Other non-players were invited to contribute their thoughts including former USM President Aubrey Lucas and former Ole Miss football coach Billy Brewer.

USM Former President Aubrey Lucas

President of USM from 1975-1996 through Carmody's coaching days at USM both as an assistant and as head coach, Aubrey Lucas subsequently returned to USM as interim president when USM was seeking a new president in 2012. I met him at the Natchez Literary Festival, and he offered the following interesting observation:

"Jim Carmody was one of the smartest coaches I ever worked with and the very best I ever worked with in terms of the use of the language. A lot of coaches talk with their muscles, but Jim was very articulate and very smart. I wish he had been more articulate with our alumni. We had to let him go, you know, because of poor attendance. But he was smart."

Billy Brewer

Billy Brewer and Jim Carmody had much in common. Both coaches were intense, highly competitive, keen recruiters, motivators, disciplinarians, and both hated to lose. Both also had to deal width chief administrators who had large egos. Billy has said that Carmody was the most intelligent coach he ever worked with. "He never wore headphones on the sidelines. He had the whole game plan in his head." As competitive as both men were, Billy should be admired for talking Carmody into joining his staff as defensive line coach after their bitter rivalry and after Carmody's comments about Billy back in 1987. The two worked well together, the famous 1992 goal-line stand against Mississippi State being a prime example.

Former Players

Jim Carmody had a major impact on players he coached at all levels — high school, college, and professional. He had, perhaps, the greatest impact on those players who were not at the All-American or Heisman Trophy levels, players who had to use 150 percent of their talents in order to succeed, those players who were in the trenches, who used grit and determination to enhance the athletic skills they were born with, those players who could be motivated to succeed. The impact he had went far beyond a football game or season but, rather, lasted twenty, thirty, forty, or more years. There have been many anecdotes and testimonials related to his impact, and many appreciate the influence he had on their lives. A few of these tributes are given here in their own words.

Larry Boyd — USM Punter from Columbus, Georgia, Lettered, 1983

"Coach Carmody always seemed to understand his players and be able to communicate with us individually. Two stories I will share, and you have my permission to reprint.

"It was the last Wednesday before our first game of the year. *The Clarion Ledger* had announced in a story in the paper that day that was saying I was going to be the starting punter for the 1983 season. Coach Carmody had not said anything to the team or me yet about who was starting. As we headed off the field after practice, Coach Carmody called me over. He said he had read in the paper that morning that I was the starting punter. I told him I had read the article as well but that I thought he might have some say so about who started. He chuckled a bit and then did something that I remember to this day. He put his arm around my shoulders pads and said 'Boyd, you are my punter. And, I don't care if you kick the first one straight up in the air, you're still my punter.' Somehow he knew that was what I really needed to hear. That no matter what happened he believed in me and that I was his punter. That meant a lot to me.

"Later on that year, several games in to the season, I finally got the nerve to ask Coach a few questions. One thing I had always wondered about was why I was supposed to catch and punt the football in 1.3 seconds, as Coach reminded me daily. Over and over, every day it was 1.3, 1.3. He would time me to make sure I was getting the punts off in 1.3 seconds or less. So finally one day I asked him 'Why is 1.3 the magical number?' He tried explaining to me that the entire process was supposed to take 2.1 seconds and that the center snap was supposed to take 0.8 seconds, and so therefore, that left me with 1.3 seconds to get the punt off. I guess he saw I was still confused, so he explained it this way. He said, 'Son, there are studies out there that have determined that it takes that 240-pound defensive end exactly 2.1 seconds to get from right over there (the line of scrimmage) to right there (and he placed his finger in the middle of my chest)! Do you understand now?' I said 'Yes, sir, I do, and you can best believe the ball will be punted in 1.3 seconds or less.' Again, he knew how to communicate with his players."

Johnny Desler — UM Defensive Back, Lettered 1993, 1995-96

"The year is 1993, 100 years of Ole Miss football; I'm a true freshman playing on kickoffs, and kickoff returns, and Coach Carmody's special team. On the punt return I was the up-front blocker for returner Ta'Boris Fisher. I also saw a lot of playing time at right and left corner, nickelback or free safety. So, it's about one-third the way into the season, and we are like 3-1. During a hot Tuesday practice Coach Carmody, aka 'Big Nasty,' and I were standing on the sidelines going over plays. Big Nasty is pumping me up, giving me all these incredible compliments about me as a freshman corner, and he's telling me, Johnny D is the best I've ever seen, and if I keep this up I'll play four years with Ole Miss, forty-plus games, and just lifelong stuff you'll never forget. This is all in a three-minute conversation. Then a 6'5", 230-pound incredible specimen, a defensive end, from a very tough Los Angeles neighborhood, who was actually going through a defensive end walk-through, comes up to us, barges into our conversation and taunts me. 'Johnny D, you the man,' he said. He's standing about five yards from Coach and I. It was obvious that Coach did not like this guy barging his way into our conversation, so Carmody fires back at him something like, shut up and mind your own business. That really took the guy by surprise and really pissed him off. So the player steps up to Coach Carmody, basically face-to-face, and the player says something like, 'What's up, Coach?' while getting into Carmody's face. It's pretty damn intense. Coach Carmody says, 'Son, I've seen you play football; you can't scare me a bit!' That player just melted, turned around, and went on. I got so nervous my knees buckled! But Coach was right — that player never played and was a bust."

Harper Donahoe — UNC Defensive Lineman, 1972

In 2015 Carmody received a Father's Day card from one of his former players, Harper Donahue. He was a defensive player who did not play much. Probably never got in a game. He played on the scout team three years. But Carmody liked him and asked him to help him coach. On the card was printed this note to Coach Carmody:

"Coach Carmody, I wanted to tell you on Father's Day how much you have meant to me. I am now retired after 40 years as a teacher, coach and high school principal. Much of my success in my career is a direct result of the mentoring, dedication, and hard work I learned as a player at UNC under you. I cannot express how much you have meant to me."

Brett Favre

Favre has great respect for Carmody. In an interview with Jackson *Clarion-Ledger* sports writer Robert Wilson, before the second meeting of Mississippi State and USM in 1990 when Carmody was coaching State's defense against Favre, Favre credited Carmody for giving him a chance to play college ball. "Coach Carmody made the final decision of getting a scholarship to USM. He gave me an opportunity to play." When Favre was hospitalized following an automobile accident the summer of 1990 he remembers getting a call from Carmody: "Coach Carmody called me when I was in the hospital. He wished me all the luck in the world and a speedy recovery."

Favre recalled how Carmody motivated the Golden Eagles in the 1987 USM-Mississippi State matchup. "Coach Carmody is a great motivator, especially this week of the season. We played the State fight song all week long during practices. He got us fired up for the Bulldogs." Then Favre recalled the last-minute motivation just before the game. "We were in the dressing room, and Coach Carmody brought out this big box. It was a box of old colored panties with Southern Mississippi players' numbers on them. He gave them out and had a saying for each one. Like No. 99 was Sidney Coleman, and it said he couldn't tackle a such-and-such grandmother. No. 43 was Shelton Gandy, and it said he couldn't run his way out of a wet paper bag." USM, fired up, went out and beat State 18-14.

Preston Hansford — USM Tight End from
Maylene, Alabama, Lettered 1986-89

"Brian, I'm glad you asked for the email. I loved your dad. He signed me in 1985. I played tight end for him, and he was always fair to me. I always heard about how tough Coach was, and I'm sure you boys witnessed it growing up. I redshirted in '85 and I started almost every game his last two years '86 and '87. He loved players who where tough and aggressive. I was always told that the Nasty Bunch was named after him, Big Nasty. I can tell you that he hated to lose, and that one year, I believe it was '86, we went full pads, even on Friday for two weeks because we didn't play well in the games. The winter workouts were the toughest to me.

"One time in practice during two-a-days I got in a fight against a defensive player as a true freshman in '85. The next day I had moved up on the depth chart. That's the kind of aggression your father liked. I have always loved and respected your father."

Billy R. Jones, Ph.D. — Ole Miss, 1993

"Coach Carmody had recruited me some in high school from the Mc-Comb, Mississippi, area when he was at another school in 1991. I reconnected with Coach Carmody after walking on at Ole Miss in the spring of 1993. During that spring, Coach Carmody was the defensive line coach for Ole Miss. I was not one of Coach's star players. I was simply a scrub he had a great impact on personally.

"One thing I learned in a hurry was that Coach Carmody was tough. He received respect from players and from other coaches just by the sheer power of his presence and demeanor. He had very high expectations of everyone, whether you were a high draft pick (like Norman Hand), or a scrub (like a walk-on like me!). I gained a great deal of respect for him because of this. At that time in my life, I was going through a tough time personally. Coach Carmody made an effort to check in on me from time to time. If you worked hard, gave a 110 percent, and were a little mean (like him), you were one of 'his' guys, and you knew that by the way he treated you.

"I remember he would send us (third stringers, etc.) over to work with the O-line during practice some, and we took a great deal of pride in going a 110 percent against the O-line, even when Coach was not there. We knew that Coach Carmody did not expect us to be blocking dummies. He expected you to play every play like it was fourth and one in the national championship. He didn't have to say that; you just knew it by the way he acted and treated you. It was funny because usually the O-line coach would get so mad because we were being so effective, he would send us back to Coach.

"Every so often the defensive line and offensive line groups would come together to work on one-on-one pass block/pass rush. The offensive line coach was very proud of his guys. So you would have these two single file lines facing each other. One guy on one side was offense — so his objective was to pass block, and the other guy was one of Carmody's defensive linemen, so of course his job was to get to the QB. Well, during the course of this drill, one of our reserves on the D-line found himself matched up with one of starters on the O-line. Let's just say it was not going to be a fair match. To make it worse, the offensive coach yells, 'Okay, so and so, rip his freaking head off!'

Well, you could have heard a pin drop when Coach Carmody said, 'Hold on here. Norman (referring to Norman Hand who went on to play in the NFL), get in here... now, let him try to rip his freaking head off!' Needless to say, Norman bull-rushed the guy, knocking him back and over the dummy used to symbolize the QB. The drill ended after that.

"We would have some serious battles in Vaught-Hemingway with the offensive team. If you were down on the depth chart, getting 10-20 or more plays in the scrimmage was a big deal in the filmed scrimmage we would have in the stadium. The day that I think that I kind of won Coach over was the day that I was in going against the first 'O,' and one the offensive tackles that rotated in got mad because I had made a tackle for a loss or maybe a sack. So the next play, well after the whistle had blown — this guy comes flying from down the field while I am turning to go back to the huddle and spears me in the back, knocking me 15-20 feet on the ground away from the blow. Well, I never stopped moving while sliding away from the hit... I wheel around and come after the guy, and we get into a big fight. I don't know if you have ever been in a fight when wearing full pads, but it really depletes all your energy when you are done. Instead of 10-20 plays that day, Coach left me in like 50 or 60. Needless to say, I was dead when he subbed me out. When I ran off to the sideline, he tapped me on the helmet and gave me a big smile. Never said a word. I knew I made the club because I had shown that toughness he desired. The toughness he exhumed.

"Technique-wise, Coach Carmody was a very good teacher. He is a very intelligent person. This came out in his coaching. He gave great feedback on how to improve each step of the move you were trying to perform. He could take in several pieces of information at once and give you an accurate assessment of what you needed to improve almost instantly. He taught football like a great teacher would teach a class. Again, it didn't matter where you were on the depth chart; he wanted everyone to get better. He wanted you to be the best. As I coached for 10 years afterwards, I truly came to understand just how talented of a coach that Carmody truly is.

"Because of an injury, I could not play football anymore. In the spring of 1994, I returned to the team as a student-assistant coach with Coach Carmody. Coach Carmody was the first person to ever call me 'Coach.' He not only cared about you as a player, he was concerned about you as a human being. He shot you straight and was quick to do it. You know exactly where you stand with Jim Carmody; there is no gray area. The world is a better place for me because he took an interest and he gave me some of his time. Coach Carmody is the one person that I wanted to emulate as a coach. Smart, tough, and demanding the best every time. Like I shared in a speech I gave recognizing Coach before one of our ballgames a few years ago, There is a special relationship that develops between a player and a coach. If you were tough and gave a 110 percent — whether you were an All-American or a scrub like me — you were one of Coach's guys, and that meant a lot to you. At a time in my life when things were pretty bad personally, Coach took time with me, and he did not have to do that. For that I am forever grateful."

More Billy R. Jones:

"Jim Carmody is without a doubt one of the most highly skilled tacticians the game has ever known. Like Bum Phillips famously said, 'He could take yern' and beat hisn', and he could take hisn' and beat yern.'"

Tony Pogue — USM Linebacker, Lettered
1986-89

"I played for Coach Carmody 85-87. At the very first team meeting before two-a-days, there were 100 players present — including walk-ons. Coach told us that only 1 percent of college players make the pros. [He said,] 'That means only one of you in this room will make it to the NFL. So the rest of you better go to class!'"

Mike Schiro — USM SS from New Orleans,
LA Lettered 1980-83 "Early Days"

"Coach Carmody is a huge influence in my life. Not only my football life, but also my day-to-day life as a husband, dad, business owner, etc. It is an honor to try to add a little insight on what it was like to be a part of the Carmody's football and personal life.

"The obvious start would be to share how much he made us realize as individuals, what we were capable of. I will not bore you with this information, for I am sure you have all the stories you need to fill three books of inspirational stories Coach has provided for his players. So with that in mind, I will share with you a few stories that might be unique. At least for his sake, I hope so.

"My first encounter with Coach was when I walked on and tried out for the team in 1979. Up until then, everything to do with sports came easy to me. I matured faster than the kids in New Orleans, and for the most part was head and shoulders above my competitors. The sport did not matter. Whether it be football, track, baseball, or basketball. I was awarded the parish MVP award of the parish for basketball when I was in seventh grade. I was told baseball was my sport and to focus on that in high school. When my parents and coaches realized I would not entertain the thought of quitting football to pursue baseball, I was instructed to enroll at a small high school so I would be able to compete. My choice was Brother Martin that happened to be the largest school I could find that was closest to my house. The powers to be instructed me to play defense because I would never make it as a running back. I started at the safety position my sophomore year because I was ineligible as a freshmen. Coach Conlin started me at running back my junior and senior year. An injury sidelined me when we played St. Aug, the team that won state that year, my senior year. Brother Martin went on to lose that game in overtime. It might have been the fact that I did not participate in that game that kept all scholarship offers far away. I had not planned to attend college until no offers came in. My teammates would call when they received offers. I was sincerely proud and happy for them. When the dust settled, and I had no offers to reject, there was only one thing to do in my mind and that was to go earn a scholarship. I was motivated, hungry, and more importantly, angry. USM was the only school that offered me a visit. I didn't even know there was a University of Southern Mississippi until I visited. I hope this does not seem braggadocious. I want you to understand the mind set of this eighteen-year-old that was about to tangle with Big Nasty.

"As a walk-on, you are asked to basically be a live blocking dummy. I'm not sure of the statistics, but I would be willing to bet that there would be less than a handful of players that made the team via this route the five years I attended USM. In hindsight, I can see why coaches and players did not care to take the time and effort to nurture and develop these players. Most were searching for that last hurrah. That last chance to put the pads on. For most, it was a desperate attempt to hold on to a sport they did not want to relinquish. For some reason, and maybe it was just my imagination, I felt like Coach showed me a little more interest than the other scrubs. It was not spoken, but there was a certain aura Coach had. When he spoke, he had everyone's attention. When he walked or glanced at me, I felt he was reading me. There was an uneasy feeling that would wash over me. Not in a bad way. More like when my grammar school principal would walk in on my second-grade classroom. Along with feeling a little intimidated, awkward, or wondering what did I do now, there came other feelings. Comforting, confidence, I have your back, I am here for you, and you can count on me.

"It was not uncommon for a Brother Martin practice to come to a stop, so I had time to tie my cleats so I would not hurt myself. The first live USM scrimmage for me included uniformed referees, chain gangs, cameras, the kicking game, and the whole package. It was an overcast day with light drizzle. About ten plays into the scrimmage, I tackled someone from behind. His foot came up and hit my facemask. It stunned me a little, but I did not think much of it until I took my place in the huddle. The ref took one look at me and said, I quote, 'Jesus, son, take a knee.' My nose started bleeding, and I guess the extra water from the drizzle spread the blood that covered my face. Again, not much pain, but the reaction on ref's face and my teammates looking at me like they felt sorry for me, I must admit, I started to get a little concerned. Right about the time I was in that mental sweet spot where I just knew everyone would feel sorry for me, I was helped to my feet by Coach Carmody by way of my hair. Yes, he pulled me to my feet by pulling the back of my hair with the enduring words of, 'Get your ass back in the huddle. This is no sissy Catholic high school league. If you ever kneel on my field again, I will make sure it will be the last time.' At the time I had no idea he played for that same Catholic high school league in New Orleans. There are few windows of opportunities in a man's life when the next decision he makes could possibly substantially define who he is. I think that moment was a window for me. There were two choices. One was get back in the huddle because this crazy coach might kill you, or go home. I remember feeling that he could not wait to see what my reaction would be. Again, it might just be my imagination, but I think he took great satisfaction when I decided to get back in the huddle. To this day, I use that tactic at least once a week in my business life. I challenge my employees sometimes so hard, they will either quit or become better individuals.

Winter Workout

"Another story includes dreaded winter workouts. After surviving my first football season, we began winter workouts. There were horrifying rumors about the grueling, often-debilitating, winter workouts. I knew they lasted only sixty minutes; how hard could they possibly be? The silver-lining time constraint kept me optimistic.

"My first day of winter workout involved class, a special lunch of pizza, a short nap, and then I arrived in my required sweat suit on the practice field. While I knew the workout would be punishing, I had no idea the extent of the punishment. There was confirmation the first day of winter workouts. There is no offseason in NCAA football.

"The first twenty minutes of exercises were tolerable. Eventually, the physical demands caught up with me. As I proceeded to the station where jumping a bag repeatedly was the objective, I began to feel very indisposed. I began violently vomiting while trying to maintain my composure and finish the drill. Big Nasty approached me and unsympathetically said, 'Throw up on your own time; this is my time.' The consequences of this statement unfortunately affected me and my teammate holding the vomit-covered bag.

Game Day

"Coach and I had a unique unstated bond, having both been raised in New Orleans. Another commonality was our hatred for Ole Miss and their Archbishop Shaw High School's star quarterback. Often Coach would make statements during the opposing stadium walk-throughs that would get the team riled up. During the Hemingway Stadium visit, the statements included: 'Look how nice the locker room and stadium is"; "They probably eat better than you"; "Look how these guys live"; "Ole Miss didn't even want you"; and "These boys even dress better than you with all with their plaid shirts, khakis and bow ties." Undoubtedly, Coach's objective was to plant the seed of deep hatred and unequivocal resentment. His genius was to make us hate them for having so much instead of us wondering why we do not have the nicer things in life. Our mentality was that it was truly us against the world. He made us feel that each and everyone of us were that most important person on the team, and we treated each other with that respect.

"Game time arrived and my emotions were at a 'code-red' level, thanks to Coach Carmody. Unfortunately, this was at the expense of Ole Miss' tight end. One of the first plays of the Ole Miss game was to level the tight end. He was knocked out cold, and my instinctive actions, thanks to Coach, were to stand over the fallen player and get the crowd riled up. This practice could likely be frowned upon in the current athletic arena.

"Golden Eagle stickers were provided for players who made extraordinary plays. Consequently, a new category was developed after watching film of the Ole Miss game, and I received a sticker. He said, 'Ski, you knocked his dick in his watch pocket.' At the time, I had no clue what that meant, but I assumed it was a good thing. Big Nasty's pep talk and inspiration was the driving force behind this particular play."

Selling Shrimp

"On a lighter note, one summer I used my entrepreneurial spirit to sell shrimp. For some reason, Mrs. Carmody, unbeknown to Big Nasty, was kind enough to assist me with sales. She called assistant coaches' wives, friends, and family and enthusiastically let them know that I would be coming with several hundred pounds of fresh shrimp straight from my brother's boat. Not only did she do that, she invited me to weigh and sell the shrimp at her house in the front yard. Of course her kind heart wouldn't allow me to sit outside in the heat, so let's just say there was plenty of shrimp juice that led from the front yard to the kitchen. It sounded like a kind, harmless gesture until the flies showed up. Who would have known flies would show up in the middle of summer in Hattiesburg, Mississippi? When Big Nasty returned from work that day and saw Mrs. Noonie and me in the middle or our unsuccessful attempt to remove the flies and smell with bleach and anything else we could get our hands on, he just stared at us. I am not sure if he was trying to intimidate us or he was just purely shocked. After he finished his evil looks, Mrs. Carmody said, 'Lighten up, Jim; the boy is trying to make a little money.' Coach just shook his head and sat down in his lounge chair and started watching television. At that point, the cat was out of the bag. He might be Big Nasty, but Noonie was the boss. The funniest thing of that event to me was that Coach never brought it up. I'm not sure if he did not want to make me feel embarrassed or maybe he was instructed not to bring it up. Being married to a strong woman myself, I am pretty sure it is the latter.

A Needed Ride

"One early Mardi Gras morning I was heading to Lafayette Square in downtown New Orleans. My motorcycle stalled on Interstate 10 right by the Canal Street exit. Lucky for me, I was able to coast down the exit and pulled into a convenience store parking lot. Within a few seconds, I found myself surrounded by six gentlemen who obviously did not want me in their neighborhood. After realizing there would be no way of talking to these guys and discussing options peacefully, I punched the smallest gentleman and started running up the exit ramp in a hurried fashion. Thankfully, no one followed me. The horrific traffic was bumper to bumper. After hitchhiking for ten minutes, finally, out of the tens if not hundreds or thousands of people that come to Mardi Gras, one person was kind enough to make eye contact with me. You guessed it. It was Big Nasty. He lowered his window and said in a monotone voice, 'What's up, Ski?'

'Nothing much, Coach.'

'Looks like you need a ride.'

'Yep, it appears I do.' I sat in the back seat with an assistant coach and his wife and was ordered, 'don't say a word.' Coach dropped me off at my destination without one single question about how or why I was hitchhiking on the interstate at 8:00 in the morning. That is what our relationship had evolved to — unconditional love. He knew I had a few wild oats to sow, and he was okay with it."

He's Back!

"The year Coach took the job with the Buffalo Bills was the worst year of my sports career. I felt that I was on an island and misunderstood by the other coaches. There were more days than not when I wanted to walk out and head back to New Orleans. The never-quit attitude instilled in me by my parents was tested every day that year. The promise to never quit anything I started was honored. Once that year was finished, there was no doubt that would be my last.

"The announcement that Coach Carmody was headed back to Hattiesburg to be the head coach was another life-changing event for me. He was the reason I was there in the first place. It was so exciting and brought such happiness, several teammates and I went to the airport to welcome him back with signs. This unlikely event allowed me to finish my last years at USM with great pride and joy."

Life Lessons

"Coach Carmody always preached about how sports teaches you life lessons. As an eighteen-year-old I had no idea what that really means. At the age of 55, it has become crystal clear what he meant by that. Please know that it is understood that this book is about Coach and not me. This is my way of letting you know what it meant to learn and play for him.

"My 24-year-old law school student son had liver cancer at the age of six months. He had a six percent chance of living. The lessons taught were never to hang your head, just deal with the circumstances in front of you. My wife and I were on an emotional and financial roller coaster for many years. We went from being on top of the world to its lowest point. Coach's lessons and voice never left my thoughts. My 25-year-old is opening his own business in Houston. He is at the top of his profession. Coach Carmody and his family had a great deal of influence on my life and what I have been able to share with others including my fifty employees, friends, and family. He taught me to fight, scratch, and claw to get what I want. Nothing is owed to me. Earn everything and most importantly be a good teammate.

"One of my favorite sayings from Coach is, 'You can always fool your parents. You can sometimes fool your coaches. You can never fool your teammates.' This has been an invaluable lesson for me. He should take great pride in the way our team was a family. We were close because of his leadership and more importantly, his actions. We would, and still would do, anything for each other on or off the field. What more could you ask for as a coach? I can only imagine if he means this much to me, how many other people's lives he has influenced. Directly or indirectly."

Rhett Whitley —USM Defensive End, Lettered 1977-81
Original Member of The Nasty Bunch

"How it began. I don't remember who we were playing, but it was a home game. It was the first play of the game in 1978, and I was starting as a redshirt freshman. I was a bucked-toothed, knobby-kneed, freckled-faced Alabama and Auburn reject from Bluff Park, Alabama. Coach Bear Bryant said, 'We don't need you, Rhett Whitley' in a letter that I still have to this day. Maybe that was part of the Nasty Bunch being Nasty, at least, I know it was motivation for me.

"Back to that home game at USM. Thad Dillard always got nervous before the game and lost his stomach. On this day, it rested on the football before the center came to snap the ball to the QB. We were all laughing at Thad as he did it, but history took place that day, when that center said, 'You are NASTY.' We loved it, and in practice it stuck, as we started calling our fearless leader, Coach Carmody, Big Nasty and the Nasty Bunch.

"That is the way I remember it starting, but you know, after so many licks to the head, these stories probably got more embellished as the older we got, but who cares. I have two brothers who played football. Chuck Whitley, a Hoover High School coach with tons of championships, and my brother Ryan Whitley played at Auburn then transferred to USM as a center.

"The next story has two versions I am aware of, and I believe you can get this out of the Memphis paper from 1978 sports page. It goes like this: the quarterback was rounding my end, and Ron Brown or Cliff Lewis and I all did a nose dive to hit him as he was diving in the dirt to miss our hit. Cliff and I pick him up after the play, and the QB said, 'This is just a game.' We replied, 'This is not a game; it is war.' I believe the paper said, 'This is not a game; it is life.' (Carmody recalls the players saying, 'Maybe it's a game to you, but it's a way of life to us.') Either way, we made our point.

"And it wasn't a game to us. We were out to prove we were number one in the country. USM hadn't been to a bowl game since 1956. But we were, according to Coach Carmody, Big Nasty himself, the leftovers, the Ole Miss, Miss State, Alabama, Auburn, Georgia rejects. Every day in practice he reminded us of that. It was not subtle. We took that statement seriously, and we had something to prove to those that did not pick us.

"We played Alabama three times while I was there. We lost two and tied one. But I had the privilege to play in the East West All-Star game in 1982. I had always told my mom I would play for the 'Bear' one day. She said, 'You will.' Well, he coached that game and told me, 'I never should have let you out of Alabama.' I owe those words to Coach Carmody.

"Coach Carmody used war-type analogies to keep us revved up and NASTY. Although we didn't win all our games, we certainly made a name for ourselves on the gridiron. I use to tell Coach Carmody, if he called us at midnight to get on our uniforms, go to the top of the stadium, spread out our arms like wings, and we would fly to the ground, unhurt, we would have done it. We believed in him. If he said it, we just did it. His game plan was faultless. I always felt sorry for the offense, because our preparation was so intense, I felt like we had prepared so well that we knew what plays they were going to run better than they did. We watched so much film, and Coach Carmody had us so well prepared that we would not lose. We were the Nasty Bunch. People feared us. Our own scout team feared us. I lost a tooth at the Ole Miss game one year and left it out on purpose because it made me look nastier.

"Coach Carmody used psychology against the offense. If the Nasty Bunch was on the field at the end of a quarter, no matter how tired we were, we would get down in our stance and sprint by the offense, go to the new line of scrimmage sometimes 90 yards away, and Coach said, 'Do not let them see you breathing hard, or tired.' They freaked them out as we ran by them screaming like a bunch of wild animals.

"Coach also told us: 'You never take yourself out of the game; we will tell you when your hurt. Don't show pain, ever.'"

More Rhett Whitley

"Open the door, Big Nasty, open the door, open the door, Big Nasty, open the door… We were in the stadium in Jackson, Mississippi, where the locker room was underneath the fans. The stadium was filled to capacity that day, and I believe Ole Miss was expecting to win, easily. This was the year Too Tall Tillman made three sacks at the end of the game to push Ole Miss back to the fifty-yard line, after lining up inside the twenty. (This may have been Mississippi State win at USM, my freshman year, 1978.) Either way, it went as follows:

"As I recall the story, we were in the locker room and foaming at the mouth to get out on the field. The vocal leader on our team was Mike 'Crazy' Crenshaw from Mobile, a defensive back who had broken his helmet against an Alabama player on the kickoff this same year. USM didn't have a spare helmet in those days, so he borrowed an Alabama helmet and finished the game with it on as well as taking it home as a souvenir. Back to the previous story, Crazy was training me to be Nasty and Crazy. We both were jacked up and started to yell, 'Open the door, Big Nasty, open the door,' and no one would let us out. Coach Carmody had blocked the door. We couldn't get out. So, the whole Nasty Bunch ran to the door and started banging our helmets on the door. We were yelling, 'open the door, Big Nasty, open the door,' and then bang our helmets twice on benches, on doors, on walls, but it was putting us in a frenzy. We played in a frenzy. Finally, Big Nasty opens the door, and we fell all over each other getting out of that locker room."

Bo Russell (former MSU player)

In 2009, Jim Carmody was elected to the Mississippi Sports Hall of Fame. On July 27, 2009, just prior to the induction ceremony, Rick Cleveland, executive director of the hall and noted sports writer, wrote a column in the Jackson *Clarion-Ledger*: "Few could beat Carmody, so

---

dear rick,

great article on coach carmody. i played for him in 1989 and it was the best year i ever experienced in football. not many people know about it, but he gave one of the best pregame speeches i have every (sic) heard before we played usm in 1989. on the friday before we played southern, he took the defensive players who would be traveling to the game to the south end zone of scott field. he made all the coaches leave including coach felker. he started off telling us how good southern was and what the game meant to them. he reminded us how they had whipped our asses the past 15 years and that none of the southern players were offered a scholarship by an sec school; and that they would remember that every minute of the game. he told us how hattiesburg and the surrounding area was a tough blue-collar town and usm epitomized its community.

he went on to tell us he recruited all the southern players, that they had fought many great battles and they were his boys. that is when he paused and a tear rolled down his face. he then told us we were his boys now, that we were not going to lose this game. we would leave hattiesburg a winner. you could have heard a pin drop. i don't think anyone said a word on the bus trip to hattiesburg.

i remember him leading us out of the dressing room and the fans yelling "big nasty" and some other not so nice words. i noticed the southern players gawking at him. i knew then we were going to win. during warm-ups he was as cool and calm as i had ever seen him. he was definitely in his element.

when you play for coach carmody you never lay on the field. if you have a broken leg you hobble off on the good leg. in the first quarter against southern i broke three ribs on a sweep play. i continued to play another series but had a hard time breathing. they thought i had punctured a lung. i wasn't going to leave coach carmody. instead, coach carmody grabbed a highway patrolman who was guarding coach felker and told him to get me the hell out of here and to a hospital. he was tough but he also had compassion. the er doctor at forest general confirmed that i had 3 broken ribs but no punctured lung. i made it back for the 4th quarter to watch us pull out the win.

after the game i remember seeing reggie collier come into our locker room and hug coach carmody. they greeted each other like long lost friends. that told me a lot about the relationship he had with his players. once he was your coach he was always your coach.

on the bus ride back to starkville he made me sit with him. funny thing is we never discussed the game, instead he knew i was going to be taking the lsat for law school during our open date the next weekend and we discussed where i was going to law school the next year. he talked about his son who was a lawyer and his experience with law school. he thought i should go to ole miss. i told him i hated ole miss. 4 hours later we arrived in starkville and i was making plans to attend law school at ole miss. he had that kind of influence on young men.

he only coached me one year. i learned more that one year, than in my entire life prior to then. he is a hell of a man. a man's man.

he is not ole miss's coach, he is not southern's coach, nor is he state's coach. i consider him mississippi's coach.

bo russell

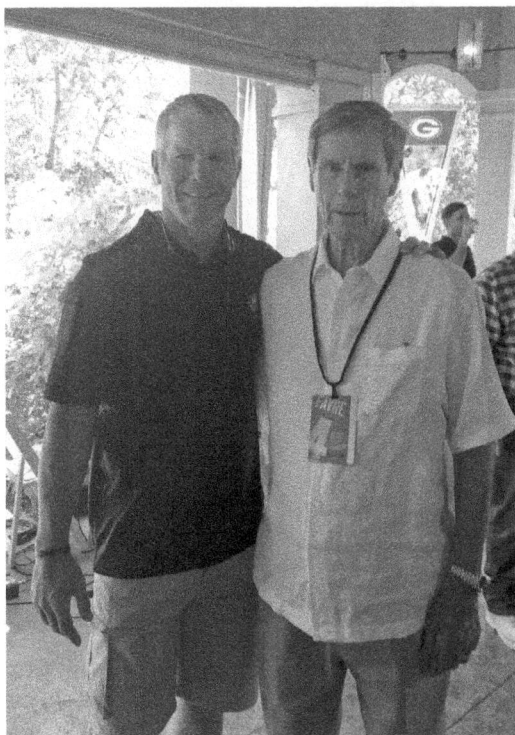

Brett Favre (USM) and Jim Carmody

they hired him," paying tribute to Carmody's career. Bo Russell, who played one year for Carmody at Mississippi State as a defensive back, emailed Cleveland to compliment and thank him for the article. (Note: the original letter was written entirely in lower case and is reproduced as it was sent)

More Brett Favre

Favre was elected to the National Football League Hall of Fame in 2016 and was inducted with Tony Dungy, Kevin Greene, Marvin Harrison, Orlando Pace, Eddie DeBartolo, Jr., Ken Stabler, and Dick Stanfel. Stabler and Stanfel were selected by the senior committee while DeBartolo was elected as a nominee of the newly formed contributor committee. The group was inducted on August 6, 2016. Favre invited Carmody to attend the induction festivities, and Jim and two of his sons, Steve and Keith, and grandson Connor went to Canton, Ohio. The first coach Favre thanked, after his father, of course, was Jim Carmody.

POSTGAME
AUTHOR'S NOTES

It was my intention to write a story about the life of a football coach, not to simply write another football book containing material found in media guides. Jim Carmody, aka, Big Nasty, came to mind. Carmody had an amazing football career, playing or coaching at the high school (Holy Cross), community college (Copiah-Lincoln Community College), Armed Forces (Korea), Division I Universities (Tulane, Kentucky, Mississippi State, North Carolina, Ole Miss, Southern Mississippi), Division II College (Mississippi College), and professional NFL (Buffalo Bills) levels while ending his career as a professional scout for the NFL Arizona Cardinals. Surprisingly, he held only one head-coaching job in his nearly sixty-year playing and coaching football career. One can speculate that this has more to do with him personally rather that athletically. Jim is not, like many head coaches, a shoe salesman, but rather a man who speaks directly, telling his listeners and players not what they want to hear but the truth. Jim has known acquaintances who were his biggest supporters when Carmody and his teams won but who would suddenly disappear after a loss. Carmody would closely measure his friendships. Nevertheless, one has to admire not only the longevity of his career but also the successes he achieved, personally and professionally, during that career.

Several interviews were held with Coach Carmody at his home in Madison, Mississippi, and form the basis of his quotations in the text. Most of these interviews were tape recorded. In writing this biography, I used several newspaper sources as the basis for many of the quotations from players, coaches, and other individuals. Rather than number each reference source in the text, which can be rather distracting in a biography, the sources utilized in each chapter are summarized in a section named "Sources" at the end of the book.

This biography attempts to capture the human nature of a football coach and not just a recounting of the statistics and the wins and losses he compiled during that career. His competitiveness hopefully makes itself known throughout this biography. For example, Jim took the intrastate rivalry between Ole Miss, Mississippi State, and Southern Mississippi seriously whether he was the assistant coach or head coach. If he was coaching at Ole Miss, he pointed to games against State and USM. If he was coaching at State then Ole Miss and Southern were his two biggest rivals, and when he coached at Southern, then State and Ole Miss were his biggest rivals. Carmody posted a 22-14 record in these rivalry games. Unfortunately, Ole Miss and Mississippi State decided to end the series against USM in the 1980s.

Jim's Nasty Bunch at USM left an impression on University of North Carolina faithful in addition to fans at USM. The following appeared in a UNC internet story about Tar Heels' head coach Larry Fedora, who came to UNC in 2011 from USM: "The issue of defense prompts an interesting 'what-goes-around-comes-around' element between Fedora, Southern Miss and Carolina. One of Bill Dooley's early lieutenants in Chapel Hill in the late 1960s was a defensive line coach named Jim Carmody. Carmody left Chapel Hill after a few years and later joined another former Tar Heel assistant, Bobby Collins, at Southern Miss. As defensive coordinator at Southern Miss under Collins and later as head coach in the 1980s, Carmody was known as 'Big Nasty.' The 'Big Nasty' moniker stuck and was applied to Golden Eagle defenses throughout the next three decades, sometimes with more accuracy than others. 'It's blue-collar, smack-you-in-the mouth defense,' Fedora says. 'That's the tradition here.'"

When USM hired David Duggan away from UNC as its defensive coordinator in 2013, after Duggan coached under former USM head coach Larry Fedora, and more recently UNC, his return to USM was hailed by the student newspaper, the *Student Prinz*: "Southern Miss fans, get yourselves ready for the revival of 'The Nasty Bunch.'"

Bob Ghetti, host of the radio talk show Eagle Hour Super Talk, based in

Hattiesburg, recalled during a recent radio interview the attitudes of Golden Eagle fans as Ellis Johnson, who succeeded Fedora as USM head coach, ended his first and only season as head coach. The Eagles were enduring a 0-12 season, and the fans were frustrated and angry. Ghetti recalls seeing a professionally made sign set up at a USM football tailgate that said, "He's Tan, He's Rested, He's Ready. Bring back Big Nasty!" Carmody was gone, but not forgotten in the hearts and minds of loyal USM fans.

I first met Jim at Ole Miss and Oxford in 1974 when he came to Ole Miss as an assistant football coach, and I was a professor. We had much in common: we were both from New Orleans, and we went to Catholic high schools who were bitter rivals — he to the Holy Cross Tigers and me to the Jesuit Blue Jays. We knew about the same New Orleans haunts and even had friends in common. He played football at Holy Cross High School, but I never participated in high school athletics — I was the second shortest boy in my eighth-grade elementary school class and the second tallest after my freshman class. My awkward, tall, lanky body did not lend itself to athletics until years later, but I loved sports nonetheless. Holy Cross and Jesuit have played football every year since the rivalry began in 1922, including the year of Katrina, one of the longest high school rivalries in the nation. I remind Jim that Jesuit leads the series 57-38, and he reminds me that Holy Cross never lost to Jesuit in the four years he played for them (1948-51). He and I both enjoyed playing golf and have played many rounds together, in Oxford and elsewhere in Mississippi. We would team up in various tournaments, and I cannot remember how many times I heard him say, "Play hard when you're ahead, and never give up when you're behind." Blue Jay feathers have been found in my golf cart and, most recently, on my automobile when we got together for a beer at his favorite watering hole in Madison. Which reminds me, we also both love to have a cold beer now and then.

I have known Jim Carmody through the good times of his career and the not-so-good times. There were certain words that are not in his vocabulary, words like "quit," and "give up." Years ago I coached his third son, Keith, in an 11- to 12-year-old Oxford city tackle football league. Early in the schedule Keith suffered a mild head injury, and I immediately removed him from the game, fearing a serious injury. I suggested to Jim that perhaps Keith should not play anymore, even though that meant losing one of our best players. His answer was to get a helmet worn by former Ole Miss player Stump Russell from the Ole Miss football equipment room for Keith to use. "He'll be all right," Jim said, "just let him play." He did and we went on to an undefeated season. This incident occurred many years before the recent emphasis on avoiding and treating concussions in football.

Knowing Jim for over 40 years puts me in a position to write about the man, the coach. I was witness to many of his ups and downs. I was in Jackson for the stunning Ole Miss upset victory over Notre Dame in 1977. After the game I met him outside the Ole Miss locker room, and he told me, "Borne, I did not think we were that good." I was in the South End Zone of Vaught-Hemingway Stadium for the great goal-line stand against Mississippi State in 1992 and celebrated the victory with him on the Square. A group of regulars was holding a "seminar" at the upstairs bar of the Gumbo Company (which later became City Grocery) the day he was notified that Steve Sloan decided to bring in his own coaching staff, despite the fact that Jim was

Jim Carmody and Ron Borne (Photo provided by the Mississippi Sports Hall of Fame)

the only member of the former staff who continued recruiting for Ole Miss. Instead, Jim was obviously bitter. Sloan brought his entire staff from Texas Tech, including his defensive coordinator. This turned out to be not only a disappointment for Jim but was a big mistake for Sloan since his defensive coordinator accepted a head coaching job elsewhere after accepting the Ole Miss position. Sloan brought his former Alabama roommate in as defensive coordinator, and the Ole Miss program was marked by weak defenses during Sloan's entire tenure as head coach.

Jim and I were in the Shiloh Falls pro shop the day he figured out he would not be named interim head UM coach as he had hoped he would be when Billy Brewer was fired in 1994. As we were signing up to play, Ole Miss defensive coordinator Joe Lee Dunn came in accompanied by Mississippi sports station owner Steve Davenport. Carmody understood immediately that Joe Lee had been appointed interim head coach and had been escorted out of Oxford until the announcement could be finalized. Jim was obviously in a lousy mood as we played, and he released some of his anger when a couple of golf course employees came up to us on the 14th hole, noted my Ole Miss golf bag, and offered, "Would you all like a tip? Get rid of that Ole Miss golf bag!" Carmody went up to them and angrily said, "I'll give you all a tip — get your asses out of here!"

Jim had many career highlights in his nearly sixty-year football career, covering the period when he played for Holy Cross High School to his retirement as a scout for the NFL Arizona Cardinals. Some of these highlights include:

- Induction to the Mississippi Sports Halls of Fame (2009) and Southern Mississippi Sports Halls of Fame (2009) and the Copiah-Lincoln Community College Hall of Fame (1993) and his selection as Co-Lin Alumnus of the year (2014);

- Serving as associate coach in the 1985 East-West Shrine game;

- Being chosen by the American Football Coaches Association as a member of the All-American Team Selection Committee in 1986.

Jim was a strong advocate of the student-athlete concept rather than just the concept of being a just a college athlete. In the six years he served as a head coach none, that's right, none of his student-athletes were declared academically ineligible — a rarity. Working with Hattiesburg Senator Jim Bean, he initiated an Athlete Agent Bill in the Mississippi Legislature. This bill, (No. 88-607) was designed to regulate agents by having them register with the office of the Mississippi Secretary of State. The bill was passed in 1988 and is a landmark in the state of Mississippi. As revised in 2011 the bill provides greater protection to Mississippi's student-athletes and educational institutions by requiring greater accountability from athlete agents operating in the state. The new law contains numerous amendments affecting how athlete agents conduct business in Mississippi and clarifies the secretary of state's role in regulation and oversight. The revised act now includes high school athletes and their scholarship negotiations with a prospective university or college.

Taking advantage of his experiences in journalism, Jim has written numerous articles for various national football organizations and served as a guest lecturer at coaching clinics nationwide.

Jim Carmody is a man's man, a coach's coach, and, as stated by one of his former players, Bo Russell, — Mississippi's coach. His story is one that deserves to be shared with anyone interested in athletics or in just living a disciplined life. The testimonials by his former players recorded here provide evidence of the effect he had on his players, on and off the field. Perhaps the 1986 Southern Mississippi media guide summed up Carmody's career best when it stated that Carmody "continues to enjoy the reputation among his peers of having a keen football mind, and is well known for his ability to sustain long hours of hard work and for his attention to organization and detail." They do not make many coaches, or men, any more like Big Nasty!

ACKNOWLEDGMENTS

This biography would not have been possible without the assistance of many individuals. Deborah Freeland, to whom this book is dedicated, provided much encouragement and support to the author in addition to providing considerable expertise in areas of graphic design, photograph replication, and correcting the author's numerous computer problems.

Thanks to Rick Cleveland, one of the nation's best and most highly respected sports writers and executive director of the Mississippi Sports Hall of Fame, for writing the introduction to this biography. Rick was a close friend of writer Willie Morris, now deceased, who is quoted throughout this biography. Rick knows and understands Mississippi sports better than anyone else, and his introduction sets the tone for this biography.

Also, the biography could not have been completed without the complete cooperation of the Carmody family. Jim's mother had compiled several scrapbooks containing newspaper articles about her son's career dating back to high school. Noonie kept the scrapbooks up to date later in his career. Noonie shared her experiences as a beauty queen growing up in New Orleans and the Carmody sons, Steve, Brian, Keith, and Chris, were extremely helpful in recalling their experiences of growing up with their father. Steve was especially helpful in clarifying issues involved in the Sorey v. Kellett lawsuit, and Brian was especially helpful in providing information about the Carmody family history and in inviting stories about Big Nasty from former players.

Neil White, creative and energetic author and owner of Nautilus Publishing Company, was supportive of this biography from the outset. He also encouraged me to write and invited the author to attend a two-day workshop he conducts on writing and publishing books.

Several Oxford friends including Dr. Steve Wooten, Oxford dentist, avid sports fan and a warehouse of sports memories; and Marquis Sledge, local banker and long-time friend; were gracious in providing advice and insight. Marquis worked in the sports information office at Ole Miss during the Brewer-Carmody era and was very helpful. He accompanied me on several trips to Jackson to interview Jim Carmody and JSU Coach W.C. Gorden and was very helpful. Bill Cusumano, assistant manager of Square Books in Oxford, is a walking encyclopedia of information about literature, publishing, and sports. Bill provided suggestions and encouragement in pursuing this story. Despite being a Michigander, he has an amazing knowledge of Mississippi sports. Slade Lewis, also of Square Books, was also very supportive and provided key ideas for the biography.

Special appreciation to the classy, retired JSU gentlemen: head football coach W.C. Gorden, athletic director Walter Reed, and sports information director Sam Jefferson. On October 10, 2016, Coach Gorden invited me into his home to meet with these men to discuss the origins of the historic USM-JSU football game in 1987. I was accompanied by Marquis Sledge, who was a student worker in the Ole Miss sports information department. All aspects of that game, including the details of how the matchup was secured and the game itself, were discussed. I am deeply appreciative.

Noted local writers and outstanding Ole Miss professors Dr. David G. Sansing, professor emeritus of history at the University of Mississippi, and Dr. Jere Hoar, professor emeritus of journalism, were constant sources of encouragement and inspiration. Their friendship and support are greatly appreciated. Dr. Sansing was particularly helpful in his discussions of the intense Ole Miss-Mississippi State rivalry and in his comments regarding the historical significance of the USM-Jackson State University game in 1987. His contributions are deeply appreciated.

Curtis Akey, associate athletics communication director at Tulane University, graciously and promptly provided photos of Carmody during his days at Tulane. Jack Duggan, Assistant athletic director for athletic communications at the University of Southern Mississippi, was very helpful in securing photographs and providing information regarding the USM-JSU game. Jack was an intern in the S.I.D. office at Ole Miss during the Brewer-Carmody era. Kyle Campbell, associate athletics director in charge of media and public relations, was also helpful in providing information regarding the hiring of Tommy Tuberville at Ole Miss in 1994.

John Meibaum, Carmody's buddy at LSU and Co-Lin, was generous in providing information in a telephone interview about their adventures in leaving LSU for Copiah-Lincoln Community College, also known as Co-Lin JUCO.

Senior Federal Judge Neal B. Biggers of the Northern District of Mississippi and long-time friend and golfing buddy provided insight and assistance in interpreting legal issues that affected Big Nasty at the University of Southern Mississippi.

Thanks to former Ole Miss players and coaches and members of the Mississippi Sports Hall of Fame former Ole Miss athletic director Warner Alford and former Ole Miss head Football Coach Billy Brewer, who were especially helpful in providing insight into Carmody's recruiting and coaching efforts at Ole Miss.

Special thanks also to former Jackson State University head football coach W.C. Gorden, who graciously agreed to be interviewed via telephone regarding the historic USM-JSU game in 1987. Coach Gorden is one of the greatest football coaches in the history of Mississippi and is a class act.

Leo V. Seicshnaydre, Jr., retired resident of Bay St. Louis, Mississippi, fellow Jesuit High School classmate, class of 1956, connoisseur of hog head cheese and liver cheese, and big-time LSU fan, was very helpful in helping me attempt to secure documents related to the trial of USM player Don Horn, which was moved from Hattiesburg to Gulfport. Arthur McIntosh, Oxford lawyer and friend, was also helpful in these attempts. Arthur also put me in contact with Gulfport attorney Cy Faneca. Cy and his paralegal staff helped in the attempts to secure legal documents regarding the Don Horn trial from the Harrison County Courthouse. No record of the trial could be easily found in either the Harrison County or Forrest County Circuit Clerk Office. Special thanks are due to Ms. Rhonda Creel of the Forrest County Circuit Clerk Office and Ms. Donnie Patterson of the Harrison County Circuit Clerk Office for their efforts in attempting to locate the case disposition of the Don Horn trial, which was moved from the Forrest County jurisdiction to the Harrison County jurisdiction in 1983 or 1984.

Lonn Ellzey, social studies department chair, assistant head football coach, head golf coach, and summer camp director at Holy Cross High School, was very helpful in providing information and photographs of Carmody's days at Holy Cross. Also very helpful was Charles Illanne, alumni director, at Holy Cross.

Megan Halsband, reference librarian at the Serial and Government Publications Division of the Library of Congress, was particularly helpful in helping Deborah secure photos of the Korean Armed Services, particularly the photographs of Korean President Syngman Rhee attending the EAS-COM-Zama championship football game in Seoul, Korea, and the action photo of the game itself.

Former president of the University of Southern Mississippi, Dr. Aubrey Lucas, was gracious in providing insight into Carmody's days as head coach at USM.

Thanks for sharing their experiences of being coached by Carmody and paying tribute to Carmody for his influence on their football experience and post-football lives are due to former USM players Larry Boyd, Rhett Whitley, Preston Hansford, Mike Schiro, and Tony Pogue, former player at the University of North Carolina Harper Donahoe, former Ole Miss players Johnny Desler and Billy R. Jones, and former Mississippi State player Bo Russell.

Ole Miss All-American Ben Williams graciously agreed to a telephone interview about his days at Ole Miss and his relationship with Carmody at the Buffalo Bills. Ben's wife, Linda, was especially helpful in setting up the interview.

A student in the University of Mississippi J.D. Williams Library Microfilm department, Ms. Louise Boston, went out of her way to assist me in operating and securing microfilms and equipment. Thanks are given to her for providing help when I most needed it. Another library employee, Jackie Reed, helped immensely in scanning the photograph of coaches Carmody and Gorden shaking hands at midfield after the USM-JSU football game. The scan was important because the original photograph from the Jackson

Clarion-Ledger newspaper November 1, 1987, edition could not be located.

Bob Gheti, host of the Eagle Hour Sports Talk radio show, and his co-host, Jim "Stump" Taylor, interviewed me on their show and provided interesting insights into Jim Carmody. Taylor, who was a place kicker for USM from 1988-91, said he never heard another player say anything bad about Big Nasty.

Throughout my life, professionally and personally, I have been fortunate to have the support and love of my three children, Debra Price, Dr. Michael J. Borne, and MerriBeth Catalano, and my nine grandchildren, Rachael, Baker, Taylor and Bess Borne; Mary Katherine and Jason Price; and Madison, Jordan, and Cole Catalano. I have also benefited over the years from the encouragement and support of my colleagues in the Department of Medicinal Chemistry, the School of Pharmacy, and the University of Mississippi. I am deeply grateful.

APPENDICES

APPENDIX A. Carmody Timeline

August 24, 1933	Born, Shreveport, LA
1948-51	Played at Holy Cross High School
1952	Graduated from Holy Cross High School
1953-54	Played at Copiah-Lincoln Community College
1954-55	Played at Tulane
1956	Graduated from Tulane, B.A. History
1956	Enlisted in the U.S. Army
1956-58	Served in Korea
August 1958-June 1961	Coached at Holy Cross High School
Jan. 2, 1960	Married Earlyn "Noonie" Regouffre
June 1961-July 1963	Coached at Tulane
July 1963-July 1964	Coached at University of Kentucky
1965	M.Ed. Degree, Tulane, Guidance and Counseling
July 1964-Jan. 1967	Coached at Mississippi State University
Jan. 1967-April 1974	Coached at University of North Carolina
April 1974- Jan. 1978	Coached at University Mississippi
Jan. 1978-Jan. 1981	Coached at University of Southern Mississippi
Jan. 1981-Jan. 1982	Coached with Buffalo Bills, NFL
Jan. 1982-Dec. 87	Head Coach, University of Southern Mississippi
Jan. 1982-Dec. 87	Semi-Retired
Dec. 1988-June 1991	Coached at Mississippi State University
July 1991-Dec. 1991	Coached at Mississippi College
Dec. 1991-July 1995	Coached at the University of Mississippi
July 1995-June 2003	Area Scout NFL Arizona Cardinals
July 2003-June 2005	Western Regional Scout NFL Arizona Cardinals
June 2005	Retired

Appendix B. Carmody Head Coaching Record at USM

1982 (7-4)

9/4/1982	Louisiana-Monroe	W 45-27	
9/11/1982	@ Mississippi	L 19-28	
9/18/1982	@ Auburn	L 19-21	
9/25/1982	Florida State	L 17-24	
10/2/1982	Memphis	W 34-14	
10/9/1982	Mississippi State	W 20-14	@ Jackson, MS
10/16/1982	@ Tulane	W 22-10	
10/23/1982	Louisville	W 48-0	
10/30/1982	Louisiana-Lafayette	W 36-0	
11/13/1982	@ Alabama	W 38-29	
11/20/1982	Louisiana Tech	L 6-13	

1983 (7-4)

9/3/1983	Richmond	W 32-3	
9/10/1983	@ Auburn	L 3-24	
9/17/1983	Louisiana Tech	W 28-10	
10/1/1983	@ Mississippi	W 27-7	
10/8/1983	Mississippi State	W 31-6	@ Jackson, MS
10/15/1983	@ Memphis	W 27-20	
10/22/1983	Tulane	L 7-14	
10/29/1983	Louisiana-Lafayette	W 31-3	
11/5/1983	@ Louisville	W 27-3	
11/12/1983	@ Alabama	L 16-28	@ Birmingham, AL
11/19/1983	East Carolina	L 6-10	

1984 (4-7)

9/8/1984	@ Georgia	L 19-26	
9/15/1984	Louisiana Tech	W 34-0	
9/22/1984	@ Auburn	L 12-35	
9/29/1984	@ Memphis	L 13-23	
10/6/1984	Mississippi State	L 18-27	@ Jackson, MS
10/13/1984	@ Tulane	L 7-35	
10/20/1984	Mississippi	W 13-10	@ Jackson, MS
10/27/1984	@ Louisiana-Lafayette	L 7-13	
11/3/1984	Northwestern State	L 0-22	
11/10/1984	@ East Carolina	W 31-27	
11/17/1984	Louisville	W 34-25	

1985 (7-4)

9/7/1985	Louisiana Tech	W 28-0	
9/14/1985	@ Auburn	L 18-29	
9/21/1985	Mississippi State	L 20-23	@ Jackson, MS
9/28/1985	Northwestern State	W 14-7	
10/5/1985	Louisiana-Lafayette	W 38-16	
10/12/1985	@ Louisville	W 42-12	
10/19/1985	@ Memphis	W 14-7	
11/2/1985	East Carolina	W 27-0	
11/9/1985	@ Colorado State	L 17-35	
11/16/1985	@ Alabama	L 13-24	
11/23/1985	Tulane	W 24-6	

1986 (6-5)

9/6/1986	Louisiana-Monroe	W 28-19	
9/13/1986	@ Alabama	L 17-31	@ Birmingham, AL
9/20/1986	Mississippi State	W 28-24	@ Jackson, MS
9/27/1986	@ Texas A&M	L 7-16	
10/4/1986	@ Kentucky	L 0-32	
10/18/1986	Memphis	W 14-9	
10/25/1986	@ Tulane	L 20-35	
11/1/1986	@ East Carolina	W 23-21	
11/8/1986	Louisiana-Lafayette	W 17-0	
11/15/1986	@ Florida State	L 13-49	
11/22/1986	Louisville	W 31-16	

1987 (6-5)

9/5/1987	@ Alabama	L 6-38	@ Birmingham, AL
9/19/1987	Tulane	W 31-24	
9/26/1987	Texas A&M	L 14-27	@ Jackson, MS
10/3/1987	@ Louisville	W 65-6	
10/10/1987	Florida State	L 10-61	
10/17/1987	Mississippi State	W 18-14	@ Jackson, MS
10/24/1987	@ Memphis	W 17-14	
10/31/1987	Jackson State	W 17-7	
11/7/1987	Louisiana-Monroe	L 24-34	
11/14/1987	East Carolina	W 38-34	
11/28/1987	@ Louisiana-Lafayette	L 30-37	

Appendix C. MSU vs UM vs USM

Assistant Coach MSU 1964-66		
	UM (1-2)	USM (3-0)
1964	W 20-17	W 48-7
1965	L 0-21	W 27-9
1966	L 0-24	W 10-9
Assistant Coach UM 1974-77		
	UM (0-2)	USM (2-0)
1989	L 11-21	W 26-23
1990	L 9-21	W 13-10
Assistant Coach MSU 1989-1990		
	MSU (1-3)	USM (3-1)
1974	L 13-31	W 20-14
1975	W 13-7	W 24-8
1976	L 11-28	W 28-0
1977	L 14-18	L 19-27
Assistant Coach UM 1992-94		
	MSU (1-2)	USM (0-0)
1992	W 17-10	DNP
1993	L 13-20	DNP
1994	L 17-21	DNP
Assistant Coach USM 1978-80		
	MSU (3-0)	UM (2-1)
1978	W 22-17	L 13-16
1979	W 21-7	W 38-8
1980	W 42-14	W 28-22

Head Coach USM 1982-87		
	MSU (4-2)	UM (2-1)
1982	W 20-14	L 19-28
1983	W 31-6	W 27-7
1984	L 18-27	W 13-10
1985	L 0-23	DNP
1986	W 28-24	DNP
1987	W 18-14	DNP

Sources

Author's Notes

Warm-Up
- *Rock Solid: Southern Miss Football*, by John W. Cox and Gregg Bennett, University Press of Mississippi, 2004.

- "No Fluke: USM Beats Alabama," by Lee Ragland, The Jackson *Clarion-Ledger*, November 14, 1982, p. 1D.

- "Alabama Players Say Collier was the Key to the USM Victory," by Roscoe Nance, The Jackson *Clarion-Ledger*, November 14, 1982, p. 4D.

- "In Moment of Truth, Golden Eagles Put Up," by Roscoe Nance, The Jackson *Clarion-Ledger*, November 14, 1982, p. 4D.

- "Dear Bubba, It was Great," by Orley Hood, The Jackson *Clarion-Ledger*, November 14, 1982, p. 4D.

- "Carmody: USM's Victory over Alabama was Simply the Greatest," by Paul Borden, The Jackson *Clarion-Ledger*, November 15, 1982, p. 1C.

Chapter 1
- "Jesuit-Holy Cross Football Rivalry Dates Loaded with History," by Ron Brocato, September 8, 2010; sportsnola.com/Jesuit-holy-cross-football-rivalry-dates-loaded-with-history.

- "Notre Dame All-Time Roster List," http://www.und.com/sports/m-footbl/archive/players/c.html

- "Wild Gas Well in Caddo Field Was Stopped by M.B. Carmody," Shreveport Journal, September 21, 1911.

- "Method of Closing in Wild Gas Well," The Natural Gas Journal, Vol. 5, Periodicals Publishing Co., 1911, p. 31.

- *A Man About the Campus*, The Notre Dame Scholastic, Vol. LXIV, p 402, January 16, 1930.

- "Jesuit vs. Holy Cross: Mardi Gras on Marconi," Jaynotes, Vol. 42, Fall/Winter 2015, p. 40.

Chapter 2
- John Meibaum, Personal Telephone Communication, November 23, 2015.

- http://www.und.com/sports/m-footbl/spec-rel/100715aak.html, "Victories Have Defined Notre Dame's Tradition on the Gridiron," by Todd Burlage, Oct. 7, 2015.

Chapter 3
- "Loggers Tabbed as Choice for F.E. Crown," by PFC Tom, Gregory, The Pacific Stars and Stripes," November 25-26, 1957, p. 19.

- "Korea Loggers Thump Zama's Ramblers," by PFC Al Drake, The Pacific Stars and Stripes," November 25-26, 1957, p. 21.

Chapter 4
- *Rock Solid: Southern Miss Football,* by John W. Cox and Gregg Bennett, University Press of Mississippi, 2004, p. 191.

Chapter 5
- *Tulane: The Emergence of a Modern University, 1945-1980,* by C.L.Mohr and J.E. Gordon, Louisiana State University Press, 2001, p. 259-260.

- "Tommy O'Boyle Calls it Quits as Tulane Boss," *The Florence Times Daily,* Nov. 25, 1865; www.news.google.com.

- Tulane University Official Athletic site, http://www.tulanegreenwave.com/sports/m-footbl/archive/history.html.

- *The Thin Thirty,* by Shannon Ragland, Set Shot Press, 2007.

- Bob Lee, http://bobleesays.com/author/boblee, 2015.

- "Occasionally a Column Worthwhile to Coaches," by Jack Hairston, The LakelanddLedger, Dec. 7,1972.

- "State Finally Beats Ole Miss," by Wayne Thompson, The Jackson *Clarion-Ledger,* December 6, 1964.

- "State Upsets Florida 18-13," by Carl Walters, The Jackson *Clarion-Led-*

ger, September 26, 1965.

- "Rebs Hope to Spoil Bear's Birthday," by John Stamm, The Jackson *Clarion-Ledger*, September 11, 1976.

- "Rebels Stopped Tide Bread 'n' Butter," by Bernard Fernandez, Jackson Daily News, September 10, 1976. http://www.olemisssports.com.

- "Rebels Stomp Bear's Birthday," by Kohn Stamm, The Jackson *Clarion-Ledger*," Septmber 12, 1976.

Chapter 6
- "Weather History for KJAN," http://www.wunderground.com/history/airport/KJAN/1977/9/17/DailyHistory.html?&reqdb.zip=&reqdb.magic=&reqdb.wmo=&MR=1

- Rick Cleveland, "25 Years Later, Win Over Powerhouse Notre Dame Still a Defining Ole Miss Moment," Clarionledger.com, April 5, 2012.

- Robert Markus, "Irish Title Hopes Wilt at Sultry Ole Miss," *Chicago Tribune*, September 18, 1977.

- John Adams, "Rebs Play Like No. 3 in Wiping Out Irish," Jackson *Clarion-Ledger*, Nov. 18, 1977.

- Tom Patterson, Jackson *Clarion-Ledger*, November 18, 1977.

- "Tim Ellis: Giant Slayer," by John Davis, Rebel Nation, *Rebel Nation Magazine*, May/June 2014.

- "Ole Miss' First Black Starting Quarterback Passes," *The Mississippi Link*, Vol. 19, No. 17, February 14-20, 2013, www.mississippilink.com.

Chapter 7
- "Rebel Defense Rises to Help Cooper Cause," by Mike Fleming, *Commercial Appeal*, Oct. 15, 1977.

- "Ole Miss' Cooper Quits Under Fire," Associated Press, *Daytona Beach Morning Journal*, December 1, 1977.

- Bill Winter, AP Sports Writer, *The Lewiston Daily Sun*, Jan. 17, 1974. AP story, Morning Journal, Daytona Beach, FL Dec. 1, 1977.

- *Rock Solid: Southern Miss Football*, by John W. Cox and Gregg Bennett, University Press of Mississippi, 2004, p. 166-183.

- "Hale's Tackle Brings back Cotton Bowl Memories," by Bernard Fernandez, The Jackson *Clarion-Ledger*, October 1, 191.

- *Treasured Past, Golden Future: The Centennial History of the University of Southern Mississippi*, by Chester M. Morgan, The University Press of Mississippi, 2012, p. 125.

- "Helmet Hut — University of Southern Mississippi, 1977-81 Golden Eagles," http://helmethut.com/College/USM/MSXUSM7781.html.

- Rhett Whitley, Personal Communication.

- "Beeb, Beep! USM-McNeese Have Roadrunners," by Barry Lasswell, Jackson *Clarion-Ledger*, December 12, 1980.

- "Bow, Kneel, Kiss the Turf, USM's Win Isn't a Hoax," by Orley Hood, Jackson C*clarion-Ledger*, December 14, 1980.

- "Golden …Eagles are named That for a Reason," by Clay Harden, Jackson *Clarion-Ledger*, December 14, 1980.

Chapter 8
- "The State-Ole Miss Rivalry," by David G. Sansing, Personal Communication to the NCAA. Cited with permission.

- "Hate is Ruining Great Rivalry," by Hugh Kellenberger, Jackson *Clarion-Ledger*, July 3, 2016.

- "Rebs, 'Dogs Toil in Field of Futility," by Ron Higgins, Memphis *Commercial Appeal*, November 25, 2005.

- *Rebel Coach*, by John Vaught, Memphis State University Press, Memphis, Tennessee, 1971, p. 141.

- *The Courting of Marcus Dupree*, by Willie Morris, Doubleday & Company, 1983, p. 364-65.

- *The University of Mississippi: A Sesquicentennial History*, by David G. Sansing, University Press of Mississippi, 1999.

- "Ole Miss Shelves Mascot Fraught with Baggage," by Robbie Brown, *The New York Times*, September 19, 2010.

- "A Legend Takes Shape," by Chuck Bennett, in *Favre: The Total Package*, by Editors of Sports Collectors Digest, Krause Publishers, 2008, p. 15-19.

- "Thank You, Mark McHale," by Rob Dempvsky, ^Packer Forum^, www.packerforum.com/threads/thank-you-msrk-mchale. 13289..

- "Favre Caught on Quickly in College," by Gary D'Amato, *Milwaukee-Wisconsin Journal Sentinel*, Sept. 17, 2005. http://www.jsonline.com/sports/packers/44679182.html

- *Rock Solid: Southern Miss Football*, by John W. Cox and Gregg Bennett, University Press of Mississippi, 2004, p. 182, 189 and 201.

Chapter 9
- "The History of Scouting," by Conor Orr, "Innovators of the Game," www.nfl.com/historyofscouting.

- "Carmody a Catalyst in Improving Line," by Dave Rafter, *Buffalo Bills Weekly*, December 7, 1981.

- Ben Williams, Personal Communication.

- "Carmody Honored," by Rick Cleveland, *Picayune Item*, July 28, 2009.

- "Ole Miss Recruits First Black Player," by Oxford Eagle Contributors, *The Oxford Eagle*, February 7, 2016.

The following original newspaper articles were collected into a Carmody Family scrapbook. Unfortunately newspaper publishing dates or newspapers from which the article appears were not collected:

- "'Master Craftsman' Named to Bills Staff."

- "Carmody Still Dreaming of Landing a Head Coaching Job."

- "Defensive Linemen Praise Carmody."

Chapter 10

- *Rock Solid: Southern Miss Football*, by John W. Cox and Gregg Bennett, University Press of Mississippi, 2004, p. 183-204.

- "Carmody Takes Southern Miss Job," AP, *Ocala Star-Banner*, Jan. 19, 1982.

- "Southern Miss put on Probation for Two Years," *St. Petersburg Times*, November 9, 1982, p. 3c

- "Helmet Hut," http://helmethut.com/College/USM/MSXUSM8284. html

- *The Courting of Marcus Dupree*, by Willie Morris, Doubleday & Company, 1983, p. 322.

- "Marcus Dupree Quits College; Future Unclear; Dupree Is Leaving," *The New York Times*, February 1, 1984.

- "Thank You, Mark McHale," by Rob Dempvsky, ^Packer Forum^, www. packerforum.com/threads/thank-you-msrk-mchale. 13289..

- *Favre: The Total Package*, by Editors of *Sports Collectors Digest*, Krause Publishers, 2008, p. 15-19.

- "Favre Caught on Quickly in College," by Gary D'Amato, *Milwaukee-Wisconsin Journal Sentinel*, Sept. 17, 2005. http://www.jsonline. com/sports/packers/44679182.html

- "Eagles Plunder Pirates," by Mike Christensen, The Jackson *Clarion-Ledger*, November 10, 1984.

- "USM Wins With Fantastic Finish," by Don Hudson, The Jackson *Clarion-Ledger*, November 2, 1986.

- "Eagles Prayers Answered," by Don Hudson, The Jackson *Clarion-Ledger*, November 2, 1986.

- *Brett Favre*, by Rachel A. Koestler-Grack, Chelsea House, 2013.

- "Carmody Honored," by Rick Cleveland, *Picayune Item*, July 28, 2009.

Chapter 11

- *Rock Solid: Southern Miss Football,"* by John W. Cox and Gregg Bennett, University Press of Mississippi, 2004, pp. 183-186; 193, 197-198, 200-203.

- "Bruner v. University of Southern Mississippi, Jim Carmody, Roland Dale, Dr. Aubrey Lucas, and the Board of Trustees of Institutions of Higher Learning of the State of Mississippi." Supreme Court of Mississippi, January 28, 1987.

- "Southern Miss Player Arrested in Rape Case," A.P. story, *The Gadsden Times*, February 18, 1983.

- "USM Senior and NFL Hopeful Surrenders; Charged with Rape," by Harvey Rice and Roscoe Nance, Jackson *Clarion-Ledger*, Feb. 8, 1983

- *Ted Bundy : Conversations with a Killer* First Edition, by Hugh Aynesworth, Authorlink, 2000.

- "The Famous Bitemark Case," https://sites.google.com/site/tedbundythelastbitemark.

- "Walk of Death: A Forensic Novel," by Mike Tabor, Create Space Independent Publishing Platform, 2013.

- "In Brief," *The Southerner*, Vol. 48, 1984, p. 342.

- *Treasured Past, Golden Future: The Centennial History of the University of Southern Mississippi*, by Chester M. Morgan, University Press of Mississippi, 2010, p. 152.

- "On A Highway To History Jackson State crosses Racial Barrier in Showdown At Southern Mississippi," by Les Bowen, *Daily News*, www.philly.com, 1987.

- Sorey v. Kellett, 673 F. Supp. 817 (S.D. Miss. 1987), U.S. District Court for the Southern District of Mississippi - 673 F. Supp. 817 (S.D. Miss. 1987), October 15, 1987.

- "NCAA Investigating Southern Miss Again," *The Gadsen Times*, Oct. 10, 1984. http://news.google.com).

- "Southern Miss. Fullback Dies," *The New York Times*, August 17, 1986

The Times Daily, December 18, 1985.

• *Undue Process: The NCAA's Injustice For All* by Don Yaeger, Segamore Publishing Inc., 1991, p. 171-73.

• *Undue Process: The NCAA's Injustice for All*, by Don Yaeger, Sagamore Publishing, 1991, p. 172.

• "Sherrill, Assistants Cited for Gift-Giving," Associated Press, December 9, 2003.

Chapter 12 — USM-JSU

• Coach W.C. Gorden, Personal Telephone Communications, August 11 and August 15, 2016.

• *NCAA Football: A Brief History of NCAA Football Scholarships*, by Hank Rippetoe, SB Nation, June 11, 2013, www.a seaofblue.com.

• "Jackson State-USM: May be Another Risky Done for I-AA Football," by Don Hudson, Jackson *Clarion-Ledger*, October 26, 1987.

• "USM Has Slight Edge Over JSU," by Don Hudson, Jackson *Clarion-Ledger*, October 28, 1987.

• "JSU Hexed by Unfamiliar Opponents," by Mike Knobler, Jackson *Clarion-Ledger*, October 26, 1987.

• "Tigers Profess Faith in Ability to Win Saturday," by Mike Knobler, Jackson *Clarion-Ledger*, October 26, 1987.

• "Winning: J-State's Gorden Says There is No Substitute," by Mike Knobler, Jackson *Clarion-Ledger*, October 30, 1987.

• "Sellout Crowd Sees Southern Beat JSU in Historic Game," by Mike Knobler, Jackson *Clarion-Ledger*, November 1 1987.

• "USM Escapes J-State D," by Mike Christensen, Jackson *Clarion-Ledger*, November 1, 1987.

• "R-e-s-p-e-c-t: JSU Earns More Than Just a Little Bit," by Rick Cleveland, Jackson *Clarion-Ledger*, November 1 1987.

• "USM-JSU Game one of Mystery," by Mike Christensen, Jackson *Clari-*

on-Ledger, October 31, 1987.

- "Gorden Says USM Tradition Beats JSU," Compiled from Staff Reports, *Jackson Daily News*, November 2, 1987.

Chapter 13 — Resigns
- *A Pipeline Full of Drugs*, by Bill Brubaker, *Sports Illustrated*, January 21, 1985.

- "Carmody Out as USM Football Coach," by Don Hudson, Jackson *Clarion-Ledger*, December 4, 1987.

- "Carmody Resignation is Not What It Appears," by Butch John, Jackson *Clarion-Ledger*, December 4, 1987.

- "USM's Monken Aims to Fill 'The Rock' for Home Games," by Jason Munz, *Hattiesburg American*, July 17, 2015.

- "Southern Miss Coach Todd Monken Isn't Happy with Fan Attendance Against Austin Peay," by Stephen Lassen, September 12, 2015, www.athlonsports.com

- "Carmody: 'I Won't Be Back,'" by Don Hudson, Jackson *Clarion-Ledger*, December 4, 1987.

- "Hogwash? Players Say Carmody Not to Blame," by Billy Watkins, Jackson *Clarion-Ledger*, December 4, 1987.

Chapter 14
- Rick Cleveland, http://msfame.com/ricks-writings/its-game-week-my-top-five-state-usm-memories.

- "Rewind: Re-living the Last MSU at USM Tilt, a Thriller in 1989." *Hail State Beat*, https://hailstatebeat.wordpress.com/2015/09/03/rewind-re-living-the-last-msu-at-usm-tilt-a-thriller-in-1989/

- http://forums.sixpackspeak.com/showthread.php?128484

- http://collegefootballbelt.com/1989/1989%20Game%20Summaries/Mississippi%20State%20at%20Southern%20Miss.htm.

- "Felker New Coach at Miss. State," *Gainesville Sun*, Jan. 7, 1986.

- "Under Pressure, Felker Resigns," *The Times Daily*, Nov. 27, 1990.

- "His Other Side: Sherrill's Mystique is Built on Arrogance, Insolence, but Stowers Death Made Him Let His Guard Down," *Los Angeles Times*, Oct. 21, 1991.

- "The Sidelines: Car Crash Hospitalizes Favre," *Los Angeles Times*, July 16. 1990.

- http://msfame.com/ricks-writings/its-game-week-my-top-five-state-usm-memories/

- http://forums.sixpackspeak.com/showthread.php?128484

- *Rock Solid: Southern Miss Football*," by John W. Cox and Gregg Bennett, University Press of Mississippi, 2004p. 212.

- "The Sidelines: Car Crash Hospitalizes Favre," Times Wire Services, *Los Angeles Times*, July 16, 1990.

- *Favre — The Total Package*, Krause Publications, Iola, Wisconsin, 2008, p. 18

- *Brett Favre*, by Jeff Savage, Lerner Publications, 2001, p. 17.

- *Rock Solid: Southern Miss Football*, by John W. Cox and Gregg Bennett, University Press of Mississippi, 2004p. 208.

- "Nightmare Brings Golden Eagles to Earth," by Robert Wilson, The Jackson *Clarion-Ledger*, September 10, 1989.

- "Carmody Leaves A Winner," by Billy Watkins, The Jackson *Clarion-Ledger*, September 10, 1989.

- "Bulldogs Kick No. 18 Eagles," by Rusty Hampton, The Jackson *Clarion-Ledger*, September 10, 1989.

- "Motivation: Favre Expects Carmody to Have MSU Revved up," by Robert Wilson, The Jackson *Clarion-Ledger*, 1990.

- "MSU Tops USM in Series Finale," by Joe Culpepper, The Jackson *Clarion-Ledger*, September 23, 1990.

- "State's Defense Tears Punch Out of Favre," by Mike Christensen, The Jackson *Clarion-Ledger*, September 23, 1990.

- "MSU May Play Carmody Card," author unknown, Carmody Collection.

- "Mississippi Sate's Man is Already on Campus," by Marc Kuykendall, *Dispatch*, Carmody Collection.

- "State Search Forges Ahead," by Mike Knobler, The Jackson *Clarion-Ledger*, December 1, 1990.

- "Polk Offers Carmody His Support," by Mike Knobler, The Jackson *Clarion-Ledger*, November 29, 1990.

Chapter 15

- "History of Mississippi College Athletics, " *The Official Site of the Mississippi College Choctaws*, http://gochoctaws.com/sports/2013/1/30/ADMIN_0130133512.aspx?path=admin.

- "History of Mississippi College," http://catalog.mc.edu/content.php?catoid=22&navoid=1169.

- "John Williams Leaving Mississippi College," *The Times Daily*, May 8, 1991.

- "MC Adds Carmody to Staff," by Mike Knobler, The Jackson *Clarion-Ledger*, Carmody Collection.

- "Mississippi College Handed 'Damaging Blow' by NCAA, by Gina Reynolds, *The Times Daily*, January 13, 1993.

- "Choctaws Placed on 4-Year Probation," The Associated Press, *The Rome News-Tribune*, January 13, 11993.

- "Carmody Joins MC Coaching Staff," by Renee Ambrosek, Carmody Collection.

- "Carmody Delights in Details of Game," by Mike Christensen, The Jackson *Clarion-Ledger*," Carmody Collection.

Chapter 16

- "Paul Crane is the First to Resign at Ole Miss," Associated Press, *The*

Tuscaloosa News, December 30, 1980.

- "Remembering the Immaculate Deflection," by Parrish Alford, *Northeast Mississippi Daily Journal*, November 27, 2013.

- "God Was a Rebel — The Immaculate Deflection," Associated Press, *The Clarksdale Press Register*, November 21, 2001.

- "Brewer on Carmody's Remark: Consider the Source," staff report, Jackson *Clarion-Ledger*, December 2, 1987.

- "Carmody: Comment taken Out of Context," by Don Hudson, Jackson *Clarion-Ledger*, December 3, 1987.

- "Ole Miss Hires Carmody." *Gainesville Sun*, December 15, 1991.

- "The Birth of the 3-3-5 Defense," *The Essential Smart Football*, by Chris B. Brown, CreateSpace Independent Publishing Platform," May 10, 2012; http://grantland.com/features/an-excerpt-essential-smart-football-birth-3-3-5-defense/

- "Ole Miss Found Guilty of 15 NCAA Violations," *The Seattle Times*, November 18, 1994 via the Jackson *Clarion-Ledger*.

- "Dunn Slowly Adjusting as Head Coach at Ole Miss," The Associated Press, *Ocala Star Banner*, July 27, 1994.

Chapter 17

- Larry Wells, "In the End Zone," HottyToddy.com, posted December 19, 2013.

- "Rebs Stand Tall," by Rusty Hampton, Jackson *Clarion-Ledger*, November 28, 1992.

- "Brewer's Game Ball Deserves a Spot Next to Memento," by Rick Cleveland, Jackson *Clarion-Ledger*, November 28, 1992.

- "Carmody Honored," by Rick Cleveland, *Picayune Item*, July 28, 2009.

Chapter 18

- *The History of Scouting*, by Conor Orr http://www.NFL.com/history-ofscouting.

- "Not Just Throwing Darts," by Danny Kelly, *SBNation*, April 30, 2015. http"//www.nfl.com/combine; http://www.nflcombine.net

Chapter 19
- "Big Nasty: No One Has Lived the Football Lifestyle More than Jim Carmody," by Lanny Mixon, *To the Top* Magazine,, Vol. 1, Issue 1, September/October 2011.

Chapter 20
- "Big Nasty: No One Has Lived the Football Lifestyle More than Jim Carmody," by Lanny Mixon, *To the Top* Magazine,, Vol. 1, Issue 1, September/October 2011.

- Tony Pogue, Personal Communication to Brian Carmody, 2016.

- Preston Hansford, Personal Communication to Brian Carmody, 2016

- Larry Boyd, Personal communication to Ron Borne, 2016.C
- Rhett Whitley, Personal communication to Ron Borne, 2016.

- Billy R. Jones, Ph.D., Personal Communication to Ron Borne, 2016.

- Harper Donahoe, Personal Communication to Jim Carmody, 2015.

- "Motivation: Favre Expects Carmody to have MSU revved up," by Robert Wilson, The Jackson *Clarion-Ledger*, 1990.

Author's Notes
- "Return of the Nasty Bunch," by Alan Rawls, *Student Prinz*, August 29, 2013.

- *Extra Points; What, Me Sleep?* by Lee Pace, December 12, 2011

- http://www.goheels.com/ViewArticle.dbml?DB_OEM ID=3350&AT-CLID=205488311.

- "Athlete Agent," http://www.sos.ms.gov/Regulation-Enforcement/Pages/Athlete-Agent.aspx.

INDEX

AUTHOR'S NOTES

www.ingramcontent.com/pod-product-compliance
Lightning Source LLC
Chambersburg PA
CBHW021500090426
42739CB00007B/400